SAMUEL BECKETT AND THE MEANING OF BEING

SAMUEL BECKETT AND THE MEANING OF BEING
A Study in Ontological Parable

Lance St. John Butler

St. Martin's Press   New York

Printed in Hong Kong
Published in the United Kingdom by The Macmillan Press Ltd.
First published in the United States of America in 1984

ISBN 0-312-69855-0

Library of Congress Cataloging in Publication Data
Butler, Lance St. John.
Samuel Beckett and the meaning of being.
Bibliography: p.
Includes index.
1. Beckett, Samuel, 1906-   —Philosophy.
2. Philosophy in literature. I. Title.
PR6003.E282Z579 1984   848'.91409   83-15942
ISBN 0-312-69855-0

For Godot

B. — The situation is that of him who is helpless, cannot act, in the event cannot paint, since he is obliged to paint. The act is of him who, helpless, unable to act, acts, in the event paints, since he is obliged to paint.

D. — Why is he obliged to paint?

B. — I don't know.

D. — Why is he helpless to paint?

B. — Because there is nothing to paint and nothing to paint with.

(Beckett, *Three Dialogues with Georges Duthuit*, no. III, 'Bram Van Velde', 1949)

Human reason, in one sphere of its cognition, is called upon to consider questions, which it cannot decline, as they are presented by its own nature, but which it cannot answer, as they transcend every faculty of the mind.

(Kant, Preface to the First Edition of the *Critique of Pure Reason*, 1781)

Contents

Acknowledgements

The author and publishers are grateful to Faber and Faber Ltd, John Calder (Publishers) Ltd and Grove Press Inc. for permission to reprint extracts from the works of Samuel Beckett.

Abbreviations

Beckett's own works, and the three main philosophical works considered, are referred to by the following abbreviations (editions used appear in the Bibliography):

PM	*The Phenomenology of Mind* (Hegel)
BT	*Being and Time* (Heidegger)
BN	*Being and Nothingness* (Sartre)
MPTK	*More Pricks Than Kicks*
M	*Murphy*
W	*Watt*
T	*Trilogy (Molloy, Malone Dies, The Unnamable)*
H	*How It Is*
NK	*No's Knife*
PTD	*Proust and Three Dialogues*
WFG	*Waiting for Godot*
MC	*Mercier et Camier*
E	*Endgame*
PA	*Premier Amour*
LO	*The Lost Ones*
LE	*Lessness*
PL	*Play (including Play, Words and Music and Cascando)*
ATF	*All That Fall*
IM	*Imagination Dead Imagine*
FTEYA	*For To End Yet Again*
C	*Company*
IS	*Ill Seen Ill Said*

1 Introduction

> The easiest thing of all is to pass judgement on what has a solid
> substantial content; it is more difficult to grasp it and most of
> all difficult to do both together and produce the systematic
> exposition of it.
> (Hegel)

Since at least 1960 there has been a great deal of critical attention
paid to Beckett. Besides the many articles, reviews, chapters and
paragraphs, by 1980 more than sixty books had been published
devoted exclusively to him. A lot of this critical work has been of the
highest standard and certainly it is hard to imagine how a serious
appreciation of Beckett would be able to develop without some of it.
But it is my opinion that at the heart of his writing there is an inescapable mass of involvement with the fundamental issues of
existence that has yet to be dealt with adequately. In this study I
intend to attack this central core of Beckett's work by associating it
with the discipline which, by definition, operates in the same area –
philosophy. This will demonstrate one way of reading Beckett and
may at the same time show how far philosophical analogy can illuminate a writer.

Critics who have entered this arena have tended to limit themselves to merely partial or suggestive accounts. Thus Alvarez in his
short study, *Beckett* (Fontana, 1973), has a striking conclusion (in
the original edition) yoking together *Breath* and a passage from
Kierkegaard, but this promising road is taken no further. Cormier
and Pallister's *Waiting for Death* (University of Alabama Press,
1979) claims to be a study of 'The Philosophical Significance' of
Godot but is distinctly unphilosophical: 'Beckett appears to be
saying...that man paradoxically seeks his identity and seeks to
escape his identity in society' we read (p. 45), but, in spite of
Heidegger's occasional appearance in the book, no mention is made
of the Heideggerian concepts of *Selbstsein* (Being Oneself) or *Das
Man* ('They') which are precisely analogous to this aspect of Beckett.

Some of the more widely-read critics have some very interesting suggestions, however, notably David Hesla in *The Shape of Chaos* (University of Minnesota Press, 1971) and Michael Robinson in *The Long Sonata of the Dead* (Hart-Davis, 1969) as we shall see. What seems necessary is for someone to take up the suggestions and see where they get us. Take this from Knowlson and Pilling's *Frescoes of the Skull* (Calder, 1979) for instance:

> Behind the essentially private struggle between Pim and Bom [in *How It Is*] lurks the essentially public issue of dominance and subordination, free will and determinism. (p. 74)

For Knowlson and Pilling's purposes this is adequate, but do not these philosophical hints, leading as they do directly to Hegel and Sartre among several other possibilities, cry out for further exploration? Another example:

> It is clear that for Krapp the central issue in his life is one of coming to terms with a fundamental dualism. (p. 87–8)

What is this dualism? What solution to it is possible? What is Beckett's solution? Such questions are not entirely unanswerable.[1]

Beckett's own philosophical asides and hints are something like red herrings. Descartes and his followers appear, for example, for the purposes of joke and parody. When one has learnedly pointed out what they are doing in *Murphy* and *Watt*, or what Democritus is doing in *Malone Dies*, one has merely done dully for the worse-educated what Beckett has already done well for the better-educated, which is to point out that certain real, painful issues are not much helped by a Rationalist-Idealist dialogue or by classical epistemology. But if Beckett laughs at and plays with the answers of traditional philosophy it can only be because he is concerned with the same questions. In spite of all protestations to the contrary, Beckett is working the same ground as the philosophers.

I think that we must recognize the red herrings for what they are and try to give a philosophical interpretation of Beckett without their dubious assistance.[2] This is not entirely possible, of course, and it would be unproductive deliberately to exclude, say, Zeno just because he is mentioned by Beckett. My main aim is to try to lighten the Beckettian gloom with those philosophical lamps that seem to work best. This has led me to choose one major work from each of

Heidegger and Sartre and to experiment with a less obvious source of illumination – Hegel's *Phenomenology of Mind*.

These three by no means exhaust the possible range of useful philosophical analogues for Beckett. No philosopher, anyway, is *sui generis*, and I think that every single major western philosopher has *some* light to shed both on every other philosopher and, perhaps, on Beckett. But Heidegger, Sartre and Hegel are closely related to one another and offer a wide range of the concepts that apply sub-stantially to Beckett. All three take in, develop and sometimes reject the major work of their predecessors; all three assume, for instance, the decisiveness of Descartes' work and Kant's. This puts them into a position rather like Beckett's own – he, too, has worked through philosophy up to and including the eighteenth century, but he does not refer in his published work to any philosopher later than Berkeley. It is almost as if there are two parallel developments here – the development of philosophy since 1800 on the one hand and the development of Beckett's mind since he gave up reading phil-osophers on the other.

Other modern philosophers, according to this parallel, might also have claims to be included here. A parallel between Beckett and the phenomenology of Merleau-Ponty would be valuable and that between Language Philosophy and Beckett has been suggested by several critics, for example in the proposal by Jacqueline Hoefer that *Watt* may owe something to Wittgenstein (in her essay collected in Martin Esslin's volume in the *Twentieth Century Views* series). This could be the subject of a whole book by itself, but it is not broached here. My inclination is not to miss so instructive a parallel as the *Tractatus* offers, but a thorough and detailed examination of certain philosophical works, and therefore the exclusion of everyone else, is just what no Beckett critic has yet undertaken and just what needs attempting.[3]

Above all, the three philosophers chosen display strikingly Beckettian insights. Notably, they try to escape from the *impasse* into which Descartes took philosophy and Beckett took Murphy. Descartes' *cogito*, however, is at least an admission that philosophy starts with me. Its results in the following century were, signi-ficantly, the Idealisms of Berkeley, Hume, Kant and Hegel. To paint with a very broad brush for a moment, we can say that if Greek (and Medieval) philosophy presents a picture of the *external* universe and is concerned, typically, with the cosmos, with man's relation to the cosmos and with logical categories, Descartes' decisively reverses this concern. Since the seventeenth century it has not been possible to ignore the subjective, and in general philosophy has not again tried to discuss the world without discussing the perceivers of it *as perceivers*. It is no coincidence that philosophy is no longer the 'Queen of the Sciences', that philosophers are no longer scientists. Indeed, there is a sense in which philosophy has been excluded from *all* objective disciplines, its provinces having been annexed by cosmology, biology, anthropology, sociology and psychology, that is, by the sciences of the universe, life, man, man in society and man's mind. This is a coin that has a reverse side however; when we turn it over we find that philosophy is more important than ever. No longer dealing with any specific area of knowledge and unable to escape the demands of the *cogito* it has become the moderator of the languages of knowledge and the study of the scientifically indefinable aspects of the world – being and self. It is precisely these aspects with which Beckett is ultimately concerned.

However close the parallels are we must remember that Beckett has disclaimed any philosophical achievement. He said to Tom Driver 'I am not a philosopher. One can only speak of what is in front of him, and that is simply a mess.'[4] In even more uncompromising vein Beckett said to Gabriel d'Aubarède 'I never read philosophers...I never understand anything they write' and in answer to the suggestion that 'the existentialists' problem of being may afford a key to your work' he said 'There's no key or problem. I wouldn't have had any reason to write my novels if I could have expressed their subject in philosophic terms.'[5] Some critics, however, although none has attempted a systematic comparison, have found modern philosophers useful when dealing with Beckett, as we have seen. A glance at David Hesla's bibliography in *The Shape of Chaos* will make the point (p. 245). Or we can quote Pierre Mélèse on the influence of the Existentialists: 'Parler d'influences serait, peut-être, exagéré; d'imprégnation semblerait plus justifié.' (*Beckett*, Paris, 1966, p. 120). Mary O'Hara, in a thesis presented in 1974, is able to say, 'So close is Heidegger's thinking to Beckett's that the latter's work could almost be seen as a literary exploration of Heideggerian metaphysics.' I hope to demonstrate how this 'imprégnation' and 'exploration' works in detail (Chapters 2, 3, and 4) and then use this as a basis for a new reading of Beckett (Chapter 5). The reading offered does not depend on there being any known connexion of influence between the literature and the philosophy in question. Beckett *may* be entirely innocent of Existentialist philosophy (though I would point out the contradiction between Beckett's assertions that he 'never reads' philosophers and that he 'never understands' them.) Instead I would propose that his work, especially as it becomes more remote and opaque, constitutes a series of parables which, as a matter of fact, illustrate some of the deepest, ontological reality described by our three philosophical works.[6] I do not see that Beckett's dismissal of philosophy need deter us unless we think the Intentional Fallacy unfallacious.

The detailed discussions in Chapters 2, 3 and 4 largely refer to what is generally considered the major work of the Beckett canon (the trilogy, *Godot* and some of their contemporaries such as *Texts for Nothing* and *Endgame*) although other work is not ignored. The touchstone for a reading of Beckett, however, must be the later, more difficult work and Chapter 5 tackles some of the 'residua', the short pieces produced since *How It Is* (1961). Those pieces, in particular, stand as literary correlatives of ontological insight.

NOTES AND REFERENCES

1. Other critics who have at least brushed with philosophy in their study of Beckett include Milton Rickels (in his article 'Existential Themes in Beckett's *Unnamable*' in *Criticism*, Spring 1962), Charles Glicksberg in *Modern Literature and the Death of God* (*The Hague*: Nijhoff, 1966), Martin Esslin in John Cruickshank's *The Novelist as Philosopher* (London: Oxford University Press, 1962), Olga Bernal in *Langage et fiction dans le roman de Samuel Beckett* (Paris: Gallimard, 1969) and Edith Kern in *Existential Thought and Fictional Technique* (Yale University Press, 1970). Eric P. Levy's *Beckett and the Voice of Species* (Dublin: Gill and Macmillan, 1980) makes good use of a number of philosophical notions without relating them very closely to their contemporary philosophical employers, thus 'Being' is related to Aristotle rather than Heidegger. Vivian Mercier in *Beckett/Beckett* (New York: Oxford, 1977) starts his chapter 'Artist/Philosopher' with a qualified acceptance of Beckett's anti-philosophical stance but is soon head over ears into philosophy: 'I find two dominant philosophic patterns in *Watt*: one ontological, the other epistemological... the trilogy and *Godot*... attack the problem of being and patrol the frontier between being and non-being with... ferocity...' (pp. 167–9) In the end Mercier proposes a synthesis of the roles of artist and philosopher.

2. Several critics have taken Beckett's own philosophical references (which are limited to philosophers of the eighteenth century and earlier) about as far as they can usefully go. Hugh Kenner's *Samuel Beckett: A Critical Study* (London: Calder, 1962; first published 1961) containing the delightful essay on the 'Cartesian Centaur' is an example; John Fletcher's *Samuel Beckett's Art* (London: Chatto and Windus, 1967) has a definitive chapter on 'Beckett and the Philosophers' which considers 'the philosophers who have influenced him in

chronological order, from the Presocratics to Leibniz and Hume' (p. 122). This excellent work, relying as it does only on the philosophers referred to by Beckett, has its limitations of course. It is taken a step further by, for instance, Ruby Cohn in her article 'Philosophical Fragments in the Work of Samuel Beckett' (in *Criticism*, Winter 1964) which adds Logical Positivism and Existentialism, in three pages, to Fletcher's account. More recent critics have had less to say about this topic, though see Michael Mooney's essay, 'Molloy, part 1: Beckett's *Discourse on Method*' in the *Journal of Beckett Studies*, no.3, Summer 1978.

3. It has been suggested to me that Wittgenstein might be more important for Beckett, on the question of ultimate meaning, than Heidegger. This could well be true in some points of exact correspondence, but the *general* Beckettian picture seems more Heideggerian and so it is in that direction that I point Beckett's parables. There is an element of experiment in this.

4. 'Beckett by the Madeleine', *Columbia Forum*, Summer 1961, p. 23.

5. Gabriel D'Aubarède, 'En attendant...Beckett', *Nouvelles Littéraires*, 16 February 1961, trans. C. Waters in *Trace*, no.42, Summer 1961.

6. The word 'parable' has been used before in Beckett criticism, particularly of his plays. E.g. Günther Anders' essay on Godot, 'Being Without Time', reprinted in the *Twentieth Century Views* volume on Beckett, ed. Martin Esslin (New Jersey: Prentice Hall, 1965), pp. 140–51 opens with the sentence 'All commentators are agreed on this: that it is a parable'.

2 Heidegger's *Being and Time* and Beckett

Is it true that Beckett's work 'could almost be seen as a literary exploration of Heideggerian metaphysics'?[1] What sort of a thing would 'exploration' be here? Is it formally possible for Beckett to be doing what this quotation suggests?

This Chapter will be devoted to an analysis of a series of Heidegger's concepts in *Being and Time* and an attempt to link them with similar points in Beckett. For the moment the important thing is to see if Beckett and Heidegger survive in the same world. I would claim that they do, and that they are linked by a common ontology. Beckett, and the earlier Heidegger, are suspicious of metaphysics but their interest in ontology seems to be indentical, or, rather, like two sides of the same coin. Molloy, for instance, discussing the subjects he has studied, comes out with a phrase that is pure Heidegger: 'my knowledge of men was scant and the meaning of being beyond me' (T.39). The expression 'the meaning of being' is Heidegger's own property; it is not an expression that is used in English, where we would use 'the meaning of existence', or of 'life', instead. But it has its own resonance for any reader of Heidegger. *Being and Time* has a short Foreword that haunts the rest of the work with its profundity and directness. It opens with a quotation from Plato to the effect that, in the *Sophist*, he has become perplexed by the expression 'being' and Heidegger continues:

> Do we in our time have an answer to the question of what we really mean by the word 'being'? Not at all. So it is fitting that we should raise anew *the question of the meaning of Being*. (BT.19) (Heidegger's emphasis)

The words employed in the German for 'meaning' and 'Being' ('*Sinn*' and '*Sein*') are only susceptible of this translation into English in this context. '*Sinn*' could be translated as 'sense', but not naturally here.

In the French version of *Molloy* the passage quoted above appears thus:

> Mais je n'ai jamais eu à ce propos que des idées fort confuses, connaissant mal les hommes et ne sachant pas très bien ce que cela veut dire, être. (*Molloy*, Paris: Eds. de Minuit, 1951, p. 58)

This means that Beckett, in turning the above into English, deliberately chose to compress and strengthen the philosophical connotations of his sentence. What is more, we have here a reflection of Heidegger's linking together of man (*Dasein*) and Being (*Sein*). Molloy moves straight from the idea that he is ignorant of man to the idea that he is ignorant of Being, which is a negative version of Heidegger's proposal that he must interrogate *Dasein* to reach *Sein*.

Being and Time appeared in Husserl's *Jahrbuch für Phänomenologie und phänomenologische Forschung* in 1927 with the subtitle 'First Half'. This 'first half' is in fact only the first two parts of the first half of the treatise: the third part of the first half (to be entitled 'Time and Being') and the whole of the second half have never appeared. The second half was to work on time and ontology through the media of Kant, Descartes and Aristotle.

The two parts of the work that did appear deal respectively with the Being of a special sort of entity, '*Dasein*', (roughly 'man') and with Temporality. So, in a sense, even without the section on 'Time and Being' we do have a treatise on 'Being and Time'. But the being in question is never 'Being in general' except by implication. For the most part Heidegger sticks closely to his programme and deals with the Being of Dasein. In other words, just as Beckett avoids metaphysics Heidegger never gets to them.[2] They are both 'stuck', for reasons that may not in the end be so different, 'merely' with people and worlds.

It is inevitable that this will be construed with the assistance of a spatial metaphor. The reader will now see Heidegger and Beckett as earthbound while above them and below them the heights and depths of Being go unplumbed. It is worth remembering however that *all* metaphysical and ontological language is metaphorical and, to that extent, 'not true'. We try to push this fact away from us by employing words such as 'ultimacy' and 'primordiality' but these are every bit as metaphorical as conceptions of 'God up there' or of 'profundity' or of 'the abyss'. To talk of the 'ultimacy' of a question cannot literally mean that it is the last question beyond which there can be no others; after any answer man can ask 'why?' When Heidegger talks of the 'primordiality' of Being he cannot literally mean that Being is the first number in a series.

Returning to our original point we now find that we must rephrase the question thus: Is it true that Beckett tests by literary exemplification the philosophical theses Heidegger proposes about people and worlds? Answering this will involve selecting the main theses of *Being and Time* and seeing if they appear in Beckett. In one way I have already started this process by adopting, without a by-your-leave, the expression 'People and worlds'. This does not appear in Heidegger but is influenced by his definition of 'world' as something only available to each of us personally: it is intended to delimit the non-metaphysical area of analysis.

Now, we have said that all metaphysical and ontological language is necessarily metaphorical, and indeed as we start to consider the language Heidegger uses in just this matter of 'people and worlds' we find that it too is stiff with metaphor. One of our comparisons, for instance, is going to be between Beckettian man and Heidegger's concept of '*Geworfenheit*', 'Thrownness'. There is no question but that this is a metaphor: Heidegger does not intend us to conceive of man as 'thrown' into Being literally. And when the actor in *Act Without Words* is literally flung onto the stage we automatically grope for the meaning of that flinging in just the same way as we try to seize the philosopher's concept. In other words, what we may find is that the philosopher does not necessarily only deal in literal truth and the novelist only in 'poetic' truth. They overlap.

This proposal (that philosophy can work, must at times work, by literary means) would not seem at all strange to Heidegger. Increasingly he has turned to poetry to assist him in his uncovering of Being. From the verse fragments of the Presocratics he has moved to the enigmatic beauty of Hölderlin's poetry without any sense of a discontinuity in his work. Indeed he has constantly put philosophy and poetry into the same category as the supreme mental achievements. We should thus be encouraged in our attempt to associate Heidegger's philosophy with Beckett's desperate poetry.[3]

*　　　*　　　*

DASEIN 'BEING-THERE'

Throughout *Being and Time* Heidegger uses the word *Dasein* to denominate entities that 'are there', as the etymology of *Dasein* indicates. For our purposes it is sufficient to equate this term with 'man', but Heidegger's decision to use it instead of 'man' reveals his first category: man 'is there' in a way that other things are not.

Being and Time raises 'the question of the meaning of Being' (BT,1) and it does so by making 'an entity – the inquirer – transparent in his own Being'. (BT,27) 'This entity which each of us is himself and which includes inquiring as one of the possibilities of its Being, we shall denote by the term "*Dasein*"'. (BT,27)

So the analysis of *Dasein* (which I shall treat henceforth as an English word) will lead to any possible answers about the meaning of Being in general. And Dasein is man, but man with a special emphasis, man as the entity that 'is there'. Not only that, man is also the entity that 'comports itself' towards the question of Being: Dasein is the questioner as well as the questioned – Dasein is the entity for which Being is an 'issue' and 'understanding of Being is itself a definite characteristic of Dasein's Being'. (BT,32)

Thus in fact three categories emerge from Heidegger's opening remarks: Being, Being-There (Dasein) and the 'understanding' with which Dasein already comports itself towards Being. The 'understanding' is here apparent as an 'inquiry'.

Does this have anything to do with Beckett? For Robbe-Grillet it is a way into Beckett's theatre. His 'Samuel Beckett ou la présence sur la scène' opens

> La condition de l'homme, dit Heidegger, c'est d'être là. Probablement est-ce le théâtre plus que tout autre mode de représentation du réel, qui reproduit le plus naturellement cette situation. Le personage du théâtre est en scène, c'est sa première qualité: il est là. (*Pour un nouveau roman*, Paris: Les Editions de Minuit, 1963, p. 95)

This quality of the theatre, Robbe-Grillet argues, is particularly important for Beckett. Characters in Ibsen or Shaw 'are there', of course, but they are principally vehicles – they are going somewhere, doing something – only later can we think 'he's *there*'. But Didi and Gogo in *Godot* are not going anywhere and not doing anything, they are just 'there' with a vengeance. And this quality, far from removing the tramps from our comprehension, in fact digs deeper than the purposeful qualities of traditional characters and brings us closer to human reality. Robbe-Grillet, talking of going to a Beckett play, presumably having read the novels, says 'on allait enfin voir l'homme de Beckett, on allait voir l'Homme'. (ibid., p. 95) Watching the tramps we are watching Beckettian man and seeing Man because we are having stressed for us his quality of Being-There. We are watching Dasein.[4]

This might well appear to be a special case that can be made only for Beckett's *theatre*. But the characters of the novels share this kind of contingent Being-Thereness, this 'presence'. For one thing the narrators, in the Trilogy and *How It Is* at least, keep a bizarre hold on the present (and the common etymology of 'present' and 'presence' is no accident), so that although the Unnamable is reluctant to open his wordy-gurdy with the word 'I' (= 'Present!') as Molloy and Malone did before him, he does start with three questions about the present, 'Where now? Who now? When now?' The usual emphasis here is on the interrogative half of these phrases, but the repeated 'now' is also revealing.[5]

Molloy is 'there' in his mother's bed. Malone is in more or less the same position and the Unnamable is positioned or stationed or deposited in a similar *stasis* somewhere where he can observe. It is interesting that in his early description of his place he says 'Malone is there' instead of the more natural 'Malone is here'. (T,294) But that is marginal compared to the point that underlies Beckett's choice of position for his narrators. In bed one is most nearly 'just there'. It is the position in which one's purposes and meanings are minimized. Belacqua in *More Pricks Than Kicks* moves a lot, even makes a sort of fetish of his journeyings (cf. MPTK, 39–40) although he is 'bogged in indolence' like Murphy. In spite of which Murphy also gets about, and Watt is quite a mover. But Beckett is clearly very concerned to get people to stay still. He blinds and maims them, puts them in sand, jars, wheelchairs, dustbins and mud. Progressively his characters, talking or silent, grind to a halt. Putting his narrators in bed or similar is clearly a step in the right direction. And is all this not an attempt to get rid of the spurious sense of purpose engendered by motion? To get the 'just-thereness' of a character on to paper or the stage?

Besides Being-There Heidegger's first three categories include 'Being' and 'Inquiry', the latter being a way in which Dasein comports itself towards the former.

It is rather vague to claim that Beckett is concerned with Being. In the case of both Heidegger and Beckett this ultimate concern is left to emerge by itself from an analysis of man and his world. In

Heidegger, however, Being is the stated, specific goal whereas Beckett of course has none. Since this *is* the ultimate concern, on the other hand, perhaps we too should leave it to emerge naturally and move on directly to Inquiry.

It may have been noticed that in what was said above Inquiry had two sorts of status. It had the ontological status of man's Being-towards-Being and it also had the ontical status of Heidegger's own proposal in *Being and Time*, viz. that he will inquire into Being via the Being of Dasein.

Both these meanings of Inquiry apply to Beckett. He certainly gives his characters the ontological characteristics of inquiring. Indeed it is what they do best and most often. That their inquiry is directed towards their own Being is also clear, and it is reasonable to suppose that anything they learn about their own Being implies something about Being in general. There is an element of the compulsory (as well as the compulsive) in the inquiries of the people in the novels. I would propose that this is an ontological compulsion not a moral or psychological one. 'You must go on' says the Unnamable, almost at his last gasp, and the raging question 'Why?' seems not to be adequately answered by the proposal of a moral imperative, a God who tells us to go on, nor by the proposal that we are compelled to go on by some neurosis. On the other hand an ontological answer seems a lot more satisfactory. Inquiry is the way of Being of Dasein. Inescapably we are that sort of entity that 'is there' and one of our first and inevitable modes of being there is to inquire into this matter of being there, and hence of Being.

On the ontical level too Beckett parallels Heidegger. It is often useful to see Beckett's *oeuvre* as a 'quest' or an 'exploration'.[6] Heidegger analyses Dasein as the first step along the 'trail of Being'. Beckett pushes and pushes his people into tighter and tighter corners in his search for a self that will be more than a self: clearly he does not just want to 'find himself' in the romantic cliché – he wants to find 'the Self', that is, something that will render 'the mess' intelligible, something really quite like Being, as we shall see.

*   *   *

PHENOMENOLOGY

It is worth making the point that Heidegger employs a phenomenological method throughout *Being and Time*. The aim of phenomenology is to uncover, disclose and make clear phenomena in their Being. The intention is to uncover the obvious and to disclose things in their transparency. This in itself brings Heidegger closer to a literary cast of thought, particularly to the aims and methods of the *Nouveau Roman*. It also means that he limits his horizons, eschews metaphysics and is involved in elucidating things 'as they are' rather than in placing them in positions within schemes. 'Ultimate' questions are in a sense bypassed, there is no attempt in Heidegger to construct a 'chain' of priorities that will lead up to an absolute, as in Plato or Hegel. This is one of the ways in which Phenomeno-logical–Existentialist philosophy differs most radically from earlier philosophy.

Beckett, of course, issues strong *caveats* against traditional metaphysical speculation. If his work is taken as a whole we can see that the heavily ironic treatment of philosophy in the early novels gives way to a desperation in the later work that seems rather beyond being helped by metaphysics or even logic. The point is that both Beckett and Heidegger perceive the futility of even asking many of the traditional philosophical questions. The following paraphrase of one of Heidegger's points in *Vom Wesen der Wahrheit*, made by Arne Naess, could apply equally well to the novelist or the phil-osopher:

> Man misunderstands himself when he *seeks* the light, seeks 'the meaning of his existence', or 'a goal' which will be illuminated for him. Beyond the light-giving function which man, as Dasein, himself is, there is no further source of illumination. (Arne Naess, *Four Modern Philosophers*, trans A. Hannay, University of Chicago Press, 1968, p. 239)

*   *   *

EXISTENZ 'EXISTENCE' *FAKTIZITÄT* 'FACTICITY'

Heidegger offers us, then, a phenomenological analysis of man as Dasein, that entity which already inquires into, and has some understanding of, the meaning of Being.

Dasein exists. It is unfortunate that in English we sometimes use 'exists' to mean 'merely exists' as in the expression 'He's not *living*, he's merely existing' which could be used, for instance, of someone with severe brain-damage which has wiped out all conscious activity.

In Existentialist terminology 'to exist' means precisely the opposite.

Heidegger bases his special usage of *Existenz* on the etymology of the word. Just as he breaks down the common German word *Dasein* into its component parts to emphasize the special sort of Being that man has, so he breaks *Existenz* down into the component parts of its Latin root. *Ex-sistere*, he suggests, means 'to stand out from'. Thus the first feature of Dasein's existence is that it 'stands out' from something. From what? The answer will appear more precisely when we have examined the concept of the 'world' in the next section, but for the present we can say that man 'stands out' in such a way that he is set over against his world not simply in the subject–object relation that has dominated philosophy at least since Descartes but also in a dynamic relationship that takes into account his past and his future.

Dasein's past is facticity and his future is possibility. Other sorts of entity, stones and animals for instance, have no understanding of the factical situation in which they find themselves and have no possibilities genuinely open before them; this means that they do not have temporality, a stone does not have an authentic past or a possible future But this is anticipating later points. Dasein, then, alone 'exists'. Dasein alone 'comports' itself towards its possibilities and has some sort of understanding of them. Until Dasein has chosen among them it cannot be said to have any 'essence', but it always already has an existence, whence the important thesis, taken up by Sartre as a sort of war-cry, that 'Existence precedes essence'. It is perhaps imperfectly understood that this thesis appears in Heidegger, as for example when he refers to 'the priority of "*existentia*" over "*essentia*"'. (BT,68)[7]

Thus Dasein's existence consists in his choosing of his own possibilities, his choosing of his own essence. 'Man makes himself' in other words. So much for the 'futural' aspect of Dasein's 'standing out', what of the past aspect which we have characterized as facticity? It is not, perhaps, strictly accurate to define facticity as the past in that we largely experience it as a limiting of our freedom to make choices about the future. Facticity is 'the way things are' (*How It Is*?). It is all that cribs, cabins and confines us but, like all such limitations, it is also the condition of the possible. It is a fact that man cannot simply extend his arms and fly; and it is a fact that I cannot afford to hire a helicopter; which means that my possibilities of getting to the top of a building are limited to the stairs or the lift. In a sense this example shows how facticity is in the future – I must

choose between the stairs or the lift by which I *shall* go up to the top
of the building because I *shall* not be able to go up another way. But
it is easier to think of this as belonging to the past: the building and
all the conditions of getting to the top of it are already 'in position'
before I make any choices. My situation is always already factical.

For Heidegger, on the trail of Being, man's Being is the first
target, and he finds in his analysis of *Existenz* that all man's 'ways of
Being' are possibilities perceived in the welter of facticity. He calls
man's 'ways of Being' 'existentials'. Dasein's Being is 'existence',
which is 'potentiality-for-Being' or 'Being-possible'. (BT,183)
Dasein projects itself upon or into its possibilities – this is its
existence.

Man's free choices, of course, are not only limited by facticity (I
cannot choose to be born a Russian if I am born English) they are
also limited by themselves. Man can only choose *one* possibility at a
time and this excludes the other possibilities; I cannot go up to the
top of the building in the lift and by the stairs at the same time.
Using the lift removes the possibility of the stairs as surely as the
shape of my arms removes the possibility of flying up unaided. Of
course, I can use the stairs 'next time', but by 'next time' the world
may so have altered that I *can* fly up unaided or *can* hire a
helicopter.

So, man 'is there', he already has some sort of understanding of
Being, his own way-of-Being is 'existence' which involves an
inevitable appreciation of facticity and a self-directioning towards
his own possibilities.

Beckett's characters may be said generally to 'exist' in the
Heideggerian way. There is, in nearly every work of his, an extreme
illustration of facticity coupled with an exploration of the wild and
fantastic attempts man can resort to in order to project himself into
possibilities. The factical situation is usually illustrated by physical
limitation – amputation, paralysis, blindness. On this level Beckett
is a pessimist if it is optimism to minimize facticity and maximise
possibility in one's account of man. Facticity also appears as the
master-servant relationship (Hamm-Clov, Pozzo-Lucky) in which
both parties are heavily mutually dependent. Projection into possibilities is largely verbal (of course, the actual projection is always a
mental process and, as such, verbal) and takes the form of the story-
telling and fantasizing that makes up so much of the novels and a
good part of the plays. The narrators of the novels are obvious
examples, but Hamm is the most revealing character in this context.

He cannot 'exist' in his physical environment except mentally and so invents an endless 'story', which, although obviously drawn from his past, in fact operates existentially in that he has constantly to choose how and where to take it within the factical limitations of his own memory. Hamm's choices are pointed up by Beckett quite clearly on the many occasions when he stops to comment on his story-telling or to improve a phrase. For example in the following passage he does both of these things:

Hamm: . . .(*Narrative tone.*) Come on now, come on, present your petition and let me resume my labours. (*Pause. Normal tone.*) There's English for you. Ah well. . .(*Narrative tone.*) It was then he took the plunge. It's my little one, he said. Tsstss, a little one, that's bad. My little boy, he said, as if the sex mattered. (E,36)

Even more striking is the way Hamm disregards his own earlier remarks. For instance he asserts that the day in question during the story was a hot day, a cold day, a windy day and a dry day. This sort of choice, like the choice of the words themselves, is the freedom that faces the creative writer. It is the pseudo-choosing of a fantasy world and, although it parallels the choices of 'real' life, it is not really governed by facticity. Thus Beckett, and Hamm, are 'really' plunged in a highly factical world – but when they tell stories they have a kind of mad freedom which automatically means that the stories are simply not 'about' the 'real world' although they are so desperately meant to be. The same applies to the narrators of the novels.

My chief example of facticity and existence in Beckett, however, apart from this general one, is taken from his first, unpublished, unperformed, untranslated play, *Eleuthéria*, written in 1947. I shall not recount the plot of this play (which can be found in Fletcher and Spurling's book *The Plays of Samuel Beckett*). It is enough simply to say that its hero, Victor, is a renegade from society who is trying to drop out of the everyday concerns of his family, friends and fiancée. The most important character in the play besides Victor is a glazier who voices Beckett's wisdom, presumably. This '*Vitrier*' tells Victor to 'define himself': '*Vous définir. . . prenez un peu de contour, pour l'amour de Dieu*' (p. 62 of the typescript) and he explains, '*Vous n'êtes tout simplement rien, mon pauvre ami*'. But this request that Victor should choose an essence and not simply hover in suspended freedom (*eleuthéria*) over his possibilities is precisely what he is trying to avoid. He replies, '*Il est peut-être temps que quelqu'un soit tout simplement rien*'.

Eleuthéria is a play about the tension between individual *Existenz* and the two things which place this in jeopardy; first, facticity (in the shape of Victor's friends and family) and second, choice itself – only by choosing not to choose can one remain free. This tension is also apparent in *More Pricks Than Kicks* and *Murphy*.

*   *   *

IN-DER-WELT-SEIN 'BEING-IN-THE-WORLD'

Dasein 'is there' already, it has some understanding of its Being which reveals to it that it 'exists' in a factical way. In Beckettian terms we can translate this summary of our position so far thus: Beckett's characters 'are there', statically and solidly present, with some understanding of themselves and an inescapable feeling of Being which manifests itself in the almost overwhelming facticity of the situation; but it is only 'almost' overwhelming – they continue to 'exist', to 'stand out from' everything else much though they would like to sink down into the unconsciousness of objects. We can think of Didi and Gogo, just 'there' somewhere, certainly understanding enough to keep them miserable, somehow aware of Being, but hopelessly enmeshed in the toils of facticity represented above all by the curtailment of their freedom occasioned by having to wait for Godot. They 'exist' constantly, projecting themselves into questions about the future, considering the possibilities.

The question now arises, if man is 'there', *where* is he? Where is 'there'? Heidegger's answer is that man is 'in-the-world'. But he uses this in a specialized sense; he does not simply mean that man is in an objective universe in the same way as a chair is in a room. The chair does not 'exist', it is simply 'present-at-hand' ('*Vorhanden*'). As such it is present-at-hand inside another present-at-hand entity, viz. the room. Dasein, however, exists and can truly be said to *be in* its world. (BT,78–80) To make this distinction clear Heidegger uses the example of the chair and the wall. He analyses the statement 'The chair "touches" the wall' as follows:

Taken strictly, 'touching' is never what we are talking about in such cases, not because accurate re-examination will always eventually establish that there is a space between the chair and the wall, but because in principle the chair can never touch the wall, even if the space between them should be equal to zero. If the chair could touch the wall, this would presuppose that the wall is the sort of thing 'for' which a chair would be *encounterable*. (BT,81)

Dasein, however, can 'encounter' walls and chairs, can 'touch' things. Dasein can really 'be' in the world. 'Being-in' is 'the formal existential expression for the Being of Dasein, which has Being-in-the-world as its essential state'. (BT,80)

The table, the chair and the wall, however they are disposed, are 'worldless', whereas Dasein is always in-the-world. Here Heidegger is determined not to be mistaken: he insists that 'Being-in' (and 'the world') is not something that is added to Dasein, not 'a "property" which Dasein sometimes has and sometimes does not have, and *without* which it could *be* just as well as it could with it'. (BT,84) Dasein is already 'in-the-world', the ontological definition of Dasein's Being must include this 'Being-in' as an essential state.

Are Beckett's characters 'in-the-world' in this sense? Do they particularly manifest 'Being-in' as an essential state of their Being?

Certainly Hamm specifically describes his own limited environment as 'the world'. He orders Clov to wheel him round the room/stage of *Endgame* with the phrase 'Right round the world!'. (E,23) There is a strong feeling that Hamm *is* only because he 'is in' this world of his. 'Outside of here it's death!' he proclaims towards the end of the play. (E,45)

And if we take, for instance, Malone's room as being more than literally intended we can read his description of his 'present state' as applying to his 'world' too: 'This room seems to be mine. I can find no other explanation to my being left in it'. (T,183) In fact this is the worst possible explanation of Malone's being in the 'room'; how on earth would *he* be able to possess a room unless this room is his own in an inalienable way, that is, unless it is his world? We shall have more examples to give of 'Being-in-the-world' in Beckett when we discuss *Geworfenheit*, below.

Dasein is already in-the-world. And it is involved in the world (its world) in a manner so intimate that subject–object dualism is rendered irrelevant. Heidegger here provides an answer to Murphy's Cartesian schizophrenia:

When Dasein directs itself towards something and grasps it, it does not somehow first get out of an inner sphere in which it has been proximally encapsulated, but its primary kind of Being is such that it is always 'outside' alongside entities which it encounters and which belong to a world already discovered. (BT,89)

Curiously it is in *Murphy* itself that we find Beckett adopting this at-least-partial solution to the dualism of the 'inner' and the 'outer'. When we first meet Celia's grandfather, Mr Kelly, he is mending the tail of his kite and imagining what it will be like to fly it. 'Already he was in position, straining his eyes for the speck that was he, digging in his heels against the immense pull skyward'. (M,23) Here the kite *is* Mr Kelly in a manner that is unintelligible except along the lines of our Heideggerian epistemology. Mr Kelly 'grasps' the kite 'outside', up there 'alongside' it, not from some 'inner' sanctum. This is clearly not Beckett's last word on this subject and we shall have to look more closely at the whole question of dualism in the two writers in a separate section.

For our present purposes we must develop Heidegger's alternative to dualism, 'Being-in-the-world', to illuminate further the concept of 'the world'.

Things which are not Dasein are not all merely 'present-at-hand'. In fact Dasein's primary way of encountering entities is in their 'readiness-to-hand' (*'Zuhandenheit'*). We do not meet a chair (or a kite) as something 'just lying about', we meet it first as an article of 'equipment' (*'Zeug'*) which is ready-to-hand. We see a chair as something to sit on before we see it as a 'brute' object. In other words 'concern' is closer to us than mere bare perception. (BT,95) Dasein's way of Being towards entities encountered within-the-world is 'praxis', that is, concernful dealing. Even the things of 'nature' are not exempt from this; the tree is 'equipment' for making chairs; the mountain is an obstacle, a likely source of a stream, a place of refuge; the south wind 'means' rain.

All this 'equipment' is inextricably interrelated and the world is the totality of this 'equipment'. Thus 'Being-in-the-world' amounts to absorption in the totality of equipment. (BT,105) This becomes clearer when we consider that all equipment refers back to Dasein. The south wind 'means' rain, which 'means' the growth of crops, which 'means' food, which is for Dasein to eat. Thus my world extends out as far as these 'chains' of reference go. (BT,116)

Does Beckett make the distinction between *'Vorhanden'* and

'*Zuhanden*', between objects which are present-at-hand and those which are ready-to-hand? Perhaps we have here a distinction that will make some sense of that event, 'of great formal brilliance and indeterminable purport', the visit of the Galls to Mr Knott's house in *Watt*. Perhaps it will also shed light on Watt's inability to say, of a pot, 'pot, pot' and be comforted. The Galls come to tune the piano and their visit disturbs Watt. He describes his disturbance thus,

> the scene in the music-room, with the two Galls, ceased very soon to signify for Watt a piano tuned, an obscure family and professional relation, an exchange of judgements more or less intelligible, and so on, if indeed it had ever signified such things, and became a mere example of light commenting bodies, and stillness motion, and silence sound, and comment comment. (W,69–70)

In other words Watt's world has broken down. It is precisely the '*Zuhanden*', equipmental interrelationships that constitute Dasein's world that fall away from Watt's memory of the incident, leaving only his appreciation of the merely '*Vorhanden*' aspects of the incident. 'Meanings' such as judgements and family relations break down until Watt can only perceive his memory of the incident as an abstract design, the meaninglessness, the absurdity, of the merely present-at-hand.

The merely present-at-hand is incapable of being, or having, a world. As Beckett indicates in the *Three Dialogues with Georges Duthuit*:

> All have turned wisely tail, before the ultimate penury, back to the mere misery where destitute virtuous mothers may steal bread for their starving brats. There is more than a difference of degree between being short, short of the world, short of self, and being without these esteemed commodities. (PTD,122)

The 'ultimate penury' is the gazing at the empty and absurd object perceived as 'just lying there'. It is the nausea experienced by Sartre's Roquentin as he gazes at the famous root of the *maronnier*, it is just 'there', meaningless and worldless.

The episode in *Watt* where the hero finds himself unconvinced by using the word 'pot' to refer to a pot (W,78) may also be based on the ready-to-hand/present-at-hand distinction. When an object slips over from one of these categories to the other it becomes uncanny and disturbing. Heidegger talks about 'The helpless way in which we stand before' a piece of broken equipment – the breaking robs the thing of its readiness-to-hand and thrusts it, before our very eyes, into the merely present-at-hand. This is what seems to be happening to Watt's pot, 'It was in vain that it answered, with unexceptionable adequacy, all the purposes, and performed all the offices, of a pot, it was not a pot'. (W,78) Watt's pot, although not broken, has slipped across the divide and is only acting or masquerading as a ready-to-hand pot; but it is not that, it is some other thing, some merely present-at-hand object to which the name 'pot' (which implies its ready-to-hand function) cannot be given. Heidegger returns to this phenomenon later when discussing understanding. 'When we merely stare at something', he says, 'our just-having-it-before us lies before us *as a failure to understand it any more*'. (BT,190) And he comes very close to describing the effect on Watt of both the Galls and the pot when he starts drawing his conclusions about understanding and meaning. '*Only Dasein can be meaningful*', we learn, 'all entities whose kind of Being is of a character other than Dasein's must be conceived as *unmeaning. . . And only that which is unmeaning can be absurd*. The present-at-hand, as Dasein encounters it, can, as it were, assault Dasein's Being' (BT,193, Heidegger's italics). Watt's pot is absurd, and the Galls' visit 'assaults' his Being.

There is a strong identification made in Beckett between the narrator and his space – the latter is quite clearly his Heideggerian 'world'. Malone, for example, thinks that his body *is* the world and that he has swollen to fill the universe (T,235) as indeed he has, or rather, his world and universe have contracted to the limits of his body, or at least of his 'room'. Similarly he points out that, like Miss Carriage in *Murphy* whose personality is extended, via a lead, to her Dachshund, he is extended to his possessions: 'I say my pots, as I say my bed, my window, as I say me'. (T,253) This cuts both ways of course, either Malone's world of objects is himself and he is their 'formative agent' or he is an object not really in possession of himself and thus 'utterly subject' to his factical environment.

The 'space' which Malone, in particular, occupies is Heideggerian space in that it is personalized. Science measures space objectively as the separation of things merely present-at-hand but Dasein primarily occupies space in terms of the connexions of the ready-to-hand. Heidegger gives a striking illustration of what this means when he says that my glasses are 'environmentally more remote' than the picture I look at through them. (BT,141) The picture is 'closer' to me in my world than the glasses, which I do not notice as I look through them. I construct my world out of the ready-to-hand and thus learn about space, I do not 'first' know about space and then set up my world within it. (BT, 136ff.) 'Space is not in the subject, nor is the world in space'. (BT,146) For a subject such as Malone or Watt the problem is precisely this: there is an ultimate disjunction between rational, scientific space (which separates things 'present-at-hand') and 'my' world which is arranged according to the entirely different principles of the 'ready-to-hand'.[8]

REALITAT "REALITY" DUALISM

So Dasein exists in its own world and encounters that world first as 'ready-to-hand'. The concept of Being-in-the-world (the 'essential state of Being' of Dasein) does away with dualism, as we have seen. Being-in-the world is something that Dasein always is already, it is its Being. This is an idea that Heidegger may have found in Husserl for whom consciousness is a 'noetico-noematic' correlation. That is to say that the 'noema' (the object perceived) is part of the nature of the 'noesis' (the perception). The non-mental object is as much a condition of consciousness as the mental subject. Thus for Husserl and Heidegger consciousness is no longer interior and self-sufficient.[9] This is the burden of our argument, above, *in re* Mr Kelly's kite.

Heidegger claims that the apparent insolubility of the problem of dualism is based on a misleading *'Fragestellung'* (posing of the question). If we 'put together' a present-at-hand Subject and a present-at-hand Object and then ask how they can be bound together in consciouness we naturally prevent any possible answer. 'Not only do we lack the "cement"; even the "schema" in accordance with which this joining-together is to be accomplished, has been split asunder . . . What is decisive for ontology is to prevent the splitting of the phenomenon'. (BT,170) Not surprisingly a substantial section of *Being and Time* is devoted to a comparison between Existentialist and Cartesian ontology (sections 19, 20 and 21).

The question now is whether Heidegger has not, in closing the door on dualism, opened it on the even more pernicious (and highly Beckettian) realm of subjectivism. If Dasein's world is always its 'own' world, if a 'world' is something that is always 'mine', what price a common world in which we all exist? No amount of analysis of merely present-at-hand objects 'within-the-world' will afford us a way out of this dilemma:

> Neither the ontical depiction of entities within-the-world nor the ontological Interpretation of their Being is such as to reach the phenomenon of the 'world'. In both of these ways of access to 'Objective Being', the 'world' has already been 'presupposed'. (BT,92)

A scientific analysis of objects within-the-world will not allow us to understand 'worldhood'. Science likes to proceed from the certainty of the inert present-at-hand to the ready-to-hand 'uses' to which it can be put. But Heidegger insists that Dasein does the opposite of this, 'readiness', for him, is not merely a sort of 'subjective colouring' added to presence. On the contrary, readiness precedes presence. Does this mean that we can have no objective standards and that 'the world' is mine to do as I like with?

Heidegger is well aware of this difficulty and he goes out of his way to explain himself by adopting the traditional ontological category 'Reality' and discussing it in the light of his own ontology. In doing so he is able both to re-assert his rejection of subject–object dualism and to refute charges of subjectivism. This discussion (section 43 of *Being and Time*) can be put alongside Beckett's treatment of the same problem. In the case of Beckett we shall have to look at *Murphy*, especially the famous Chapter 6 of that novel and the Mr Endon episode, and then at his later developments in this area.

In traditional ontology, according to Heidegger, 'Being' is always conceived in terms of the present-at-hand. The present-at-hand thus gains the name 'Reality' because it is, indeed, made up of *res*, Things. What, above all, characterizes Things is their substantiality, so the Real is the substantial, and Being is treated as though substantiality were its basic characteristic. To overcome this Heidegger enters into three arguments.

First, can the 'Real' world, the 'external world', supposedly 'outside' our consciousness be 'proved'? This is the classic Cartesian question and it is the point beyond which Murphy does not try to get when he pictures his mind, as described in Chapter 6.

In so far as Reality has the character of something independent and 'in itself', the question of the meaning of 'Reality' becomes

> linked with that of whether the Real can be independent 'of consciousness' or whether there can be a transcendence of consciousness into the 'sphere' of the Real. (BT,246)

> Thus Murphy felt himself split in two, a body and a mind. They had intercourse apparently, otherwise he could not have known that they had anything in common. But he felt his mind to be bodytight and did not understand through what channel the intercourse was effected nor how the two experiences came to overlap. (M,77)

For Murphy even his body is part of Reality and he has no notion how it is connected with his consciousness. He even proposes the Cartesian solution of some supreme third party, beyond body and mind, who holds them together.

Kant has a solution that purports to bind together body and mind, Reality and consciousness. He observes that Time, as consciousness of change, is 'in me' and that for me to be conscious of change there must be something 'outside me' that is permanent. The trouble with this argument, in Heidegger's view, is that it merely yokes together two present-at-hand entities (consciousness and the Real) in the same way as Descartes' argument, and that this is not enough. 'The Being-present-at-hand-together of the physical and the psychical is completely different ontically and ontologically from the phenomenon of Being-in-the-world'. (BT,248) This is precisely where Murphy, (not Murphy's creator) has gone wrong. 'There was the mental fact and the physical fact, equally real if not equally pleasant'. (M,76) Murphy cannot see how the twain can meet any more than Heidegger can see how Kant can make them meet. This is exactly the point brought up in our discussion of Being-in-the-world: two merely present-at-hand entities, such as a chair and a wall, cannot 'touch', cannot 'meet', cannot 'encounter' or be encountered by each other. Unless we grant Dasein a kind of Being (Being-in-the-world) that is different from the Being of the present-at-hand we inevitably end up in Murphy's obviously false position.

Let me repeat that this is not the position of Murphy's creator. Beckett is looking for a way out of dualism, too, and our position is now this: both Heidegger and Beckett establish the inadequacy of the premises from which Descartes, Kant and traditional ontology start; Heidegger offers an alternative; does Beckett? Heidegger's alternative is that:

The Real is essentially accessible only as entities within-the-world. All access to such entities is founded ontologically upon the basic state of Dasein, Being-in-the-world . . . Being already in a world — as Being alongside entities within-the-world. (BT,246)

Beckett is at least aware of a possible alternative to dualism in his essay on Proust. He points out that the Proustian moment of vision, when the involuntary memory and the perception of the present come together and thereby bring us into contact with our lost selves, overcomes dualism. The memory is Ideal and imaginative while the present situation that stirs it up is Real and empirical. The double-act involved in this moment of truth is 'at once an evocation and a direct perception, real without being merely actual, ideal without being merely abstract, the ideal real'. (PTD,75) 'The ideal real' has certainly beaten dualism. But this has not got very much to do with Heidegger's solution. Heidegger dismisses dualism as a false question in a way that is a lot more radical than this example from *Proust*. Does Beckett get beyond it?

Readers of the trilogy will notice that the dualism *motif*, so strong in *Murphy*, has almost entirely disappeared in *Molloy*. Indeed it is not at all prominent even in *Watt*. The impression given is that other, more urgent considerations have intervened and take up the narrators' energy. True, in *Watt* there is the debated question of the significance of the compounds fenced-off in the asylum where Watt meets Sam. If we take these compounds to be symbolic of the limitations of perception then they show us Beckett still aware of the 'outer' and the 'inner' (the 'big world' and the 'little world' of *Murphy*) but he now seems to be accepting the possibility of a passage from one to the other. Watt and Sam can get through the holes in their respective fences in a way that seems to mark an advance over Murphy's total inability to communicate with Mr Endon.

But by the time of the trilogy such problems have been superseded by considerations of a more fundamental sort. For instance, who is 'narrating' whom? Who determines how much communication there can be between people? Is the entire business a fiction of Moran's, of Malone's, of Beckett's? Certainly the last of course. There is a sort of hankering after the old Murphyesque obsession in places after *Murphy*, but it appears either less painfully or just differently. In *Godot* Estragon asks Vladimir, 'We always find something, eh Didi, to give us the impression we exist?' (WFG,69) which is something of a joke compared to the more violent and serious issues in the play. It is only too painfully obvious that the tramps exist: they suffer, therefore they are. In *Play* the spotlight commands each head to speak of its own experiences, isolated from the others, but this is not an ontological isolation so much as a psychological and emotional one. In *How It Is* there is the 'public' world of the meetings with the other figures that crawl through the mud and the 'private' world of memories about life 'up there' in the light. This is perhaps the definition of how dualism appears in later Beckett. The Real appears as a painful if ambiguous Here and Now. The Ideal appears as memory and fantasy. But we can never be sure which bits of the Real are not in fact memories or fantasies more or less thoroughly disguised. As a result, particularly in *How It Is* and *The Unnamable*, the Real and the Ideal merge as they do in the Proust essay, outer and inner are one and Beckett has achieved, *ipso facto*, the integration and homogeneity of Heidegger's Being-in-the-world.

Throughout Beckett's work after *Watt* his characters are plunged in their worlds irrevocably and their worlds are indistinguishably real-and-ideal; their mental life, far from being cut off in some way from their physical existence, is so intimately bound up with it that we could claim that the two are one. In *Endgame*, for instance, Hamm's world is very definitely Hamm's complete world and questions as to its status according to the Dualist criteria seem irrelevant. When Clov reports on the outside world he may or may not be imagining it: when the reports reach Hamm he is obliged to imagine their details (the greyness of the prospect for example) because he is blind, but the passage of information via Clov's verbal (and therefore mental) descriptions to Hamm's imagination does not in itself affect the real or imaginary status of that information. The prospect may well not be gray but the play does not permit us to know this: as far as the play is concerned the imaginary is the real, but it may be real as well. *Endgame*, indeed, can be read as an extended metaphor about perception but if it is so read it must be admitted that the question of dualism is simply *not posed* and this not-posing is what Heidegger wants us to do with this question.

The question of whether the 'external' world can be proved is the first of three headings under which Heidegger chooses to attack the errors of traditional ontology. The other headings are 'Reality as an ontological problem' and 'Reality and Care'. The second of these we cannot fruitfully discuss until we have met the concept of 'Care' in the next section (below). The first (discussed in BT, pp. 252–5, i.e.

also in the section nominally about 'Care') sets about trying to use the illegitimately-employed concept of Reality properly. Heidegger borrows Dilthey's idea of Reality as fundamentally being 'resistance' but establishes that 'The experiencing of resistance – that is, the discovery of what is resistant to one's endeavours – is possible ontologically only by reason of the disclosedness of the world'. (BT,253) Here Heidegger is using 'disclosedness' in a special sense that ties in with all his other usages. Dasein is the entity that 'discloses' the world by existing (i.e. 'Standing-out' from it) and by 'behaving' towards it and understanding it to some extent. The condition for standing-out, disclosing and so on is obviously that the world 'already' exists. So resistance can only be experienced because Dasein is already 'there', disclosing the world and 'endeavouring' to do things in it. So Reality is not a primordial entity that needs to be proved 'first'. In so far as it can be, it is.

This second phase of Heidegger's attack on traditional ontology has its parallel in Beckett. In the trilogy, in *How It Is*, and in many of the texts, there are constant references to a past life, to an area, a world already 'given', with an accompanying impression that the narrator and his creations are churning about memories of this given past life. It is all they have in their minds, all they can pass the time with, it is irredeemable. 'Yesterday is not a milestone that has been passed, but a daystone on the beaten track of the years, and irremediably part of us, within us, heavy and dangerous'. (PTD,13) None of the characters appears at anything like a beginning; they are already *'en situation'*. The likes of Malone can say, 'The search for myself is ended. I am buried in the world'. (T,199)

This leaves us with one unresolved question. We asked earlier whether Heidegger, having avoided dualism, does not fall into subjectivism. The answer to this will have to appear in the course of our analysis of Heidegger's concept of Being-with-others. Meanwhile we must put his concept of 'Care' in its place.

*   *   *

SORGE 'CARE'

Early in *Being and Time* Heidegger explains that the kind of Being that Dasein has when we consider it as Being-in-the-world is 'concern' ('Besorgen'). Our way of Being-in is to have 'concern', which is thus a definitive term for all our activities with the world conceived as the ready-to-hand. For example, 'Producing something, attending to something and looking after it, making use of something' and so on. (BT,83) And the Being of Being-in-the-world is 'concern' because 'the Being of Dasein itself is . . . *care*' ('*Sorge*'). (BT,83–4) This 'has nothing to do with "tribulation", "melancholy" or the "cares of life". . . These – like their opposites, "gaiety" and "freedom from care" – are ontically possible only because Dasein, when understood *ontologically*, is care'. (BT,84)

Thus, Dasein is 'in-the-world' in a concernful way because it is itself care. Heidegger devotes an entire chapter (Book 1, Chapter 6) to the elucidation of this concept. In this chapter he works round and with the idea of care in a way that takes in the concept of Angst and has reference to several other ideas which we have not yet dealt with. For our present purpose it is enough simply to point out how care itself is defined. Heidegger recapitulates the points that we have so far covered. Thus, Dasein 'exists' and understands its existence; understanding is 'self-projective Being towards its ownmost potentiality for Being'. (BT,236) This means, as we saw in our discussion of '*Existenz*' above, that Dasein is 'ahead-of-itself' or, more fully, 'ahead-of-itself-in-already-being-in-a-world'. This does not mean that Dasein is busy out there 'welding together' the objects that are present-at-hand into a world. No, Dasein's 'ahead-of-itself-in-Being-already-in . . . , is primordially a whole'. (BT,236) In other words Dasein, its existentiality and its facticity are equally primordial. Naturally this totality that Dasein is includes its 'concern' with the world and its 'Being-alongside' and using of the ready-to-hand. Heidegger considers that this description of Dasein's Being is in fact what the word 'care' means.

This may not be immediately perspicuous and the fault here may be partly Heidegger's. He allows the term 'care' to be used in a way that at times seems to rely on his own special definitions and at times seems simply to require the conventional colloquial interpretation. This being the case I think an attempt at clarification is in order.

Care is what men have but tables do not. If you burn your table, or chop it up, or sing to it, it cannot 'care'. Burning, chopping up or singing to a man (an entity with the character of Dasein) must result in some reaction; even if it is the negative one 'I don't care' this is clearly ontologically different from the table's 'not caring'. In a sense Heidegger is looking for the most fundamental difference between Dasein and 'Reality' and he is using Socratic–Aristotelian methods, albeit disguised. Care is the 'basic' difference between men and other things. Because man cares he is in a world. That is to say, the table is worldless, meaningless until we see it as part of our world. Tables do not have worlds of their own; it is because of us that they are revealed as tables. Because man cares he exists. That is to say, because I 'care' I can project myself into my possibilities. Tables have no possibilities, no future, no existence. And because man cares there is facticity. That is to say, my world and my existence inevitably already include the factical, and the factical only *is* factical because I can care about it. Care, in other words, is the basic condition for there being such a thing as Dasein existing in a factical world.

Much later in *Being and Time* we learn that 'the care-structure includes the phenomenon of Selfhood'. (BT,370) But we can leave this point to our discussion of the Self, below, and turn now to consider whether Beckett employs anything like 'care' in his work.

In one way, of course, Beckett must be working within the framework of something like care. If Heidegger's analysis is correct, and it is very hard to quarrel with a definition of man as the 'caring' entity, then all literature, in so far as it is concerned with Dasein, is concerned with 'care', and Beckett is no exception to this. So our inquiry boils down to this, we must ask whether Beckett takes any special trouble to emphasise aspects of existence that reveal 'care', perhaps in view of the fact that such a concept is so fundamental as to be easily overlooked.

One of Beckett's most succint and often-quoted dicta on the difficult art of writing appears in the *Three Dialogues with Georges Duthuit*. When asked what alternative he offers to the 'plane of the feasible' that he has rejected, Beckett replies that he prefers

> The expression that there is nothing to express, nothing with which to express, nothing from which to express, no power to express, no desire to express, together with the obligation to express. (PTD,103)

Perhaps the most opaque of the clauses in this quotation is the last. Why is there an obligation to express? And why does Beckett keep returning to this point throughout his later work? To give only two examples, there is Molloy's

Not to want to say, not to know what you want to say, not to be able to say what you think you want to say, and never to stop saying. (T,28)

Here it is clear that Molloy is somehow driven on to 'say'. Then there are the many occasions in *The Unnamable*, especially in its closing pages, when the narrator insists 'you must go on'. And it is not merely a question of Beckett and his characters making comic statements about being obliged to go on talking. The whole motive force behind the 'whey of words' is clearly some sort of serious compulsion. Malone must go on telling his stories, saying something, until the end; even the creatures in the mud of *How It Is* build up the impression that they must go on 'quoting' – 'I say it as I hear it' (H,*passim*). And Beckett himself is in the grip of the same ineluctable command, he too must 'go on'.

I would propose that this obligation, which seems at once quite normal and quite arbitrary, is an expression of Heideggerian 'care'. We feel that we understand Beckett's inability to fall silent, perhaps because the state of unconsciousness (= wordlessness) is inconceivable to us, but if asked to explain why there is an 'obligation to express' we cannot do so adequately. This ambiguity reflects exactly the ambiguity of something which is a really basic assumption, something like 'care' in fact.

The obligation to 'say' is the obligation to be involved with, to 'produce, attend to, make use of' and so on (Heidegger on 'concern' as quoted above). The narrators in Beckett would dearly love to do 'nothing', as we shall see, but they must go on 'churning'. Their words are the objective correlatives of Care, they exemplify and symbolize man's inability to escape from his situation as the caring entity: even 'not caring' is evidence of Care seen ontologically and Beckett's compulsion to 'go on' represents this ontological fact. If it did not, it would be adequate to object to Beckett by saying 'Surely you don't *have* to paint' or 'Why not just fall silent?' or 'Just stop, then!' But these objections, operating as they do at the *ontical* level, are clearly inadequate; they are too obvious not to have been considered and dismissed as irrelevant. Beckett is thus working on an *ontological* plane where these objections have no force. He is depicting what actually is the ontological state of Dasein, of 'Being-there'. Being-there already means being involved with. Dasein *is* care. Not prescriptively, of course; that is where we make our mistake when we try to 'explain' the 'obligation to express'. It is not a prescriptive law 'handed down', it is a descriptive law, like gravity.

Man is obliged to care by being man and this is symbolized in literature by the obligation to express.

SELBSTSEIN 'BEING-ONE'S-SELF'

We shall deal with the Self as such in a separate section, below.
Meanwhile, the next step is to outline briefly Heidegger's preliminary definition of what it is to 'be-one's-self'. Dasein exists
understandingly in a factical world that is primarily ready-to-hand,
rather than just objectively 'real', and his way of being in that world
is care. To this Heidegger must add some account of who Dasein is.

As so often, the answer is contained in the question. Dasein is that
sort of entity of whom we can ask the question 'who?'. Of other
things we must ask the question 'what?'. And the answer to 'who?' is
always 'I myself'. Dasein is characterized by *'Jemeinigkeit'*, 'in-each-
case-mineness'. Dasein is always 'me' and the question 'who?' can
only be answered by a 'me' or on behalf of a 'me'. It is thus a 'subject'
or a 'self'. (BT,150)

But Heidegger is a lot warier than Descartes about seizing on this
apparently indisputable starting-point. Dasein is indeed 'I', but the
'I', the self, is not an object present-at-hand within the world which
can be analysed and described in the same way as a table. 'In
clarifying Being-in-the-world we have shown that a bare subject
without a world never "is" proximally, nor is it ever given'. (BT, 152)
The Self is already in the world and if we conceive of it as isolated
from the world it must 'be understood only in the sense of a non-
committal *formal indicator*'. (BT,152) The Self just is not any
'given' thing, like another arm or leg say, there is no 'nature' for the
Self to possess, no 'essence' except, of course, Dasein's special kind of
essence which is 'existence'. So the Self is existential, 'Dasein is its
Self only in existing'. (BT,152)

The burden of this is that the Self exists (Dasein is already 'I' and
already exists) and that means it exists in a world. But the world
contains 'Others'. I have quoted the passage in which Heidegger
points out that the 'bare subject' is never 'given' without a world. His
very next sentence runs 'And so in the end an isolated "I" without
Others is just as far from being proximately given'. (BT,152) The
'Others' are already 'there with us' in the world. This important
point (a crucial part of all existentialist philosophy, especially that
of Buber and Sartre) will be discussed in the next section. For
the moment we should see if this preliminary stage, that of

Being-one's-self, appears in Beckett.

In general Beckett's work reveals the unsatisfactoriness of beginning with the Cartesian 'Ego' as the fixed point of speculation. The word 'I' must appear a record number of times in his *oeuvre*, but there is a feeling of insane repetition about it, of hollowness and unimportance. As in Heidegger, man can say 'I', and indeed in all situations he is obliged to be in his own world, the world that must be 'mine', but this is only a formal, contentless sort of condition-for-existence. As Kierkegaard says, 'One keeps on saying "*Ich-Ich*" until one becomes. . .ludicrous'. (*The Concept of Dread*, trans. Lowrie, Princeton University Press, 1944, p. 136)

In *Eleuthéria* Victor explains himself thus: '*D'abord j'étais prisonnier des autres. Alors je les ai quitté. Puis j'étais prisonnier de moi. C'était pire. Alors je me suis quitté*'. (p. 115 of typescript) These marvellously-balanced sentences, if they are not just rhetoric, show us a character realizing that he is already in the world with Others and putting his escape from them on exactly the same level as his escape from himself. Being-with-Others and Being-one's-Self are equiprimordial conditions of Dasein's existence.

Above all, the Self in Beckett, as we shall see, is specifically more than just a matter of this saying '*Ich-Ich*'. Unless we adopt Heidegger's view of the 'I' as a mere formal indicator we are hard put to it to explain the constant appearances, especially in the trilogy, of sentences in the first person describing waiting or seeking the Self. Molloy, for instance, says

> And as for myself, that unfailing pastime, I must say it was far now from my thoughts. But there were moments when it did not seem so far from me, when I seemed to be drawing towards it. (T,163)

In other words 'I' is inadequate, in both Heidegger and Beckett, as a term for the Self, merely indicating in both cases that we are dealing with a 'who?' not a 'what?', that is with Dasein for whom the world is always 'mine'.

*   *   *

MITSEIN AND *MITDASEIN* 'BEING-WITH' AND 'BEING-THERE-WITH'

By these two terms Heidegger expresses the two aspects of Dasein's Being-with-Others. On the one hand I am always already in a world 'with' others, my Being-in-the-world is a Being-with, and on the other hand Others are 'there' with me in the world.

My world is primarily composed of the ready-to-hand. The ready-to-hand is equipment ('*Zeug*') and equipment, by definition, is referential, it is always equipment 'for' something. And the thing to which a piece of equipment refers always refers to something else in turn. Thus a 'chain' is automatically built up from anything ready-to-hand, a chain of references that always leads back to the entity for which '*Zeug*' is ready-to-hand, Dasein. Thus, the hammer is for mending the roof, the roof is for excluding the rain and the rain is excluded because Dasein prefers to be dry. In this way other Daseins are revealed to us, we see the equipment in our world being used by others, we follow back chains of reference to their originators – men like ourselves. And of course our own world is full of others, 'The world is always the one that I share with Others'. (BT,155)

Even when I am alone I still have 'Being-with' as an ontological characteristic. I am aware of being alone only because I have that sort of being for which an Other can be missing.

Dasein has been defined as 'care' ('*Sorge*'). The sort of care I have for the ready-to-hand has been called 'concern' ('Besorgen'), and now we encounter another sort of care, the care I have for other Daseins, for which Heidegger employs the term 'solicitude', ('fürsorge'). As with all Heidegger's terms the 'solicitude' carries no ethical weight. Even when I ignore a fellow Dasein I am displaying 'solicitude', but in a 'deficient mode'. (BT,158) The point is that only Dasein can 'ignore', and Dasein can only do this because it is Dasein's ontological character to be able to be solicitous.

> Being with Others belongs to the Being of Dasein, which is an issue for Dasein in its very Being. Thus as Being-with, Dasein 'is' essentially for the sake of Others. This must be understood as an existential statement as to its essence. Even if the particular factical Dasein does *not* turn to Others, and supposes that it has no need of them or manages to get along without them, it *is* in the way of Being-with. (BT,160)

I think we have here an ontological thesis that can help us to understand Beckett. There is a sort of painful, inescapable bond between the Self and the Other, between Dasein and Dasein, throughout Beckett's work. The tramps in *Godot* say that they don't need each other but they are bound together just as much as Lucky and Pozzo or Hamm and Clov. And what is Heideggerian about this binding is that it is ontological, something to do with the tramps' Being, and not social or psychological, or at least not fundamentally social or psychological. Their inability to separate is deeper in their natures than a simple need for company or love, they sound when they talk as though they are a single person 'talking to himself'. Lucky's increasingly close connexion with Pozzo exists in spite of the latter's avowed intention of selling him. And Clov states simply to Hamm, when asked why he doesn't leave, 'I can't leave you'.

Selecting almost at random from the *Texts for Nothing*[10] we find a mountain of similar evidence. Here is some of the opening of the fourth Text.

> It's the same old stranger as ever, for whom alone accusative I exist, in the pit of my inexistence, of his, of ours. . .
> I'm not in his head, nowhere in his old body, and yet I'm there, for him I'm there, with him, hence all the confusion. . .
> He wants me there, with a form and a world, like him, in spite of him, me who am everything, like him who is nothing. And when he feels me void of existence it's of his he would have me void, and vice versa, mad, mad, he's mad. . .
> He thinks words fail him, he thinks because words fail him he's on his way to my speechlessness. . . .(NK,87)

Here we have a tearing tension between the nominative and the accusative, a fierce struggle that can be taken as being between the author and his character. No doubt this is a fair interpretation, but it does not completely satisfy; we feel that the 'I' has a less nebulous existence than that of a fictional character, that this is less trivial than the sort of joke between author and character indulged in by Fielding or Thackeray. More significantly we have here two Daseins, the Self and the Other, labouring for clarity in the mind of the Self. I exist for the Other, he exists for me, 'in the pit of my inexistence' (see above, on Being-one's-Self and below on the Self *tout court*). 'All the confusion' arises because he and I are inseparable. If he needs me he needs me with a 'world' (here used in a sense very like Heidegger's). Sometimes I am 'everything' and he is 'nothing', as in the quoted passage, and sometimes vice versa, which reads very like a gloss on Heidegger's analysis of 'just standing around'. This is the minimum mode of existence, the least Dasein-like state that Dasein can be in, barring death as we shall see, but it is still quite different from the Being of something merely present-at-hand.

Even if we see the Other 'just standing around', he is never apprehended as a human-Thing present-at-hand, but his 'standing-around' is an existential mode of Being – an unconcerned, uncircumspective tarrying alongside everything and nothing. (BT,156)

When Hackett and the others see Watt standing by the tram stop he is *almost* like a roll of tarpaulin or a carpet. But not quite. Even Watt, stationary in the gloaming, just 'standing around', is Dasein and has to be dealt with as such.

Throughout the majority of the fiction Beckett's characters are alone. But alone precisely in the Heideggerian way of being alone, alone because their Being is a Being-with-Others. Molloy is always trying to avoid or escape from people (like Buster Keaton in *Film*). He says he could have followed 'A or C' and spoken to them, and he wanted to, but he didn't, he stayed in his 'observation post', 'But instead of observing I had the weakness to return in spirit to the other, the man with the stick. Then the murmurs began again'. (T,13) Molloy wants to stop, to cease to exist, to go silent. But he is in the world and Being-in-the-world is a Being-with-others and others mean 'murmurs' as we see. He then tries to avoid being accosted when he goes into his town, and all he wants is for the police to leave him alone, but they don't. And he tries to escape from Lousse's house and eventually succeeds, and so he goes on. But besides the physical presence of Others, he carries within him the imperative of that first Other, his mother. And Moran, who follows him, is not only accompanied by his son for most of his journey (and has constant skirmishes with physical Others) but carries within him his images of his quarry, Molloy, and Gaber's instructions, and Youdi's authority.

Malone, as his name implies, is alone, but not alone in the ontological sense: his Being is not that of the isolated present-at-hand. He is very clearly in a world and his whole Being appears as Care both in the positive sense that he is 'concernful' about his 'possessions' (ready-to-hand, while he can still reach them at least) and 'solicitous' about the Others who actually are his stories. If the reader confuses Malone with his fictions he is to be forgiven, Beckett intends it, 'Dasein "is" essentially for the sake of Others'.

The Unnamable is even more explicit. 'Why did I have myself represented in the midst of men?' he asks. 'It seems to me it was none of my doing'. (T,299) Indeed, it was not. He speculates on how he knows what he knows and illogically decides that, although he has never had any contact with anyone, 'they' gave him 'lectures'. 'They. . .gave me the low-down on God. . .But what they were most determined for me to swallow was my fellow-creatures'. (T,300) Which is Beckett's way of expressing the inescapability of Being-with-Others.

For Beckett Being is the first inescapable (suicide is pointless and unsuccessful, cf. *Molloy, Godot*, etc). In parallel with Heidegger Beckett learns that Others are inescapable;[11] Heidegger says that Dasein's Being *is* Being-with, Beckett expresses the same thing *passim*, especially in *Film* where the Other is carried 'within', like a character in an author. But Being, for Beckett, is also that traditionally inescapable situation, Hell. This can be illustrated from several places, but a brief consideration of the title and contents of *The Lost Ones* should be enough. All of which adds up to a familiar conclusion – that hell is other people.

*   *   *

GEWORFENHEIT 'THROWNNESS' *ENTWURF* 'PROJECTION'

Dasein 'is there'. But it does not choose the time or place of its arrival. Whatever man does or thinks or feels it is obvious that, first, he is already there. This gives rise to a metaphor that describes man as 'thrown' (*'geworfen'*) into Being. (BT,174) Man always has a 'mood', or a 'state of mind', a basic component of which is this feeling of having been thrown into the 'there'. The 'there', of course, is facticity, and we have seen that facticity is the negative aspect of possibility. Dasein's Being is its Being-possible and the 'fundamental existentiale' that is the Being of this potentiality is understanding. From my 'state of mind' I look backwards, as it were, at my thrownness into facticity; from understanding I look forwards into my possibility.

Understanding has the structure of *'Entwurf'*, projection, which is a keeping-open of possibilities. 'Understanding is the existential Being of Dasein's own potentiality-for-Being; and it is so in such a way that this Being discloses in itself what its Being is capable of'. (BT,184) The etymological connection between this projecting (*'entwurf'*) and thrownness (*'Geworfenheit'*) is no accident. Man is thrown into Being and throws himself into his own Being. Does anything like this appear in Beckett?

Perhaps the *locus classicus* of thrownness in the modern theatre is Beckett's *Act Without Words I*, which opens

Desert. Dazzling light. The man is flung backwards on stage from right wing. He falls, gets up immediately, dusts himself, turns aside, reflects. (E,57)

It will be noticed that reflection here follows thrownness. As we gaze at the creature flung before us, 'there' in the dazzling light, we feel the force of Heidegger's query 'Has Dasein as itself ever decided freely whether it wants to come into "Dasein" or not, and will it ever be able to make such a decision?'. (BT,271) All the many further stage-directions, in *Act Without Words I*, to 'reflect' are examples of projection. The man tries to seize his possibilities, which are given to him by his understanding, and quickly learns the factical limitations of his situation. This short play can be seen as a perfect Heideggerian parable for *Geworfenheit* and *entwurf* with the Beckettian rider that seizing possibilities is harder than it looks.

Other examples abound. Both Murphy and Watt are plonked down into our ken without a by-your-leave. Watt, especially, is just thrust off the tram into the story. But the best examples appear later. Molloy, for instance, is just thrown into position: 'I am in my mother's room. It's I who live there now. I don't know how I got there'. (T,7) In *Cascando* 'Voice' speaks of 'him' as 'a ton weight' who is 'stuck in the sand' (*Cascando*, p. 41) rather like Winnie in *Happy Days* who has been thrust into the sand and is jerked back into 'life' daily by her alarm-clock. In *The Expelled* the 'hero' arrives at the beginning of the story by being flung down some steps. He makes it clear that he is frequently flung out like this, and usually pursued and beaten, but on this occasion, 'For once, they had confined themselves to throwing me out and no more about it'. (NK,10) At the first line of *How It Is* we are plunged *in medias res*, that is, into the mud alongside the creature who, like all Beckett's creatures, is 'already' there. Malone is in much the same state as Molloy, 'One day I found myself here, in the bed'. (T,183) The Unnamable is even clearer about this and often refuses to accept that he was ever anywhere else, as for instance, 'I have been here, ever since I began to be' (T,296) and all he says about how he got there is implied in his reference to the 'signing' of a 'life-warrant'.

'They' sign the warrant and we are flung into Being.

So much for thrownness. What of projection? Here Beckett seems to be parodying Heidegger – all his moribunds project wildly, aimlessly, artificially. Malone is the best example. He draws up a plan of what he is going to do before he dies (cf. 'Being-towards-Death' below) and makes a determined effort to fulfil his last remaining possibilities, that is, his abilities to tell stories, to talk, to list things. To some extent he achieves his project. To some extent the brevity of life, the poorness of memory and the interventions of the unexpected conspire to thwart him. But he cannot do other than project. Nor can Beckett avoid filling his own time by inventing stories.

We can now construct a preliminary list of the 'equiprimordial' existentials of Dasein. Dasein is 'there', thrown into factical existence, already in-a-world, already with-others, already concerned with the ready-to-hand, already solicitous about others, already with understanding and in a state-of-mind, and only thus can Dasein be-Itself. None of these constitutive items 'precedes' or explains any of the others, they are equiprimordial, part-and-parcel of Dasein's existence and generally to be subsumed, if at all, under the heading 'Care', which is the meaning of Dasein's Being. We are beginning to see how Beckettian man has many of these features too.

* * *

DAS MAN 'THEY' UNEIGENTLICH EXISTENZ 'INAUTHENTIC EXISTENCE'

'Das Man' roughly means 'the they' or 'people'. It is the crowd, the herd, rather than the individual. In 'everyday Being-with-one-another "Dasein" stands in *subjection* to Others. It itself *is* not; its Being has been taken away by the Others'. (BT, 164) Dasein is its possibilities; my existence is my understanding projection of myself into my possibilities, but in 'average everydayness' Dasein's 'possibilities of Being are for the Others to dispose of as they please'. (BT,164) Heidegger gives the examples of employing public transport or reading the newspaper that is also read by so many others. My 'own' existence is subordinated to a public existence that is not mine. In our average everydayness, 'We take pleasure and enjoy ourselves as *they* (*Man*) take pleasure; we read, see, and judge about literature and art as *they* see and judge' (BT,164).

'The Self of everyday Dasein is the *they-self*, which we distinguish from the *authentic Self* – that is, from the Self which has been taken hold of in its own way'. (BT,167) Thus existence dominated by 'them' is inauthentic existence, and inauthentic existence is the Being-in-the-world of everyday Dasein.

Perhaps surprisingly this is another constituent part of Dasein's primordial Being-there. 'Dasein has, in the first instance, fallen away from itself as an authentic potentiality for Being its Self, and fallen into the 'world'. (BT,220) Here 'world' is in inverted commas to indicate that it has the denotation of the ordinary usage rather than Heidegger's special meaning. So it means 'world' rather as in the Christian conception of 'the devil, the world and the flesh' – Dasein 'falls' into the world, that is, into the 'they'. And Dasein is constantly 'tempted' by the 'world' and by the relative ease of only being its 'they-Self'. Once we have fallen into the world we become 'tranquillized' by it, but this implies nothing static, rather we are driven into 'hustle' and hurry that drives us along, 'alienating' us from ourselves. But this 'worldly' 'they-Self' we fall into is not really 'Other', it is still 'myself', so in falling we become 'entangled' in ourselves; we can never become Other however inauthentically we behave. 'Dasein plunges out of itself into itself, into the groundlessness and nullity of inauthentic everydayness'. (BT,223)

The primordiality of the 'they-Self' is established in the following passage, which also serves as Heidegger's summary of his position up to this point:

As something factical, Dasein's projection of itself understandingly is in each case already alongside a world that has been discovered. From this world it takes its possibilities, and it does so first in accordance with the way things have been interpreted by the 'they'. This interpretation has already restricted the possible options of choice to what lies within the range of the familiar, the attainable, the respectable – that which is fitting and proper (BT,239)

If Dasein only consults its 'they' possibilities it remains blind to its *own* possibilities or it resorts to mere 'wishing' about them and wish-states-of-mind, daydreams, are really the opposite of a genuine grasping of possibilities. 'They' never choose, 'they' have always already chosen, and to exist inauthentically is to let their choices operate for *me* too. (BT,345) Inauthentic Dasein is 'carried along by the nobody'. (BT,312) Listening to the voice of 'they', Dasein fails to hear itself. (BT,315)

Do we find any of this in Beckett? Do his characters suffer under 'the dictatorship of the "they"?'. The second *Act Without Words* appears to be a comment on the 'everyday' Being of man, and is a good place to start in its clarity.

In *Act Without Words II* a goad, emerging from the wings of the stage, prods into life two men in sacks. They go through the motions of a daily routine, dressing, eating, undressing and so on, in alternation, and Beckett creates the impression that the goad, like Winnie's alarm clock, will go on goading until there is nobody left to torment. Thus each player in this mime appears to exemplify an endless and deadening routine and to conform unquestioningly to habits imposed upon them. Significantly 'A' and 'B', as they are called, go through their routines quite differently, thereby giving the *impression* of choosing their own possibilities and consequently of existing authentically. But the overall structure within which they exercise this freedom makes a mockery of it. Their conformity to what the goad clearly expects of them is absolute; to emphasize the point, they wear the same clothes (not merely similar clothes, the very same garments) and eat the same carrot. Here we have two people under the tyranny of the 'they', this last being represented by a goad. And in fact the goad is a better illustration of '*Das Man*' than a crowd of people would be, for Heidegger is at pains to emphasize that 'they' are no particular group of people or individuals, 'they' must only be the indefinite, collective neuter. Something like an impersonal goad, in fact.

Act Without Words II can be seen as an illustration of the situation that we feel all through the trilogy and that appears unambiguously in *How It Is*, the situation of being compelled to 'go on'. It is no coincidence that, scattered all through the fiction after *Watt*, there are references to the source of this compulsion as 'they'. In the *Texts for Nothing* for instance we find the following,

> We seem to be more than one, all deaf, not even, gathered together for life. Another said, or the same, or the first, they all have the same voice, the same ideas, All you had to do was stay at home...(NK,71–2)

And Molloy has this aside:

> All the things you would do gladly, oh, without enthusiasm, but gladly, all the things there seems no reason for your not doing,

and that you do not do! Can it be we are not free? (T,36)

It is the 'they-Self' that prevents us from doing what is not acceptable to 'them', although there 'seems no reason' to refrain. Later Molloy talks about the spurious relief of getting lost in the 'they' and of coming back again:

> Yes it sometimes happens and will sometimes happen again that I forget who I am and strut before my eyes like a stranger. Then I see the sky different from what it is and the earth too takes on false colours. It looks like rest, it is not, I vanish happy in that alien light, which must have once been mine, I am willing to believe it, then the anguish of return, I won't say where, I can't, to absence perhaps (T,42)

Here we have Beckett's old trick of splitting the Self and having 'I' talking about 'me', a split that seems to be along the lines of the 'they-Self' and the authentic Self. They are both me but the condition of passage from the latter to the former is that I must 'forget who I am'. And, as we have seen, this will put me in 'alien', or 'alienated' light which looks like 'rest' ('tranquillity') but 'is not' (it is 'hustle'). Getting back to me ('myself') is going to feel like getting back to an 'absence' after the excitements of the 'they-Self'.

The Unnamable is constantly talking about 'them' and what 'they' want. 'They', for instance, try 'to make me believe I have an ego all my own, and can speak of it, as they of theirs'. (T,348) This underlines the irony of Heidegger's position – in being exhorted to 'be ourselves' we are presented with an impossibility, for if I 'am myself' at *your* bidding then I am, again, bowing to the dictatorship of the 'they'. 'They' are bound to fail, as the Unnamable implies, by definition, in the attempt to 'make me believe' anything about myself, although 'I was like them, before being like me'. (T,382)[12]

Once again we find ourselves back at the problem of Beckett's narration. Who is narrating what to whom? And once again Heidegger provides some illumination. Take the following crux from the fourth *Text for Nothing*:

> He has me say things saying it's not me, there's profundity for you, he has me who say nothing say it's not me. All that is truly crass. If at least he would dignify me with the third person, like his other

figments, not he, he'll be satisfied with nothing less than me, for his me. (NK,88)

Here the tension between 'him' and 'me' can be seen as that between author and character. But there is another level that emerges from our Heideggerian considerations, a level on which the 'everyday' Self, the 'they-Self' is talking about the authentic Self. On this level we can gloss this passage as follows. The authentic Self ('He') seems to be the origin of the 'they-Self' and makes it 'say things' such as 'it's not me' (the self-rejection of the alienated 'they-Self'). There's profundity if you like: I, who don't say anything because my voice is drowned in the voices of the 'they' manage here to say something. An apparently stupid situation. It would be better if 'he' (my authentic Self) would talk about me (who is after all only a puppet of the 'they') in the third person as he does with his other 'figments', that is, with the other objects of his perception or imagination. But no, he won't treat me like Tom, Dick or Harry (he can't, he *is* me), when he talks about me he must talk about me as 'his me'.[13]

*   *   *

EIGENTLICH EXISTENZ 'AUTHENTIC EXISTENCE'
GEWISSEN 'CONSCIENCE'

Authentic existence is, of course, the reverse of the inauthentic existence described in the last section. To exist authentically is to exist as Self and not as 'they-Self'. Heidegger borrows the term 'conscience' to describe the power that calls us out of the 'they-Self' and into the Self. It is Dasein's own conscience that does this, so it is I who demand my Self from my 'they-Self'. Conscience is an 'appeal' from one to the other, 'and because only the *Self* of the they-self gets appealed to and brought to hear, the "*they*" collapses'. (BT,317) It may collapse, but it does not disappear. Dasein has Being-in-the-world quite as much when it exists authentically as when it does not; as Heidegger points out earlier, '*Authentic Being-one's Self* does not rest upon an exceptional condition of the subject, a condition that has been detached from the "they"'. (BT,168) The call of conscience passes over all the considerations of the 'they', of introspection, of psychoanalysis, of anything that treats the Self as an object. It calls 'solely to that Self which, notwithstanding, is in no other way than Being-in-the-world'. (BT,318) So authentic existence is not detached from the world and the 'they'; Murphy's mistake is to make a bid to shut out 'the world' and to 'come alive' in his mind, but 'the appeal to the Self in the they-self does not force it inwards upon itself, so that it can close itself off from the "external world"' (BT,318) We are in no way discussing solipsism or subjectivism here.

Conscience, in calling to the Self, strictly says, 'nothing', but it calls Dasein forward into its 'potentiality-for-Being-its-Self', that is, it calls on Dasein to exist authentically. And it discourses 'solely and constantly in the mode of keeping silent'. (BT,318) Here the 'caller', conscience, sounds remarkably like a Beckettian character, not simply because it talks by keeping silent in a manner that echoes Beckett's paradoxes on this subject, but in its ambiguous anonymity:

> The caller maintains itself in conspicuous indefiniteness. If the caller is asked about its name, status, origin or repute, it not only refuses to answer, but does not even leave the slightest possibility of one's making it into something with which one can be familiar when one's understanding of Dasein has a 'worldly' orientation. On the other hand, it by no means disguises itself in the call. (BT,319)

The point here, as in Beckett, is that the Self calls to its Self from its Self. And at least one, if not two, of these terms is anonymous and indefinable. The 'they-Self' we can perhaps define, but what are we to say of the Self 'itself' or of the conscience that calls to it? They are both 'me', undisguisedly, but we can say nothing of them.

The call of conscience 'comes *from* me and yet *from beyond me*'. (BT,320) Once again we are back at the 'First Person'–'Third Person' problem, discussed in the last section. This calling conscience, at once me and not me, sounds very like the 'I'–'They' tension in, say, *How It Is* or the *Texts for Nothing*. If we are tempted to call the 'them', in Beckett, God, we find Heidegger positing the same possibility. The 'Scribes', 'up there' in *How It Is*, bending over the prone forms of the mud-creatures, dictating; or the 'He' of the fourth *Text for Nothing*, seem to be external powers and yet within the narrator. As Heidegger says, one can take 'the power itself as a person who makes himself known – namely God'. (BT,320) But he has a better explanation, and one that I think will fit Beckett better too. 'The fact that the call is not something which is explicitly performed *by me*, but that rather "it" does the calling, does not justify seeking the caller in some entity with a character other than that of Dasein'. (BT,320–1) The caller is an 'it', but it is also me, a 'who'. 'In its "who", the caller is definable in a "worldly" way by *nothing* at all. The caller is Dasein in its uncanniness: primordial, thrown Being-in-the-world as the not-at-home – the bare "that-it-is" in the "nothing" of the world'. (BT,321) The caller is 'alien' because nothing could be more alien to the 'they-Self' than the Self. And Heidegger repeats: 'The call does not report events; it calls without uttering anything'. (BT,322) There is no possibility of my being mistaken as to who is calling when I hear this silent call – I know it is me. I know myself in my 'uncanniness', that is, in my individuality, and I recognize myself unmistakably when I call myself out of the 'they-Self' into my own potentiality because I am 'Care'. 'Conscience manifests itself as the call of care: the caller is Dasein...The one to whom the appeal is made is this very same Dasein'. (BT,322) If Dasein interprets the call of conscience as the voice of God it is merely slipping back into the world, into the 'they-Self', hiding in the Objective, resting in inauthenticity. If the voice of conscience is not *my* voice then it is a public voice, 'God's voice', the voice of the 'they'. *Vox populi, vox dei.* But thus it must be *my* voice for it is precisely the voice that calls me *away* from the 'they'. (BT,323)

We should now be in a position to understand the following comment of Heidegger's that summarizes this basic state of authentic existence. 'In understanding the call (of conscience), Dasein is *in thrall to its ownmost possibility of existence.* It has chosen itself'. (BT,334) This is how 'man makes himself'.

It will be seen that this question of authentic existence is bound up with the question of selfhood, which in Beckett appears as the quest for Self. I have already made some points about Beckett *en passant* and the bulk of this discussion must be left to our direct approach to the Self in the section so-entitled, below. For the present I shall give some examples of Beckett's references to the quest for the Self that will perhaps read a little more clearly with Heidegger in mind.

Arsène, for instance, describes the mystery of Watt's arrival at Mr Knott's house thus: 'he knows he is in the right place at last...he will be in his midst at last, after so many tedious years spent clinging to the perimeter', he will be able to taste 'the long joys of being himself'. (W,39) We now have a chance of understanding this and not merely admiring it aesthetically. The 'right place' is the authentic Self which is 'in our midst', the 'perimeter' to which we cling is the they-Self. Only in the former can we be ourselves.

Frequently through the *Texts for Nothing* we come across similarly arcane statements that seem a little clearer with Heidegger's help.

> I don't know, I'm Here, that's all I know, and that it's still not me, it's of that the best has to be made (NK,85)

> To be judge and party, witness and advocate, and he, attentive, indifferent, who sits and notes. It's an image, in my helpless head... (NK,91)

> One, meaning me, it's not the same thing (NK,91)

> The ears straining for a voice not from without (NK,91)

> That other who is me...because of whom I'm here (NK,109)

In each of these examples there is a 'me' and some other who is also 'me', a calling from the one to the other, an oscillation between two selves. If these appear susceptible of a non-Heideggerian interpretation (which is possible, though I suspect it would end up being a very similar sort of interpretation) what can be made of the following from *The Unnamable* without our Heideggerian view?

> What I say, what I may say, on this subject, the subject of me and my abode, has already been said since, having always been here, I am here still...I greatly fear, since my speech can only be of me and here, that I am once more engaged in putting an end to both. Which would not matter, far from it, but for the obligation, once rid of them to begin again, to start again from nowhere, from no one and from nothing and win to me again, to me here again...(T,304)

The 'nowhere' and 'nothing', here set up against the 'me' and the 'here' to which the Unnamable aspires, are at the heart of Heidegger as they are at the heart of Beckett.

*   *   *

ANGST 'ANXIETY' *NICHTS* 'NOTHING'

Dasein 'falls' into inauthenticity. It 'flees' from itself into the 'they'. This fleeing is not the same as the fleeing of one afraid. If I am afraid, it is of a definite entity within-the-world that threatens me, but when Dasein 'flees' into the 'they' it is fleeing from itself. Hence we need a term other than 'fear' to describe the state-of-mind that brings about this fleeing. This is especially so as Dasein, when it flees from what it fears, is in fact totally orientated towards the 'fearsome' thing (Heidegger gives no examples, but this physical one is clear enough: when I run away from a fierce dog all I do has reference to the dog, I can think of nothing else, my whole being is involved with the dog, albeit in the negative mode of trying to avoid it). But when Dasein flees from itself into the world, into the 'they', it is quite unable to say definitely what it is fleeing from. So it is even more important to find a term that will differentiate this from fear.

Heidegger adopts Kierkegaard's word *'Angst'* which we will translate 'anxiety'; it has also been rendered as 'dread', which is perhaps too strong. Just as 'concern' and 'solicitude' are both made possible by the fact that 'care' is Dasein's fundamental Being, so fear and its related emotions are made possible because anxiety is one of Dasein's fundamental *existentialia*. Fear is fear of what threatens us from within-the-world. Anxiety is anxious about no specific entity but about 'Being-in-the-world as such'. (BT,230) 'In anxiety one does not encounter this thing or that thing which, as something threatening, must have an involvement . . . That in the face of which one has anxiety is characterized by the fact that what threatens is *nowhere*. Anxiety "does not know" what that in the face of which it is anxious is'. (BT,231)

We are anxious in the face of the 'nothing and nowhere' that is the world. If this seems incomprehensible it is perhaps worth considering that 'the world' cannot mean this or that entity within-the-world nor can it mean the aggregate of all such entities; it must be defined as the *possibilities* of the ready-to-hand. And possibility is precisely 'nothing-yet, nowhere-yet'. In fact we have now followed Heidegger to the point where we can see that his concept of *Angst* coincides with Kierkegaard's. In discussing original sin in *The Concept of Dread* Kierkegaard explains Adam's position by saying that *Angst* is awoken in him by the prohibition to eat the fruit of the forbidden tree. The *Angst* is aroused precisely because Adam is being offered a choice and therefore is confronted by possibility. Kierkegaard goes further and specifically defines this possibility as 'nothing'. Adam 'dreads' in the face of 'nothing' (*The Concept of Dread*, pp. 38–40).

Because Dasein turns away from itself, its Self is 'disclosed' as

being 'there'. (BT,229) Thus, paradoxically, the fleeing into inauthenticity is the condition for authenticity. I flee because I am
anxious; I am anxious in the face of my Being-in-the-world, in the
face of the 'nothing' of my possibility; *my* possibility, as we have
seen, *my own* Being-in-the-world, is my authentic existence. Thus
Angst is a condition of authentic existence, it 'discloses' Dasein to
itself.

> Anxiety makes manifest in Dasein its *Being-towards* its ownmost
> potentiality-for-Being – that is, its *Being-free-for* the freedom of
> choosing itself and taking hold of itself. Anxiety brings Dasein
> face to face with its *Being-free for*...the authenticity of its
> Being...Anxiety individualizes Dasein and thus discloses it as
> *'solus ipse'* (BT,232–3)

In the face of itself and about itself, Heidegger says, Dasein feels
anxious. To put it another way, Dasein feels anxious in the face of
the 'nothing' of the world. Heidegger stresses that this 'nothing' is
not to be interpreted as a lack of something in the present-at-hand,
rather it is the condition of the world. 'The present-at-hand must be
encountered in just *such* a way that it does *not* have *any* involvement
whatsoever, but can show itself in an empty mercilessness'. (BT,393)
'Anxiety discloses an insignificance of the world'. (BT,393)

Elsewhere Heidegger asks whether anyone 'has...ever made a
problem of the *ontological source* of notness'. (BT,332) And what
emerges from all this is a picture of anxiety as a fundamental state-
of-mind, in which authentic existence is possible, and of 'nothing',
'nullity' or the 'not' as that which we are anxious about, although
not in the way of 'missing' something that is 'not there'.

The application of this to Beckett must be obvious. His fiction in
particular abounds with characters terrified of 'nothing', depending
on 'nothing', needing 'nothing' in a way that makes it quite plain that
this nothing is not just a 'not something'. And the state of mind of
the Beckettian narrator is rarely specific fear of things within-the-
world, but it is not comfort and freedom from everything like fear
either; it is *Angst*.

Watt is a good place to start to look for examples. Heidegger asks
if anyone has looked into the ontology of 'notness', and here surely is
Watt attempting it in his speculations about Mr 'Knott'. Even before
he has come properly face to face with Mr Knott, Watt's narration
(or Sam's, or Beckett's) is stiff with the word 'not'. 'Not that Watt

was ever to have any direct dealings with Mr Knott, for he was not', for example. (W,64) And the first major event of his stay in Mr Knott's house (besides Arsène's speech, of which more hereafter) is the visit of the Galls, father and son, to 'choon' the piano, which is described later as 'a thing that was nothing' that had 'happened'. (W,73) This is repeated a few pages later as though Beckett were pleased with the paradox, 'a nothing had happened'. (W,77) And it is in this connexion that he delivers himself of his oracular *reductio*: 'For the only way one can speak of nothing is to speak of it as though it were something, just as the only way one can speak of God is to speak of him as though he were a man'. (W,74) Which, of course, is Heidegger's point that 'nothing' does not always just mean a 'lack' — it can have a positive value. This throws a new light on such *dicta* of Watt's as 'Yes, nothing changed, in Mr Knott's establishment, because nothing remained, and nothing came or went, because all was a coming and a going'. (W,130) The 'nothings' in this sentence clearly denote something more than a 'lack'. Which might even suggest a new interpretation of apparently simpler statements such as 'What did he know of Mr Knott? Nothing'. (W,147) After all, the sentences that follow this are: 'Of his anxiety to improve, of his anxiety to understand, of his anxiety to get well, what remained? Nothing. But was not that something?'. (W,147) The last question goes unanswered.

All this consideration of 'nothing', we have seen, is intimately bound up in Heidegger with anxiety. 'Anxiety "does not know" what that in the face of which it is anxious is'. So it is with Watt. 'Of the nature of Mr. Knott himself Watt remained in particular ignorance'. (W,199) 'For of Mr. Knott he could not speak'. (W,214) Mr Knott would seem to be the nothing in the face of which Dasein is anxious. In the Addenda the verses that begin 'Who may tell the tale/of the old man?' conclude with the parallel interrogative 'nothingness/in words enclose?'. (W,247) The old man's tale *is* nothingness.

What is significant about this is not merely that we now have an explanation of the negativity of Mr Knott. We can go further. Heidegger's definition of the 'nothing' can be thoroughly applied to Mr Knott more extensively. We are anxious, it will be remembered, in the face of the 'nothing and nowhere' that is the world, the world here meaning that which is created by my freedom, that is, possibility. Mr Knott is just this possibility. He *is*, but he is not any one given entity. He is free possibility before it has chosen this or that. This explains his notorious systematic irregularity and unpredictability and his capacity to run through the whole range of possibilities of a given subject. Mr Knott's meals, appearance and habits are quite indefinable. As one of many examples we can consider his clothes. 'The clothes that Mr Knott wore... were very various, very very various'. (W,199) All sorts of random clothing is attributed to him, which he wears in the most random manner. This seems to symbolize possibility well enough, but what clinches the argument is the deliberately exhaustive list of what he wears on his feet. This list (W,pp. 200–1) is too long to quote *in extenso* but it is an example of one of the most striking features of the novel – a desperate ratiocination that wants to say every possibility in a given context. To explain it away as merely illustrative of an insane rationalism is inadequate; we can start to understand it properly only by taking it as it is and interpreting it in its obviousness. It is a list of possibilities. It includes *all* possibilities, it therefore puts us in a position to stand back from them, it symbolizes the pre-choice situation of Watt gazing at Mr Knott, it symbolizes freedom, Watt's gazing at the nothing ('Knott') of possibility.

If our comparison with Heidegger does no more than establish who Mr Knott is, and why Beckett adopts the technique of exhaustive enumeration in *Watt*, it has done a great deal. But 'nothingness' also figures largely in the other work. It is present in *Murphy* where the hero finds himself at peace when 'the somethings give way, or simply add up, to the Nothing, than which in the guffaw of the Abderite naught is more real'. This nothing is 'the accidentless One-and-Only'. (M,168) Then, later, there are the *Texts for Nothing* with their ambiguous title, and a scatter of references to nothingness in most of the work. From *The Expelled*, 'I raised my eyes to the sky... where nothing obstructs your vision'. (NK,13) An ambiguous sentence. From *The Calmative*, 'All I say cancels out, I'll have said nothing' (NK,26), where it is interesting to note the future tense; Beckett does not have the audacity to claim that he *has said* nothing. Then again the narrator's mind was 'always flung back to where there was nothing'. (NK,41)

These examples can all be read in a Heideggerian context; and if they are so read they acquire more meaning. Even more obviously Heideggerian is this from *Eleuthéria*: Victor, the hero, defends his liberty and when asked what he is defending it for ('pour quoi faire?') he replies 'pour rien faire'. Freedom is precisely to do nothing, to be able to choose but not to choose yet.

Molloy has an interesting aside on nothing. He claims that 'to know nothing is nothing' (T,64) in a context which indicates that the second nothing is idiomatic and the equivalent of 'easy'. The implication is that nothing, previously treated seriously as important, is now the easiest thing to grasp, which, in Heidegger's case, is paradoxically true – before anything I am faced with the nothing of freedom. Moran, like Molloy, 'stumbles' in the midst of 'nothingness' (T,123) at exactly the point when we expect him, surrounded by his house and his possessions as he is, to feel most certain of 'something'. Once again, this needs Heidegger. If we take 'nothing' as a sort of equivalent opposite of 'house', Moran's stumbling is incomprehensible. But if we see 'nothing' as possibility in the face of the world, then the house is precisely the condition of Moran's 'nothing'. And at this point in the tale Moran is specifically concerned with choice – the illusory choice of whether to obey Youdi and the real choice of how to set out and when.

It may be noticed that I am here stressing the 'nothing' aspect of this argument rather than the '*Angst*' aspect. The two are inseparable, of course; face to face with the nothing, Dasein, like Moran, *is* anxious. '*Angst*', however, does have an objective content of a sort in Kierkegaard and we may assume that this is implied in Heidegger.[14] Anxiety is 'vertigo' for the Danish philosopher, a dizzy peering into the 'abyss'. This is a metaphor for Being-towards the nothingness of freedom, the anxious peering into the 'depths'. It appears thus in Beckett too. Malone, who is as capable as any Beckettian hero of little asides such as 'the true prayer at last, the one that asks for nothing' (T,130) also has a revealing explanation: 'What I sought', he says, 'was the rapture of vertigo...the relapse...to nothingness' (T,26). And the Unnamable, in whose babble the word 'nothing' is repeated over one hundred times, after his endless repositionings of himself and his 'vice-existers', finally realizes that he is in an 'enormous prison, like a hundred thousand cathedrals' (T,413), and in 'this immensity' his voice gets lost in the 'vault' in 'the abyss' where he is 'already' (T,413). In Kierkegaard, Heidegger and Beckett freedom is a vertigo in the face of the abyss of nothingness.

*   *   *

SEIN-ZUM-TODE 'BEING-TOWARDS-DEATH' *GANZSEIN* BEING-A-WHOLE'

Dasein's Being cannot be a sort of aggregate of the Beings of his body, his soul and so on. It must be the Being of Dasein's unity. So says Heidegger. (BT,74) Being-in-the-world is shown to be unified in the section on Care. Care *is* Dasein's Being and it is defined as 'ahead-of-itself-Being-already-in-the-world-as-Being-alongside-entities-within-the-world'. (BT,237) This definition is sufficient to establish Dasein as a unity if we consider Dasein statically, but once we introduce the concept of temporality something more must be added.

It is significant that the definition of Dasein as Care quoted above refers to Dasein's 'average everydayness', that is, to Dasein in inauthenticity. At the beginning of Part Two of *Being and Time*, introducing temporality, Heidegger is at pains to point this out. He observes that in Part One he was not discussing Dasein's authenticity or totality. The two automatically appear together. Our discussion of inauthentic existence, above, depends largely on propositions from Part One of the work and our discussion of authentic existence depends on material from Part Two. Part Two is entitled 'Dasein and Temporality'.

The point is that however well we get on defining Dasein as Care and so on we cannot discover its unity or authenticity without time. Only with time are we able to understand our existential projections into the future. Also we at once discover the horizon of those projections – death. Being-towards-death reveals the totality of Dasein's possibilities and hence imposes a unity on Dasein's Being.

At death Dasein ceases to 'exist', there is nothing more 'outstanding' for Dasein to do and it becomes merely 'present-at-hand'. A dead body does not even rise to the status of readiness-to-hand, it is just brutally present. This provides a contrast with 'existence' and helps to define it. More important than this, however, is the direct pressure exerted by Being-towards-death on the Self to exist authentically. Not only is death the horizon that creates a unity for Dasein, it also forces Dasein to 'be itself' by virtue of its inescapability. We saw that inauthentic existence involved allowing the 'they' to replace 'me' as the maker of decisions, the projector of existence. Now the one occasion on which I cannot find a replacement for 'me' is at my death. If authentic existence is characterized by being 'always mine' then Being-towards-death is guaranteed authentic. (BT,283–4)

Then again, we are always old enough to die. Death is always impending, another possibility among the many, an indefinite but undeniable element in the factical. (BT,289) The 'they' tranquillizes itself about death, but thereby only proves that Dasein's Being is

Being-towards-death; the tranquillizing is Being-towards-death in a negative mode. (BT,295) Death is Dasein's 'ownmost possibility'. (BT,303) The authentic state of mind of Being-towards-death is *Angst*. We have seen that this 'anxiety' is a vertigo in the face of possibility, and death is the final possibility, the possibility of no-more-possibility. In the face of death *Angst* is the only authentic way of Being.

When we consider death we are, by implication, considering our lives as a whole.

Authenticity is related to totality, and we can expect the authentic only in the unified whole. However, unless we commit suicide immediately on having this thought, our Being-towards-death, that is our potentiality for Being-a-whole, will be characterized by anticipation. But then all our existential projects are characterized by anticipation, by expecting, by waiting for. (BT,349) This positive waiting is quite the opposite of the dreaming, hankering-after, wishing-for and mere willing of inauthentic existence. (BT,239–40)

It will at once be apparent that there is a good deal of this in Beckett. Malone's entire narrative, for instance, illustrates Being-towards-death. Sometimes he authentically grasps his possibilities, firmly aware of the probable limits of his existence and determined to shape his remaining time into a whole. This is the state he is in when he plans what he is going to do with his remaining time. He decides to tell certain stories in a certain order, make an inventory of his possessions, die. This is a perfect example of authentic Being-towards-death within the limits of the factical. At other times he is far away, plunged deeply into his stories about others. For him, as for the Unnamable, they are 'vice-existers', in other words they are his 'they-Self'. When he tells their stories he is letting 'them' exist for him. This, incidentally, underlines the paradox involved in the concept of free, authentic choice. Once Dasein has chosen X he is no longer free to choose Y, that is, he is no longer free. There is a clear sense, in *Malone Dies*, of Malone 'putting off' talking about himself; we feel that the narrative is away from the centre, away from the point, while we learn about the Lamberts, Saposcat and Macmann. And indeed it is, these are Malone's ways of passing the time. When *considering* his projects, Malone is existing authentically, but when *engaged* on them he is inauthentic. The issue becomes clear in *The Unnamable*, where the narrator says that he has invented Malone and the others much as they invented Saposcat and the others, and he rejects them accordingly:

> All these Murphys, Molloys and Malones do not fool me. They have made me waste my time, suffer for nothing, speak of them when, in order to stop speaking, I should have spoken of me and of me alone. (T,305)

The Trilogy becomes a striving after authentic existence when seen in this light. In *Malone Dies* this is coupled with a Heideggerian Being-towards-death, but by the time we reach *The Unnamable*, although the narrator has learnt that he must try to do without others (without 'they', without projects) if he is to be able to stop talking (that is, stop being, that is, become a whole at last) he is patently unable to stop. He 'must go on'. So here Beckett again develops a Heideggerian proposition into a picture of hell. It is all very well, he implies, to talk of Being-towards-the-end, but how are we to get to the end in a world in which Zeno's 'grains of millet' can never add up to a heap, 'the impossible heap', as Clov discovers.

This reference to *Endgame* is not fortuitous. In both the major plays, *Godot* and *Endgame*, the situation of anticipation and Being-towards-death are explored. Indeed a lot of Beckett's theatre is terminal; *Happy Days* implies an impossible third act in which Winnie is totally buried, Krapp's tape is his last, and so on. Obviously there is an opportunity here to interpret the waiting element in *Godot* in existentialist terms. I shall quote most of a paragraph from *Being and Time* which can be compared with *Godot*, perhaps especially so in the extra knowledge that in German it is entitled *Warten auf Godot*.

> Dasein comports itself towards something possible in its possibility by *expecting* it (im *Erwarten*). Anyone who is intent on something possible, may encounter it unimpeded and undiminished in its 'whether it comes or does not, or whether it comes after all'. . . To expect something possible is always to understand it and to 'have' it with regard to whether and when and how it will be actually present-at-hand. Expecting is not just an occasional looking-away from the possible to its possible actualization, but is essentially a *waiting for that actualization* (*ein Warten auf diese*). Even in expecting, one leaps away from the possible and gets a foothold in the actual. It is for its actuality that what is expected is expected. By the very nature of expecting, the possible is drawn into the

actual, arising out of the actual and returning to it. (BT,306)

In *Waiting for Godot* there is a tendency for the reader or the audience to put the emphasis on Godot. Who is this person who does not come? But, reasonable though his question is, the play itself is clearly about waiting. Now waiting is how we comport ourselves towards possibility, according to Heidegger, and for Vladimir and Estragon this is roughly the case too. And we have seen that authentic existence is best guaranteed while we remain free to choose, that is, before we have chosen. So the tramps are authentically keeping their options open while waiting for possibility. Meanwhile it is essential that they do nothing that will preclude their genuine availability for possibility. In other words they must do nothing. Which is why nothing happens in the play. Thus, when they try to hang themselves they fail and go into pointless dialogue instead, a dialogue designed to avoid action:

Vlad: Well? what do we do?
Est: Don't let's do anything. It's safer.
Vlad: Let's wait and see what he says.
Est: Who?
Vlad: Godot.
Est: Good idea. (WFG,18)

Later Estragon asks whether they are 'tied', and here is the existentialist rub – they *are* tied, tied to inaction if they are to remain authentic. In a sense, thus, they are tied to possibility – if only they would give up waiting for possibility and plunge into possibility, as Pozzo so clearly has done, then, like Pozzo, they would be free to come and go. It is Beckett's addition to this scheme that neither freedom (the tramps) nor involvement (Pozzo) brings anything more than misery. It is also Sartre's addition. As we shall see, for Sartre man is 'condemned to freedom' (the tramps) and is always in 'bad faith' (inauthentic existence, Pozzo).[15]

*   *   *

SCHULD 'GUILT' ENTSCHLUSS 'RESOLUTION'

'Dasein has, in the first instance, fallen away from itself as an authentic potentiality for Being its Self, and fallen into the world'. (BT,220)

This we now understand as Dasein's inauthentic involvement with 'das Man', 'they'. But if inauthentic Dasein is characterized by 'falling', authentic Dasein is characterized by 'guilt'. Neither of these concepts has anything to do with sin or lawbreaking. (BT,224) Guilt is primordial and precedes any 'indebtedness'. (BT,329) We have dealt with 'falling', by implication, in the section on inauthentic existence, above, and now we must examine this apparently ineluctable guilt. With it we must look at another aspect of authentic existence, one that accompanies guilt, 'resolution'.

'Dasein as such is guilty'. (BT,331) Here is yet another of the equiprimordial existentialia of Dasein. And Dasein is guilty because freedom is freedom to choose only one possibility, so Dasein always 'lacks' the other fulfilments – the possibilities it does not choose. This 'lack', which is obviously inescapable, Heidegger treats as similar to the 'lack' which is at the basis of all sorts of guilt. He interprets guilt as an 'indebtedness'. Indebtedness means not having or not doing; thus Dasein's basic inability to choose everything, which means 'not doing' most things, is an indebtedness, a lack, a guilt. 'Dasein as such is guilty'.

Conscience, we saw above, is essential to Dasein also and is defined as the call of Dasein's Self back to its Self. It is this conscience that tells us that we are guilty, for conscience is the call of Care, and Care is our Being as Being-in-the-world, and our Being-in-the-world is a matter of concernful dealing with the world, and that is a matter of choices and freedom. All this is already there in our situation.

When Heidegger says that we are guilty because we have 'fallen' into the world, into the 'they', this amounts to exactly the same thing. The way in which we fall into the world is to allow our choices to be made for us, to lack possibilities in just the way we lack them even when existing authentically because we cannot choose them all. So Dasein is responsible for what he does choose and guilty because of what he does not. (BT,332-3).

'Resolution' is the 'reticent self-projection upon one's ownmost Being-guilty, in which one is ready for anxiety'. (BT,343) This is the condition of authentic existence. Resolution is 'authentic Being-one's-Self'. (BT,344) What does this mean? Heidegger is not at his clearest here, but it would appear that this is his version of Sartre's 'choosing to be oneself'. Dasein must make the 'resolve' to want to listen to the call of his conscience and Dasein must be 'resolute' in adhering to himself if he wants to exist authentically. This decision 'to be myself' does not detach me from the world or let me become a 'free-floating "I"'. (BT,344) On the contrary it permits me to exist in my true Being, which is Being-in-the-world. 'They' are irresolute, 'they' never choose, somehow everything has already been chosen by 'them'. When I submit to 'their' choice I am doubly inauthentic – I have not chosen, and no identifiable one of 'them' has chosen either.

Two final points. 'Authentic resoluteness', we are told, 'resolves to keep on repeating itself'. Authentic existence is not merely achieved once for all, it is a permanent state of effort. Secondly, 'resoluteness is authentically and wholly what it can be, only as *anticipatory re-soluteness*'. (BT,355–6) From what we learnt of anticipation and waiting in the last section it will be apparent that resoluteness is an essential part of authentic Being-towards-death, itself a condition of authentic existence.

Here we have an example of two of Heidegger's concepts that apply usefully to Beckett because of the profound level at which the philosopher is working. Beckett's characters, for instance, seem to be endlessly self-punishing and never able to say that it is unfair or that they are 'not guilty'. I would propose that to associate their torments with, say, those of Dante's demned, is a genuine exercise in literary criticism but does not go far enough in the direction of explanation. After all, Beckett's cosmology is not Dante's; Dante intended his vision to be taken on several levels of meaning, no doubt, but first among them was something very like a literal meaning. This cannot be true of Beckett. As we shall see in the final chapter, Beckett is not devoid of an interest in religion, but he is certainly not an orthodox Christian. If we want an explanation of the pervading guilt and punishment themes we are likely to do a lot better with Heidegger's ontological versions.

In a sense this point can stand without examples. After all, there is no question but that Beckett's characters are punished for a profound guilt and that his entire *oeuvre* is created in a sort of grey light in which bitter suffering is universal and, because never complained of as such, curiously assumed to be fair. However, there is a clarity to be obtained from some of the specific points at which Beckett's characters talk about their guilt.

Malone, for instance, adopts the metaphor of the 'sin of having been born' and is specific that there is nothing unmerited about the punishment which follows such a sin.

And without knowing exactly what his sin was he felt full well that living was not a sufficient atonement for it or that this atonement was in itself a sin, calling for more atonement, and so on, as if there could be anything but life, for the living. And no doubt he would have wondered if it was really necessary to be guilty in order to be punished but for the memory, more and more galling, of his having consented to live in his mother, than to leave her. (T,240)

Later, pondering on his stories, Malone wonders if he is talking about the right Macmann. But he comforts himself with the reflection that 'So long as it is what is called a living being you can't go wrong, you have the guilty one'. (T,260)

The intimate relationship between this basic guilt and life is further stressed by the Unnamable who not only talks about 'signing' Worm's 'life-warrant' but even says that 'My crime is my punishment'. (T,372) In other words the 'crime' in Beckett, creating the 'guilt', is life and the 'punishment' is life. 'The inestimable gift of life'. As Heidegger says, 'Dasein as such is guilty'.

*   *   *

ZEIT 'TIME'

Early in *Being and Time* Heidegger promises to 'point to' temporality as 'the meaning of the Being of that entity which we call "Dasein"'. (BT,38) He points to one or two places where thinking about time has not been very clear. We are accustomed, for instance, to make a distinction between what is 'in time' and what is 'eternal' (BT,39) and we are baffled, as Kant was, because 'the decisive *connexion* between *time* and "I think" (is) shrouded in darkness'. (BT,45) But we must try to see what is really meant by these distinctions and connexions if we are to understand Dasein.

The second part of *Being and Time*, as it stands, is entitled 'Dasein and Temporality'. To some extent it is a recapitulation of the first part with the dimension of time added. It enables Heidegger to introduce authentic Being, that is, Being-a-whole and Being-towards-death. He does this in the first three sections of this part (2,1 – 2,3). In the remaining three sections (2,4 – 2,6) temporality and historicality are directly considered.

It may have been noticed that there is now an apparent rivalry for the status of 'the meaning of Dasein's Being'. We have just learnt that this is 'temporality', but in discussing 'care', above, we defined care in exactly this way too. This is deliberate. 'Temporality' is yet another of the equiprimordial elements of Dasein's existence and it *is* care. 'Temporality reveals itself as the meaning of authentic care'. (BT,374) The unity of the structure of care lies in temporality. Thus, '*Existenz*' relates to the future, I project myself existentially into my possibilities ahead-of-myself. Facticity, on the other hand is the past, the given, the 'already' into which I find myself 'thrown'. Resolute Dasein calls itself back from the factical 'they' and the possible 'then', from the past and the future, into the 'there' of *Dasein*, Being-there, that is, into the present of choice and freedom. Resolute Dasein gives, and listens to, the conscientious call of care and brings its Self back to the authentic present. (BT,375ff.)

In other words we have now put together all the equiprimordial aspects of Dasein's Being. If we select any one of them we find that it brings all the others with it, but this is only clear once time has been added to the other elements. There is no need here for us to rehearse all the categories so far discussed in the light of time, as Heidegger does. It must suffice simply to point out that everything that we have met so far takes on a new intelligibility in the light of time. 'Understanding', for instance, relates to the Future, while one's 'state of mind' relates to the Past, 'Being-in-the-world' is only possible because Dasein can 'temporalize' – indeed, just as there are only 'worlds' because of Dasein, so there is only time because of Dasein. And so on.

When Heidegger comes to discuss time itself, in isolation from his other concepts, he makes the point that time is not, as we so easily imagine, a 'succession' of discrete instants. Only Dasein is temporal, and Dasein is the 'between' of the phrase 'between birth and death'. (BT,425–6) And only for Dasein is there history – Dasein itself is the primary stuff of history, the ready-to-hand is only secondary historicality as we can see if we consider a museum exhibit which is, 'in nature', no 'older' than the glass of the case that exhibits it but which is 'old' to us by virtue of the defunct 'world' it connotes, that is, by virtue of past Dasein.

We do not experience time as an 'infinite' succession of 'nows' as in the Aristotelian definition. Time is always 'datable' and always has a 'span'. That is, 'now' always means 'now, when . . .', for instance, 'now, when I am eating lunch'. And this 'date', this 'reference', is never to a theoretical, infinitesimal 'now', it is to a 'span' of time, however brief; lunch takes time to eat. (BT,461–2) Heidegger develops this at some length, but enough has now been said to relate this to Beckett's unusual handling of time.

First we can see that Beckett is conscious of the paradoxical traditional handling of time. In the second *Text for Nothing* we read 'And now here, what now here, one enormous second, as in Paradise' (NK,78) where the equation is made between the infinite divisibility of time and the Eternal Present of God. In the eighth Text the narrator exclaims 'there will be no more time, till I get out of here' (NK,108) which makes us realize how much of Beckett's work is set in a timeless limbo. *Endgame*, for instance, is full of endings (there are no more pain-killers or bicycle wheels, the rat and the flea are killed, Nell dies) but this only underlines the situation of Hamm, whose play it is, and who is somehow hanging on, beyond time, after all the other deaths, waiting in timelessness for nothing. The exiguous leaves sprouted by the tree in *Godot* serve the same function, they are a parody of a development, of a moving time that is mocked by the stasis of the play's action. The only sort of positive time in Beckett is just that condition of authentic temporality stressed by Heidegger, as we have already seen, Being-towards-death. But in Beckett it is no cause for rejoicing. The whole matter is summed up in Pozzo's celebrated outburst towards the end of *Godot*.

> Have you not done tormenting me with your accursed time! It's abominable! When! When! One day, is that not enough for you, one day like any other day, one day he went dumb, one day I went blind, one day we'll go deaf, one day we were born, one day we shall die, the same day, the same second, is that not enough for you? (*Calmer.*) They give birth astride of a grave, the light gleams an instant, then it's night once more. (WFG,89)

Here are all the elements. *Sub specie aeternitatis* time is nothing, being either infinite or infinitesimal, so Pozzo can say that life adds up to one second, the 'enormous second' of the *Texts for Nothing*. (This is the same point as the one Beckett makes in *Breath* where the two cries separate one breath, representing minimal life, and the title seems to be an amalgam of 'birth' and 'death'). On the other hand Pozzo is also aware of the Heideggerian thesis that time for Dasein depends on finitude, Being-towards-an-end, so his examples of 'whens', of 'days', are all examples of endings – the ending of speech, sight, hearing. This is just Beckett's usual addition to Heidegger – the conditions, even of authentic existence, are hell.

It seems true, however, to say that Beckett's most frequent use of time-elements is as a parody of the Aristotelian paradox. In *Mercier et Camier*, for instance, we learn that there are days when one is being born all the time and will never die. (MC,50) *In Malone Dies* we have to make something of the opinion that a month is not much 'compared to a whole second of childishness', just 'a drop in a bucket'. (T,233) The Unnamable adds his expected twist: 'It was one second they should have schooled me to endure, after that I would have held out for all eternity'. (T,325)

So Beckett rejects, by parodying it, the traditional view of time, just as Heidegger does. Further, we have seen that he stresses the Being-towards-death (Being-towards-the-end) component in Dasein's temporalizing, again, as in Heidegger. But it is perhaps worth mentioning in conclusion that there are several non-Heideggerian aspects of Beckett's treatment of time.

There is, for instance the 'passing the time' motif which appears for instance in *Malone Dies* ('I divided, by 60. That passed the time' T,202) and frequently in *Godot*. Then there is the 'piling-up-of-time' motif represented in *Happy Days*, in the 'millet grains' of *Endgame* and in *The Unnamable*: 'Time...piles up all about you...thicker and thicker'. (T,393) Then there is the whole discussion of Proustian time in the essay on *A la recherche du temps perdu*.

I mention these to show how, as we leave Heidegger's first analysis of Dasein behind, and move into his considerations about temporality, we start to find fewer instructive parallels with Beckett. This is therefore where we should stop. However, there are two elements in Beckett's work which, although not expounded systematically by Heidegger, in his *magnum opus*, are sufficiently present at various points in *Being and Time* to merit attention. For this reason the two remaining sections of this comparison, besides the Conclusion, do not carry Heideggerian concepts as titles but have Beckettian themes instead.[16]

*   *   *

LANGUAGE AND SILENCE

When the narrators of the trilogy lose the thread of the story they are telling, or despair of it, they find themselves left with words. The words, language covering sheets of paper, appear to be compulsory, and they are undeniable, they have a sort of certainty which the stories do not. Not far behind this comes a yearning to be done with words and to lapse into silence.

Similarly, when the reader finds himself adrift on the sea of Beckett's prose he tends to try to anchor himself in the hard fact of the words in front of him; Beckett may build castles and destroy them but the stones are there on the pages of his works. He wants to lapse into silence, it seems, to stop writing, and there is an undeniable sense of relief for the reader when silence at last falls at the end of *The Unnamable*. Thus a tension between language and silence is an ever-present element in Beckett and in our response to Beckett.

A sufficiently clear example of this appears early in the trilogy where Molloy is unable to make a definitive choice between language and silence. When the man 'A' (if it *is* 'A') speaks to him he says 'I believe him, I know it's my only chance to – my only chance, I believe all I'm told, I've disbelieved only too much in my long life, now I swallow everything, greedily. What I need now is stories'. (T,13) But then 'A' leaves him and he is 'free', if that means anything, and his monologue reaches one of its occasional climaxes as he wonders what he is 'free' for: he is free 'to know', but to know

> that you would do better, at least no worse, to obliterate texts than to blacken margins, to fill in the holes of words till all is blank and flat and the whole ghastly business looks like what it is, senseless, speechless, issueless misery. (T,13)

In a dozen lines he moves from being greedy for stories to proposing the abolition of words, from language to silence. To reinforce the point he immediately observes that the trouble lies in other people and in thinking about other people; as soon as he 'returns in spirit' to 'A' he finds that 'the murmurs begin again'. Which leads to the further observation that 'To restore silence is the role of objects'. (T,13–14) Much later Moran refers to 'the silence of which the universe is made'. (T,122) Beckett's world is polarized by the hell of language and the speechless misery of silence.

Before relating this to Heidegger it is worth considering an essay on Nihilism by Stanley Rosen in J.M. Edie's collection *New Essays in Phenomenology* (Chicago: Quadrangle, 1969). This remarkable essay establishes a most interesting relationship between Ontologists and Language Philosophers which we can adopt to clarify the relevance of Language Philosophy to Beckett's obsession with language.

Rosen adopts the position that for Language Philosophy language is identical with Being. The limits of my speech are the limits of my world, and the Being of my world is revealed in my speech. This is an appropriate way into Beckett. The Unnamable says that he is 'made of words'. (T,390) There is a sense in which all Beckett's work is self-consciously a word-castle, words are the only possible way of Being, yet a sort of counterfeit Being. It may be hopelessly unsatisfactory, but words are as close as Beckett is ever going to get to Being.

That is the approach suggested by Language Philosophy. Rosen is more concerned, however, with the Ontological alternative, and here he could be speaking of either Heidegger or Beckett:

> The goal of ontological speech is not discourse about beings, but the revelation of Being. Since speech is itself an emanation of, rather than...identical with Being – i.e. since speech, as discursive, necessarily 'runs through' or is bound to the disjunctive multiplicity of *things* – speech necessarily separates us from Being. (Edie, op. cit. p. 154)

This is interestingly similar to Wittgenstein's point of view[17] and it sums up Molloy's (and Beckett's) dilemma exactly – speech, language, words are the only way we have of capturing Being, they are certainly all that an author or narrator has to use, and at the same time they are exactly what separates us from Being – whence the simultaneous talking and yearning after silence. 'The ontologist discerns more or less that it is silence he yearns for. The linguistic analyst struggles to keep talking'. (Edie, op. cit., p. 154) Beckett and his narrators, I would suggest, are both these things.

Rosen's subject is Nihilism and, since Beckett can easily appear nihilistic, we can profitably follow Rosen's move from this discussion of language and silence to his treatment of Nihilism. Nihilism, he says, contends that there is no significance in the universe, that nothing, not even human life, has a final meaning. Nihilism therefore holds that 'it makes no difference what we say, because "difference" is internal to speech and speech cannot speak about its own sense or significance'. (Edie, op. cit., p. 155) However, there is always the possibility that there exists a 'sense or significance' in the universe that is outside the limits of speech. So true Nihilism must maintain that 'evening is sayable' in order to dispose of any possible extra-linguistic 'meaning'. Beckett's narrators seem to go on in their effort to 'get it all said' as a sort of test of this proposition. Only when all that is sayable has been said can we get to the silence beyond and see if there is any 'further' meaning.[18] This, incidentally, is the burden of a good deal of discussion of Wittgenstein; the matter of 'mysticism' and of 'totalities' about which only silence is possible is brought up as an unsolved problem at the end of Russell's introduction to the *Tractatus*.

When Rosen talks of 'Ontologists' he cannot help meaning, or including, Heidegger. It is Heidegger who is concerned that man should be open to the call of Being and our job must now be to see what his Ontology makes of language in the light of this concern.

Heidegger has turned increasingly, since *Being and Time*, towards poetry and the presocratic philosophers in his search for Being. He claims that the Presocratics were open to Being and that they fulfilled the thinker's task which is to reveal Being. Since their time philosophy has tended to conceal Being. Poets, on the other hand, have remained open to it, and Heidegger has devoted a good deal of attention to Hölderlin's poetry in particular. Real thinkers, and poets, have a responsibility towards Being for, as Heidegger says in his '*Letter on Humanism*' of 1947,

> In thinking Being comes into language. Language is the house of Being. In its home man dwells. Those who think and those who create with words are the guardians of this home. (*Basic Writings* D.F. Krell (ed.), London: Routledge, 1978, p. 193)

Language is the house of Being; 'chattering' (*Gerede*) may conceal Being but genuine speaking is Being itself talking.[19]

Walter Kaufmann, in a curious essay entitled 'Heidegger's Castle' in *From Shakespeare to Existentialism* claims that Heidegger is trapped by his own words into meaninglessness. 'He thinks that unlike all previous thinkers since the early Greeks he is on the traces of Being itself, but it is language that has her sport with him.' (Kaufmann, op. cit., p. 277) This is not adequately substantiated in Kaufmann's essay, but I think it is interesting that it applies rather well to Beckett. He is on the traces of the Self, of course, and knows very well that language has her sport with him; he perhaps demonstrates the necessity of trying to capture philosophical goals in words, however inadequate words may be.

What does Heidegger himself say about language and silence in *Being and Time*? First, he considers that language is founded in 'discourse' which is equiprimordial with 'states of mind' and 'understanding' which are themselves 'the fundamental *existentialia* which constitute the Being of the "there", the disclosedness of Being-in-the-World'. (BT,203) He demonstrates this by observing that 'hearing' and 'keeping silent' are modes of 'discourse' and the Dasein that is in a 'state-of-mind' and 'understanding' the world is naturally orientated towards the world and Others in one of these modes, or in language. Here we find an ontologist attributing the same sort of position to language that Language Philosophy does. Language is Dasein's 'truth', the articulation of Dasein's 'disclosedness'. 'Discourse is existentially language, because that entity whose disclosedness it articulates according to signification, has, as its kind of Being, Being-in-the-world.' (BT,204) In other words, language is Dasein's way of 'Being-in-the-world'. Dasein is 'made of words' as the Unnamable says.

We have seen that 'keeping silent' is another possible mode of discourse for Dasein. But this in no way alters the contention that language is Dasein's way of Being-in-the-world. On the contrary, Dasein can only 'keep silent' because his Being is such that he is able to speak. We cannot say of a man born dumb that he is 'keeping silent'. (BT,208) Keeping silent, then, is not a haven of innocence for Heidegger any more than it is for Beckett. For both, and for Wittgenstein, the mystic silence would be a perfect consummation, but unless, like Victor in *Eleuthéria*, we can be dead, and see ourselves dead, we cannot achieve this. Life is words. But keeping silent may achieve more than talking a lot. Babbling away is most often '*Gerede*', 'idle talk' which instead of disclosing things covers them up. 'Idle talk' is gossip, it 'passes along' things it has learnt and it believes what it is told on authority; thus it is never in contact with the truth at all. It is the voice of the 'they'. (BT,211–13) On the other hand, 'if anyone is genuinely "on the scent" of anything he does not speak about it'. (BT,218)

This connects with what we have learnt of conscience. Conscience, the call of Care, the call of the authentic Self to the 'they-Self', discourses 'Solely and constantly in the mode of keeping silent'. (BT,318) So the silence is the condition of authentic existence. Man will only find his Self after the silence has set in, which is surely one of the clearest messages of Beckett's fiction.

We have already mentioned the frequency of the pronoun 'I' in Beckett, especially in *The Unnamable*. We are now in a position to quote Heidegger's last word on the subject of language and silence; it is a summary that could be put at the end of Beckett's trilogy; the emphases are Heidegger's.

> Dasein *is authentically itself* in the primordial individualization of the reticent resoluteness which exacts anxiety of itself. *As something that keeps silent*, authentic *Being*-one's-Self is just the sort of thing that does not keep on Saying 'I'. (BT,369–70)

*   *   *

THE SELF

'Once a certain degree of insight has been reached', says Wylie to Neary in *Murphy*, 'all men talk, when talk they must, the same tripe.' (M,44) Thus, or perhaps in the less direct tones of Heidegger as quoted at the end of the last section, we opt for silence. But Beckett refuses, notoriously, to be silent. After *Breath* came *Not I*. Why? Because when his silence falls, he has not yet attained his Self. Here lies the usual extra twist that Beckett gives to a Heideggerian proposition – he agrees that silence is the condition of authentic existence, but how can we fall silent, especially when silence is still a 'mode of discourse'? Beckett, or rather his narrator, puts it thus in the eighth *Text for Nothing*:

> I say no matter what, hoping to wear out a voice, to wear out a head, or without hope, without reason, no matter what, without reason. But it will end, a desinence will come, or the breath fail, better still, I'll be silence, I'll know I'm silence, no, in the silence you can't know, I'll never know anything. (NK,108)

The mystic silence that is more than just a 'keeping silent' is unavailable to our 'knowing' because it is by definition a cessation of Being, of discourse, of language. So we are left with words. They are the bar to whatever ultimate reality the silence represents, but they are also the only means towards it.

It is evident that in Beckett this 'ultimate reality' is, at least in one aspect, the Self. Throughout his work, and indeed on the very same page of *Texts for Nothing* from which I have just quoted, there is a desperate scrabbling to get to 'me', to say 'I' to be 'in my midst' to 'win to me' and so on. In *Text for Nothing* number eight we read 'Me, here, if they could open, those little words, open and swallow me up, perhaps that is what has happened.' (NK,108) The tension here is between the incomprehensibility of words (perhaps I have already managed to say 'me') and their obvious uselessness (if only 'me' *was me*). In some mystical way the true silence may be 'me'. Meanwhile there are only the words, and they are not me. We have seen what Heidegger has to say about the silence; we can now consider what he has to say about the Self, about 'me'.

Heidegger starts his enquiry about Being by interrogating Dasein because Dasein already has 'a vague average understanding of Being'. (BT,25) Furthermore, Dasein also has an understanding of itself, it 'always understands itself in terms of its existence'. (BT,33) This looks promising. Heidegger at least may get somewhere in his definition of the Self; we shall see.

Whatever Dasein's Self is it is not definable in Dualist terms. Heidegger refers scornfully to 'the naive supposition that man is, in the first instance, a spiritual thing which subsequently gets misplaced "into" a space'. (BT,83) He insists that man is a whole, a unity. When we come to the section entitled 'An Approach to the Existential Question of the "who" of Dasein' (BT,150ff.) Heidegger unambiguously equates Dasein with the Self. 'Dasein is an entity which is in each case I myself. . . The question of the "who" answers itself in terms of the "I" itself, the "subject", the "Self".' (BT,150)

So, Dasein is always 'Self', but Heidegger makes quite sure that, having made this point, we cannot rest comfortably on our Cartesian assumptions. He subjects the 'Self', the 'I' to a rigorous examination (BT,150–2) the burden of which is as follows.

'I' cannot be, and must not be treated as, just another present-at-hand object within the world. 'I' is Dasein, so its existence precedes its essence; we must examine it existentially. This means that 'I' can only be exhibited by exhibiting one of the definite kinds of Being of Dasein, for example Being-with-others or Being-in-the-world. I am not 'I' in isolation. If we use the word 'I' in isolation it is merely a 'formal indicator' rather than a substantive. As a 'formal indicator' 'I' does not disclose Dasein at all. So Dasein is 'I', but it is useless to examine this 'I' with a view to finding out 'who' Dasein is. What must examine is Dasein's existentiality – the ways of Being of man – to answer this question 'who?'

Dasein's existence is a Being-with. An 'I' that has meaning is an 'I' already in a situation already with-Others, in-the-world. Is this the limit of our discussion? Far from it. We have yet to consider the implications of authenticity. We saw that 'inauthentic existence' is dominated by the 'they' and that the 'authentic Self' (existence and Self are interchangeable here) is 'the Self which has been taken hold of in its own way'. (BT,167) Both of these must be taken existentially – the 'they-Self' in action is the one whose possibilities have been taken over by the 'they', the authentic Self is the one that projects itself into its own possibilities. Both of them 'really are' the Self – 'the "not-I" is by no means tantamount to an entity which essentially lacks "I-hood".' (BT,152) Knowledge of the Self 'is not a matter of perceptually tracking down and inspecting a point called the "Self", but rather one of seizing on the full disclosedness of Being-in-the-world *throughout all* the constitutive items which are essential to it.' (BT,187) Heidegger's emphasis makes my point here – the Self is to be sought as much in inauthenticity as in authenticity. After all the 'they' is defined as belonging 'to Dasein's positive constitution' (BT,167) So it is a 'constitutive item' of Dasein and as such relevant to 'knowledge of the Self'. Even though I am 'proximally and for the most part' my 'they-Self', it is my *existence*, authentic or inauthentic that defines, creates and *is* my Self.

For Beckett this suggests that his characters are 'themselves', or have 'found' their Selves, already and in spite of what they say. The novels and plays represent the 'existence' of their people, so they reveal their Selves constantly as they act and talk. The same may be said of the narrators who tell their stories and of Beckett who invents them all. This is Heidegger's cutting of the Gordian knot – 'what I do is me', as Hopkins put it, so there is no need to search further for my Self.

This common-sense approach certainly applies to Beckett up to a point. We do feel an automatic 'superior' knowledge as readers or as audience. *We* can see what Hamm is, *we* can talk objectively about Moran. We can observe their doings and so observe 'them'. But this is not, surely, a sufficient interpretation of Beckett. We cannot say that all his work is simply a demonstration of a delusion and that the Self is quite obvious all along. This can be only one aspect of the truth, and indeed it is not Heidegger's last word on the subject.

There appears to be a contradiction between this first stage of 'all is Self' and the stress laid on the importance of my 'own' Self, my authenticity. It is as if Heidegger moves from an 'empirical Ego' position (I am my desires, my body, my Bank account) to a 'transcendental Ego' position. The purely existential Self is very like the empirical Ego, it is all my actions and possibilities bound together by a 'formal' 'I'. But the 'ownness' of my 'authentic' Self seems to imply something transcendent. Is this so?

We saw, in discussing Conscience, above, that Conscience calls Dasein back from the 'they-Self' to its 'own Self'. (BT,317) Conscience says 'nothing' to the Self and by 'keeping silent' it calls us out of 'concernful Being-with-Others' into our 'potentiality' for Being our Selves. And 'the call comes *from* me and yet *from beyond me*'. (BT,318–20) The caller, we learn, is 'Dasein in its uncanniness'. (BT,321) It sounds like an 'alien' voice to everyday Dasein, it even sounds like the voice of God, all this in a highly Beckettian manner, as we have seen. But it is guaranteed to be the voice of the authentic Self because whenever we interpret it, or attribute it to anything beyond ourselves we at once find that we have turned away from it and back towards the 'they'. For example, if I interpret the call of conscience as 'universal conscience' I find I have merely defined the voice of the 'they'. Only in meeting the ineffable spirit can I match up to it and become myself.

This new level proposes, thus, some sort of transcendent self. It is even more Beckettian than our earlier empirical self; it is my 'ownmost' potentiality for Being, about which I must talk and think, but it is exactly that self-relationship that starts where words leave off.

Heidegger returns to these points in the second half of *Being and Time*. He analyzes Kant's position on the Self and concludes that Kant's 'I' is still an object present-at-hand within the world. Kant has not broken the traditional ontological mould. Heidegger does this as follows. Dasein is a unity that has some understanding of its own Being, and it is a unity that is always 'mine'. Dasein's unity is 'held together' by the 'I'. (BT,365) This 'I' is 'harboured' by Care – obviously the condition of Care is to be a subject, 'Care for oneself' is a tautology – Dasein is existentially Care by being Self and Self by being Care. When Dasein's 'I' expresses Being-in-the-world or Being under the dominion of the 'they', it 'fails to see itself in relation to the kind of Being of that entity which it is itself'. (BT,368) By this point it is apparent that Heidegger is moving towards a position in which, in spite of earlier statements, he must acknowledge that there is a sort of selfhood in the authentic Self that is lacking in the everyday 'they' Self. And, sure enough, 'Selfhood is to be discerned existentially only in one's authentic potentiality-for-Being-one's-Self – that is to say, in the authenticity of Dasein's Being *as care*.' (BT,369) Once he has reached this point Heidegger finds that clarification follows naturally – the 'constancy of the Self' is now seen to depend on authentic existence and we find a satisfaction in realizing that we have, long since, defined as *in*authentic the irresolute 'falling' into the world. So Heidegger at last chooses to unify the Self with authentic existence, which leaves us open to our most Beckettian gloss to date. We have seen that authentic existence depends on the call of conscience from the Self to the 'they-Self' and we have found this to be a call that operates in the mode of keeping silent. I would propose that this silent call is the voice of the 'little world' that calls Murphy, the silent summons of Mr Knott that brings Watt to his house and the goad or god that prods the narrators of the trilogy and the characters of the plays into further 'existence'. It is the voice that prompts the three questions that open *The Unnamable* and it is the compulsion that dictates that novel's conclusion. It calls to the 'they-Self', the inauthentic Self that has been 'dispersed' and 'disconnected' (BT,441) and it prompts Beckett's dreadful struggles for unity. In Heidegger this unity is held out as a possibility – it can grasp itself as a whole that exists between thrownness and death. In Beckett this 'loyalty of existence to its own Self' (BT,443) is never achieved.

*   *   *

CONCLUSION

Heidegger warns us of the dangers of accepting tradition instead of confronting Being for ourselves and speaks of the necessity of arriving at the 'primordial experiences' of Being that we had before philosophy. (BT,44) It is as if, like Wittgenstein, Heidegger reaches a position from which he can see that his labours to arrive there are a little beside the point. True, he proposes that philosophy, like poetry, *can* reveal Being, but the non-conclusion of *Being and Time* and the oracular nature of his later work indicate an impatience with systematic analysis, however profound, as a tool to bring man into contact with Being.

Arne Naess in his summary of this point concludes that Heidegger means man to approach Being but warns that man, to do this, will have to learn to 'exist in the nameless'. (Naess, op. cit., p. 242) I would propose that Beckett's work is an attempt to describe this 'nameless' existence.

NOTES AND REFERENCES

1. As suggested by Mary O'Hara in an unpublished thesis of 1974. Jean Onimus in his study *Beckett* of 1968 (Paris: Desclée de Brouwer) ponders the possibility of Beckett having read Heidegger's *What is Metaphysics?* on its appearance in French in 1937. He goes further: 'Beckett . . . avait peut-être alors déjà lu *Sein und Zeit*. En tous cas les thèmes principaux de Heidegger recoupent souvent ceux de Beckett.' In this context 'recouper' seems to be being used in its common sense of 'to blend' (as with wine). David Hesla, in *The Shape of Chaos* (University of Minnesota Press, 1971), seems to eschew this approach, but of the two sentences in which he does this the second seems to contradict the first: 'I am not imputing a knowledge of Heidegger to Beckett (though I would not deny it either), and am not supposing that Beckett's works are puzzles or allegories explicable only by reference to *Sein und Zeit*. I am, rather, trying to get at the "meaning" of the scene, and am using Heidegger as one of several possible ways of doing so'. (p. 140)

2. In *Being and Time*. In other works he discussed metaphysics (eg. in *What is Metaphysics?* of 1929) although it is worth stressing that Heidegger is better thought of as an Ontologist than a Metaphysician.

3. For further light on this topic cf. 'Philosophy and Poetry' and 'Heidegger's Castle' in Walter Kaufmann, *From Shakespeare to Existentialism* (New York: Beacon, 1959). For English versions of Heidegger on these topics cf. his *Poetry, Language, Thought* (New York: Harper and Row, 1971).

4. Günther Anders, in his essay in the Esslin volume already cited, calls the characters in Godot 'abstractions'; Cormier and Pallister, in *Waiting for Death* (University of Alabama Press, 1979), go further and say 'It seems more accurate to say that the play's four characters, taken together, portray universal man.' (p. 5)

5. David Hesla points out that Heidegger provides an 'accurate answer to the Unnamable's question "Who now?"' He quotes BT, pp. 152–3: 'The "Who?" is to be answered only by exhibiting phenomenally a definite kind of Being which Dasein possesses . . . man's "substance" is not a spirit as a synthesis of body and soul; it is rather *existence*.' From *The Shape of Chaos* (University of Minnesota, 1971), p. 126

6. Most of Beckett's characters are in quest of something: Belacqua, Murphy and perhaps Watt are in quest of Nirvana; Molloy is in search of his mother, Moran is in search of Molloy. All of them are in quest of themselves.

7. Perhaps, however, Heidegger offers a more subtle formulation than Sartre when he also says that Dasein's essence *is* Dasein's existence.

8. There is a jug in Heidegger's essay 'The Thing' (*Poetry, Language, Thought*, pp. 165–82) which has a strong affinity to Watt's pot.

9. For a full discussion of this topic see Aron Gurwitsch's essay 'Husserl's Theory of Intentionality' in Lee and Mandelbaum (eds), *Phenomenology and Existential-*

ism (Baltimore: Johns Hopkins, 1967). 'Being-in-the-world', however, cannot be regarded as central to Husserl's thinking.

10. The best discussion of these somewhat neglected pieces is to be found in Knowlson and Pilling, *Frescoes of the Skull* (London: Calder, 1979, pp. 41–60) where they are seen, not as the rejectamenta of the trilogy but as transitional, attempts at finding new ways to say the silence, a development.

11. Murphy's solipsism is rejected by Beckett, it seems. In *Watt* Sam and Watt are separated by the fences of their compounds (in Chapter 3) but some mysterious agency has burst holes through these fences and the two men do meet and communicate, after a fashion.

12. Hesla comments: 'Since in the trilogy speaking is identical with being, the fact that the Unnamable has no words of his own but only "their" words means that he has no being of his own but only "their" being' (op. cit., p. 126).
Hesla spends more time putting Heidegger and Beckett together than any other critic I have seen in print although even he, in the end, is suggestive rather than systematic (cf. op. cit., pp. 140–4 especially).

13. In *Premier Amour* we find this aphorism: '*c'est plus pénible de ne plus être soi-même, encore plus pénible que de l'être, quoi qu'on en dise.*' (PA, p. 21) This may reflect Heidegger's public and private selves: whatever 'they' say it's worse *not* to be oneself than to be oneself.

14. Heidegger's own notes make it clear that he adopts Kierkegaard's usage of *Angst* more or less *in toto*. Cf.BT, p. 235, n. IV and p. 278, n. VI.

15. The Being-towards-Death motif permeates Beckett's work. It is neatly summarised by Molloy: 'Perhaps there is no whole, before you're dead.' (T,27) Molloy also applies this to the whole world: 'For what possible end to these wastes where true light never was...? Yes, a world at an end, in spite of appearances, its end brought it forth, ending it began, is it clear enough?' (T,40)

16. This may appear unsatisfactory; after all, Heidegger claims in *Being and Time* that temporality is the ground and explanation of all that he has said about Dasein and, indeed, about Being itself. Among many examples here is a typical sentence: 'Within the horizon of time the projection of a meaning of Being in general can be accomplished'. (BT,278) The very title of this work seems to give Time what Heidegger would call 'equiprimordiality' with Being. If this is so are we not cheating Heidegger by playing down this essential aspect of his thought when making an extensive comparison with Beckett?
It may seem an impertinence, but I would suggest that this is not so on the grounds that Heidegger's analysis of Dasein seems to run into difficulties as it starts to tackle time: 'Division Two' ('Dasein and Temporality') is *not* exclusively concerned with this topic and many of its summarising and generalising statements make surprisingly bald claims about time that leave it unanalysed as a concept. Thus for instance near the end of the work we read 'The existential-ontological constitution of Dasein's totality is grounded in temporality'. This remains at the level of assertion as is confirmed by the sentence immediately following which is uncharacteristically tentative: 'Hence the ecstatical projection of Being must be made possible by some primordial way in which ecstatical temporality temporalises'. The three remaining sentences of *Being and Time* are all questions and they, too, indicate Heidegger's difficulty with time:

How is this mode of the temporalising of temporality to be Interpreted? Is there a way which leads from primordial *time* to the meaning of *Being*? Does *time* manifest itself as the horizon of *Being*? (BT,488)

In short, Heidegger did not offer a full analysis of time in the part of *Being and Time* that he completed and published and he never completed the part that was to have dealt with this question fully. Significantly, the many later Heidegger works do not, as far as this author knows, take up time again as a central topic. The trouble perhaps is that for Heidegger time is an empty and inscrutable *sine qua non* of Dasein's being about which nothing further can be said. In 'The Question of the Essence of Being' in *An Introduction to Metaphysics* (German ed., 1953), he observes

> We cannot say:
> There is no time when man was not. At all *times* man was and is and will be, because time produces itself only insofar as man is. There is no time when man was not, not because man was from all eternity and will be for all eternity but because time is not eternity and time fashions itself into a time only as a human, historical being-there. (R. Mannheim (trans.), Anchor Books, 1961)

Unlike Being, time is so much an essential of human existence as to become trivial.

17. There is a supposed antagonism between Wittgenstein and Heidegger (assumed, for instance, in A.J. Ayer's *Language, Truth and Logic* of 1936) but Wittgenstein's single paragraph on Heidegger, reprinted in Michael Murray (ed.), *Heidegger and Modern Philosophy* (Yale, 1978), suggests, if anything, an affinity. It also offers a possible gloss on Beckett which, in view of the mystical possibilities inherent in Wittgenstein's famous ladder image, could be extremely suggestive. The paragraph includes these sentences:

> Man has the impulse to run up against the limits of language. Think, for example, of the astonishment that anything exists. This astonishment cannot be expressed in the form of a question, and there is also no answer to it. Everything which we feel like saying can, a priori, only be nonsense...It is a priori certain that whatever one might offer as a definition of the Good [as an example of an abstraction], it is always simply a misunderstanding to think that it corresponds in expression to the authentic matter one actually means...St. Augustine already knew this when he said: What, you wretch, so you want to avoid talking nonsense? Talk some nonsense, it makes no difference! (Murray (ed.), op. cit., pp. 80–1)

Altogether it seems that a thorough Wittgensteinian analysis of Beckett would be most rewarding.

18. Rosen, of course, is also the author of the classic study *Nihilism* (Yale U. P., 1969) which, although it does not mention Beckett, pays considerable attention to Heidegger among others. Steven J. Rosen, whom I take to be Stanley Rosen's son, has written *Samuel Beckett and the Pessimistic Tradition* (New York: Rutgers University Press, 1976).

19. For Heidegger on poetry, language and art, see the English-Language collection *Poetry, Language, Thought* (New York: Harper and Row, 1971) which contains seven of Heidegger's essays on these topics.

3 Sartre's *Being and Nothingness* and Beckett

INTRODUCTORY

Sartre's *Being and Nothingness* owes something to Hegel, something to Husserl, and a great deal to the Heidegger of *Being and Time*. Several of the concepts Sartre deals with are taken with little or no alteration from Heidegger, for example '*Angst*' as the state-of-mind of man in the face of freedom. Or, again, the 'human reality' used by Sartre is a term equivalent to 'Dasein'. But more important than these points of close resemblance is the general point of structure. Sartre operated within Heidegger's framework. There are differences in emphasis, and plenty of original developments, but there are almost no ideas in the French work that do not correspond in some way with similar ideas in the German. Thus both philosophers picture man as 'there', already aware of himself, already free, already aware of a world, of Others, of facticity and so on. This means that some of this chapter will overlap with some of the preceding one. As far as Beckett is concerned, some of Sartre's amplifications of Heidegger bring him closer to our subject and I shall concentrate on these. Where Sartre either repeats Heidegger or develops him away from Beckett I shall be briefer.

It is more difficult to write about *Being and Nothingness* than about its German predecessor. Sartre's argument does not progress from point to point as Heidegger's does, his concepts are more closely woven together (in his presentation of them; not, of course, as a picture of man and the world.) Thus 'nothingness', for instance, appears in his discussions of Freedom, the Self, Consciousness, *Angst* and so on rather than being dealt with once for all. Because of this I shall first give a rapid summary of the argument of the book, putting the salient concepts into their places in Sartre's argument, and then deal with each concept in turn showing how it affects Beckett.

As with Heidegger, 'Being' is the question at issue. As with Hegel, there is a dialectical necessity of opposing 'Nothing' to 'Being'. Sartre grasps this nettle of 'Nothing' much more firmly than either of the Germans. 'Nothing' for him, is human consciousness. This does not mean that the human *mind* is nothing. 'Being' is made up of two sorts of thing, 'real' objects and our mental pictures of those objects when we imagine them. To both these sorts of 'Being' we oppose our consciousness – I am conscious of my neighbour's house when I look at it, and then I am conscious of it when I imagine it with my eyes closed. In each case there is a clearly definable object of consciousness (the house; my mental image of it) but my consciousness itself is not an object. So what is it that I 'oppose' to 'Being'? Sartre says it is 'Nothing'. Consciousness is a 'hole' in the solidity of 'Being', it 'decompresses' the otherwise total pressure of it.

'Human reality' is *'pour-soi'*. We are 'for-ourselves' while all objects are *'en-soi'*, 'in themselves'. (I shall henceforth treat *pour-soi* and *en-soi* as English words.) This reflects Heidegger's thesis that Dasein already has an understanding of its own Being. In short, I know that I am me.[1]

Knowledge is the 'presence' of a thing to consciousness. Things cannot be 'present' to the en-soi; we can remember here Heidegger's expression when he says that the table 'cannot touch' the wall. What is 'present' to my consciousness is, precisely, not me. So, as pour-soi, I 'negate' the en-soi, I am the 'Nothing' to its 'Being'. Only the known is a being, the knower is 'not apprehensible', he is nothing. Thus there is 'nothing' to separate the knower from the known. The known, being, the en-soi, is solid (*'massif'*) and contingent. 'Uncreated, without reason for being, without any connexion with another being, being-in-itself is *de trop* for eternity.' (BN, xlii) *Being and Nothingness* is Sartre's attempt to do better than either Idealism or Realism in holding together the mutually-exclusive regions of the en-soi and the pour-soi. That is, it is an attempt to explain man in the world.

Freedom is a fundamental part of this explanation. 'I' can always choose what I shall do even after account has been taken of all 'my' motives and desires. 'I' am free, even of 'me'. There is nothing to justify my choices but I do choose; the en-soi is brute contingency but I choose what values it is to have. Values 'spring up like partridges' when I act. My value-conferring freedom, as in Kierkegaard and Heidegger, breeds *'Angst'*. I am inclined to flee from the *'Angst'* and to reduce my freedom, choices and responsibility; in short I am tempted into inauthentic existence. This is like Heidegger's flight into '*das Man*' but, in Sartre, stress is laid on the fact that I am responsible for becoming inauthentic, it is 'I' who lies to 'me' when I am in 'bad faith'. Man, however, is always in 'bad faith', for the opposite, 'sincerity', means *being what you are*, and how can I ever *be* sad or happy? I can *act* sadly or happily but as for being – we have already seen that I *am* nothing. So all human action is in bad faith.

'Human reality' is thrown into a world and abandoned in a 'situation'. It can never reduce itself to en-soi, in which case it would be a definable something, but it does aspire to the 'impossible synthesis' of the for-itself with the in-itself where a 'real' self would emerge. As things are, the self is the foundation of values. My choices confer value. How close all this is to Heidegger is made clear by Sartre's summary of his arguments which he gives at the end of the first chapter of the second part of *Being and Nothingness*. (p,105) There he lists the topics he has treated: man 'negates' things by 'not being' them; his existence is always inauthentic in that he can never *be* himself; Descartes' *cogito* is not enough; man is being for-itself not in-itself; man gives rise to values and possibilities. Still Heideggerian, he goes on to say that now we must study time (the *cogito* has instantaneity but possibilities need time) to settle the main question – that of 'the original relation of consciousness to being'. (BN,105)

On the matter of time Sartre repeats Heidegger on the non-historical non-temporal quality of the en-soi; man gives time to the universe. On the other hand he adds the idea that my past is that en-soi which I am – an idea he explains by observing that the past makes me what I am 'from behind'. The pour-soi alone is present and the present alone is pour-soi. Pour-soi projects into the future. So we have here the familiar Heideggerian trio – the past is facticity, the present is man, Dasein, pour-soi, and the future is possibility.

The world is *my* world. It is only 'an ideal limitation – by nothing – of a collection of thises'. (BN,183) Space, like time, 'is not'. It comes into the world because of pour-soi.

Where Sartre develops Heidegger most successfully is in his treatment of Others. His concrete examples of the existence of others, connected with shame and similar emotions, force him to develop a third category of existence. Man exists pour-soi in a world of en-soi, but he recognizes the existence of other pour-soi beings and realizes that he exists for them. Consequently man exists 'pour-autrui'; for others. Sartre discusses this and its implications at length, as we shall have to do with Beckett in mind.

The discussion of Others leads Sartre on to discussions of the body, and love. Then a section is devoted to freedom, although this concept has been much in evidence before. Now, of course, it takes into consideration the expanded view of Others. Some of Sartre's most inspired writing appears here as he deals with the possibilities that confront pour-soi and the relationship of these possibilities to the world and to the limitations of facticity. One of the essential points of Existentialist freedom and choice is made here -- that man has freedom of choice that may or may not coincide with his freedom of obtaining. The importance of this freedom of choice appears again and again -- it illuminates spatiality (Japan only becomes distant if I choose to go there), temporality (even the past can be modified by present choices as for instance in the change in the value of the revolutionary events of 1789 when seen from the perspective of 1917) and it illuminates Others (when I choose I always discover that meanings have already been implanted into the world by the choices of Others.)

Death is treated differently by Heidegger and Sartre. For the latter, death, so far from being my ownmost possibility, is not a possibility at all. All my genuine choices imply finitude -- I will do X, not Y, and I will finish doing it within a certain time. But death, although it *is* finitude in one sense, is an 'unrealizable', infinite state for which I can have no responsibility. This leads into a discussion of man's responsibility within his lifetime which involves an Existentialist psychoanalysis according to which men do not have given characters or characteristics but choose themselves.

Sartre offers a short conclusion to *Being and Nothingness* in which he considers the metaphysical and ethical implications of his philosophy. The first of these will find its place in our final chapter.

* * *

CONSCIOUSNESS

It will be apparent from the above summary of the main theses of *Being and Nothingness* that Sartre, like Descartes, finds he must lean heavily on a clarification of what 'I' means. His starting point, and the place around which he circles and to which he frequently returns, is consciousness. The same may be said of Beckett.

But can 'I' and 'consciousness' be equated? This is the question that Sartre tackled in his first published work, *The Transcendence of the Ego*.² This essay is a development of Husserl's theory of intentional consciousness. Husserl, according to Sartre, refreshed philosophy by claiming that even such apparently purely 'mental' phenomena as mathematics and chimeras are *objects* of consciousness and thus not really 'mental' at all. This enabled philosophy to describe all things, from tables to hallucinations, as objects in their own right. Sartre concurs with this. But Husserl, according to Sartre, goes on to describe the 'other side' of the business of perception in terms that Sartre finds unsatisfactory. Husserl adopts a neo-Cartesian position which proposes a split between the subjective and objective worlds; on the subjective side of the split we have consciousness and an Ego presiding over consciousness. To bring subjective and objective together we must 'bracket out' the question of whether the objective exists or not and rely on the marriage implied in the concept of intentionality – consciousness 'intends' its objects.

In Sartre's version this is simplified. There is no Ego 'behind' or 'in' consciousness. Intentionality *is* consciousness. The 'bracketing out' of the question of the existence of objects becomes redundant because there is no real dualism here. It is impossible to 'stop' in the passage from consciousness to its object and ask 'does the object exist?' because there is no passage, no gap between consciousness and its object. Thus Sartre, like Heidegger, cuts Descartes' Gordian knot – consciousness is always consciousness of something, *cogito, ergo est*.

To be fair, Sartre does not reject the Ego's existence, only its transcendence. Husserl proposed the Ego as a transcendent 'pole' which unified experience. Sartre sees another, less mystical, definition of the Ego. For him it is another object of consciousness, like the world. When I say 'I am undecided' what I mean is that my Ego appears to my consciousness to be in the psychic state of indecision. This Ego, therefore, is an object of consciousness, not 'behind' consciousness as a subject. The Ego is not an abstract something that has the mission of unifying mental events, it is all those events put together, the 'infinite totality of states and actions which never lets itself be reduced to *one* action or to *one* state'. (op. cit., p. 57, my translation here and hereafter) Sartre compares the Ego to the world – the world is not a transcendent unity of things, merely their totality.

The implications of this constitute some of Sartre's most characteristic doctrines. If the Ego is merely a non-transcendent totality of psychic states it follows that there is no 'real me', no given Ego that is the absolute 'me' to which I must or can or should conform. Similarly there can be no 'unconscious', no hidden pool of my 'real' desires and 'thoughts'. Only when I turn the light of consciousness onto my state of mind (or any other object) and grasp it as mine can it be me or part of me.

Sartre claims here to have liberated and purified the 'transcendental field'. All that is left in it is consciousness, which is the only absolute in that it is 'nothing', merely being an 'intention' towards objects. Consciousness, alone, is inaccessible. My mental states, love for example, are as objective as chairs. There is no longer anything impenetrable about others except, by definition, their consciousnesses. Perhaps rather dangerously, considering that he is engaged in a rejection of Husserlian and Cartesian dualism, Sartre sums up his propositions by describing two spheres, the 'transcendental' sphere of consciousness, and the 'Ego-sphere' accessible to psychology, the sphere of mental states, actions, qualities. The latter is the object of the former.

Transcendental consciousness is an 'impersonal spontaneousness' which 'determines its existence at every monent without our being able to conceive of anything *before it*. Thus every instant of our conscious life reveals to us a creation *ex nihilo*'. (op. cit., p. 79) This consciousness is a monster: if at every moment it creates a new world, how can there be any unity or continuity in conscious life? 'A phenomenological description of the spontaneousness (of consciousness) would, indeed, show that it renders impossible all ideas about the freedom of the will.' (op. cit., p. 82) Thus an Ego is needed to give a coherent object to consciousness. If consciousness suddenly appears on the plane of pure reflexion ('I am I') then we are seized by a fear of ourselves and an 'absolute anguish'. This last is not an intellectual process, but a daily event.

Consciousness as a monster defeated by the Ego, consciousness as anguish (an anguish that 'we cannot avoid'), this is the price of our humanity and the agony of Samuel Beckett.

In spite of the celebrated dualism of *Murphy*, Beckett's early work shows some concern with these Sartrean problems. Subject and object are much canvassed in the essay on Proust and Beckett comes to the conclusion that direct contact between them is impossible 'because they are automatically separated by the subject's consciousness of perception'. (PTD,74) This both states Sartrean negation (I know I am *not* what I am conscious of) and, paradoxically, implies the unity of perception with what is perceived (I am not separated from objects by perception, indeed, I *am* what I perceive, but I am separated by my consciousness of that perception.)

Even in *Murphy* some of the philosophical fireworks bring the characters who indulge in them close to Sartre's position in *The Transcendence of the Ego*. When Wylie, for instance, proposes that the world is a closed system (like 'the horse leech's daughter' its 'quantum of wantum cannot vary') Neary sees why Berkeley wanted to find some escape from this static hell, 'He had no alternative. . . Immaterialize or bust. The sleep of sheer terror.' (M,43) This is reminiscent of Sartre's 'absolute anguish' in the face of *his* escape from the closed system, consciousness. It is also possible to put an Existentialist interpretation on the well-known point made in Chapter Six of *Murphy* that in the third and final zone of his mind 'he was not free, but a mote in the dark of absolute freedom'. (M,79) Here the 'absolute' is specifically not him but could be something like consciousness in which his Ego is an object, a mote in the absolute light.

In *Watt* Beckett is struggling with other problems than those of consciousness, but even here there are Sartrean elements in some passages. The picture on the wall of Erskine's room (W,126–7) of a circle and its centre, perhaps in search of one another, can be taken as an illustration of the problem of the Ego. If the circle represents the limit of everything that is 'me' (my feet, my dreams, my bank account) then the question, as tackled by Sartre in *The Transcendence of the Ego* is, what is the centre? Is it something recognizable that we must put into position at the heart of our lives, an identifiable Ego? Or is the dot in Erskine's picture not going to become the centre of this given circle? In which case is it merely a 'mote in the dark of absolute freedom'? In this latter case we find outselves faced with the dangerous 'new' dualism described above in the discussion of Sartre's 'two spheres', consciousness and the rest. The dot is consciousness, the circle 'the rest'. The dot does not belong as the centre of the circle because transcendental consciousness is 'impersonal'.

Some other examples could be given from *Watt* but it is Beckett's later work that is in more need of elucidation. Before turning to it we must see what *Being and Nothingness* has to say about consciousness.

Our time spent on *The Transcendence of the Ego* has not been wasted in that Sartre clearly incorporated its ideas into *Being and Nothingness*.[3] Sartre's development of his views on consciousness in the later work is excellently summarized in David Hesla's study of Beckett *The Shape of Chaos*.[4] Hesla reduces Sartre on consciousness to five propositions: consciousness is 'nothing', 'intentionality', 'reflexivity', 'freedom' and 'not in-itself'. (Hesla, op. cit., p. 186) All of these we can now understand, with the possible exception of 'reflexivity'. This is Sartre's term for the fact that consciousness can have itself as an object, it 'reflects' itself. Indeed, consciousness only exists as both consciousness of an object *and* consciousness of that consciousness. In *Being and Nothingness* Sartre points out that Ego can have a sort of theoretical existence 'between' consciousness and consciousness. This is not a contradiction of the thesis of *The Transcendence of the Ego* for it establishes this Ego as, precisely, nothing. 'The *self*...represents an ideal distance within the immanence of the subject in relation to himself, a way of *not being his own coincidence*, a way of escaping identity while positing it as unity.' (BN,77) Thus there is a 'nothingness' that divides me from myself, a 'nothingness' that is necessary to my identity.

So, consciousness is a 'nothing' opposed to 'being', and, within this nothing, the self is the nothing that divides me from myself in reflexive consciousness.

All this seems to be a most satisfactory gloss on the passage in *The Unnamable* where 'I' suggests

> perhaps that's what I feel, an outside and an inside and me in the middle, perhaps that's what I am, the thing that divides the world in two, on the one side the outside, on the other the inside, that can be as thin as foil, I'm neither one side nor the other, I'm in the middle, I'm the partition, I've two surfaces and no thickness...(T,386)

What is so appropriate about this as a parallel for Sartre is the fact that not only is this narrator the 'ideal distance' between consciousness (that is, no distance, 'nothing') but these consciousnesses are described as 'outside', 'inside' and 'surfaces'. Now these three concepts, technically, add up to zero. The 'outside' of something has no depth, it is another 'nothing', as is the 'inside' or the 'surface' of something. This 'nothing' is just what Sartre says that consciousness is.

Beckett has frequently worked on the idea of consciousness confronting itself. In some of the novels and plays he finds a sort of objective correlative for this by confronting characters with their own pasts. We cannot understand this fully until we have considered the Sartrean conception of time but for the moment it is illuminating to think of Krapp in *Krapp's Last Tape*, or Henry in *Embers*, as people face to face with themselves, consciousness to consciousness. Similarly the two halves of *Molloy* could be considered in this way.

Most important for Beckett, however, is the Sartrean stress on the different positions of consciousness. All through the trilogy, the *Texts for Nothing* and *How It Is* there is a tension between the narrator and his 'vice-existers'. Who narrates *Molloy*? Is it Moran? Who is the Unnamable? Who are the scribes in *How It Is*? These questions seem finally to lead us to think of all Beckett's characters and narrators, and Beckett himself, as being one and the same person. This is made possible and comprehensible by Sartre's view of consciousness. At the first level I have a 'non-thetic', 'non-positional', 'pre-reflexive' consciousness, to borrow the terms used in *The Transcendence of the Ego* and *Being and Nothingness, passim*. Then there is my consciousness of that consciousness, and then there is the possibility that the objects of these two sorts of consciousness may coincide and I become conscious of being conscious of myself. Sartre avoids 'infinite regress' here but leaves us with enough of a Chinese puzzle to help clarify Beckett. As an example we can consider the first of the *Texts for Nothing*.

> Suddenly, no, at last, long last, I couldn't any more, I couldn't go on. Someone said, You can't stay here. I couldn't stay there and I couldn't go on. I'll describe the place...How can I go on, I shouldn't have begun, no, I had to begin. Someone said, perhaps the same, What possessed you to come?...It's simple, I can do nothing any more, that's what you think. (NK,71)

This opens with a tension immediately established between 'I' and 'someone'. It is our Sartrean point that these two are the same. After a dozen lines 'someone' is again quoted and Beckett says that this someone is 'perhaps the same' as the first, and indeed it is, but time has elapsed, casting doubt (consciousness 'determines its existence at every moment without our being able to conceive of anything before it'). But all the 'someones' *are* the narrator. 'It's simple' he says, 'I

can do nothing any more' and continues, with only a comma inter-
vening, 'that's what you think'. (NK,71) The 'I' and the 'you' are
both him – his consciousness bifurcated as we have seen. And this
consciousness is not a physical or a mental thing, but distant from
and different from either of these:

> I say to the body, Up with you now, and I can feel it
> struggling...I say to the head, Leave it alone, stay quiet...I am
> far from all that wrangle. (NK,71)

So the 'I' is the pure subject, opposed both to the objective world
and objective images of that world, as in Sartre. And it is not the
Ego. 'It's not me' says the narrator when asked why he is there.
(NK,73)

But of course 'pre-reflexive', immediate consciousness is indis-
solubly linked with the object that it 'intends'. So, 'the cold is eating
me, the wet too', he says. But he goes on 'at least I presume so, I'm
far.' He is at once far and near, at once 'pre-reflexive' consciousness
of the cold and wet and consciousness of that consciousness:

> Eye ravening patient in the haggard vulture face, perhaps its
> carrion time. I'm up there and I'm down here, under my gaze,
> foundered, eyes closed...we're of one mind, all of one
> mind...(NK,73)

Indeed, the two consciousness are 'of one mind', they are 'up there'
and 'down here' and they are both 'I'.

We have thus looked at three of the Sartrean categories that
described consciousness: 'nothing', 'intentionality' and 'reflexivity'.
The two remaining are 'freedom' and the fact that consciousness is
pour-soi not en-soi.

Freedom might appear to be the one thing that Beckettian consciousness is not. 'I can do nothing' says the narrator of first *Text for
Nothing*, 'I can't go on' says the Unnamable. But this is to miss the
point about Existentialist freedom – it is not freedom necessarily to
do, it is freedom to *project*. Now the one thing that we are left with,
after the amputations, the paralyses, the reductions, the isolation,
the darkness, the silence and the mud of Beckett's mature fiction is
the babble of a freely-projecting consciousness. Even when, in *How
It Is*, we have to account for the scribes and for the constant
repetition of 'I say it as I hear it' we find we are merely pushed back

one stage further – the scribe is Beckett, the voice heard his voice. *Beckett* is free to will, to project; his fictions are entirely his own. Beckett expresses Sartre's insight – man is condemned to freedom. This will be dealt with at greater length in the two sections on freedom, below.

As for the fact that consciousness is pour-soi and not en-soi this is as clear in Beckett as anywhere else and hardly needs exemplification. But, to make the point, we can consider the following, again from the first of the *Texts for Nothing*:

> I need nothing neither to go on nor to stay where I am, it's truly all one to me, I should turn away from it all...(NK,71)

The word 'one' in 'it's truly all one to me' denotes the en-soi, '*massif*', solid, indifferent, away from which consciousness 'should' turn – feels it can turn. But consciousness, although absolutely other than being, other than en-soi, 'exists' in its nothingness only because being 'is'. The narrator will not and cannot, in fact, 'turn away'. There is no possible gap between consciousness and the objects of consciousness. 'Let them cease' says our narrator, referring to the body and the head, but answers himself, 'I can't, it's I would have to cease.' (NK,71)

*   *   *

NOTHINGNESS

Consciousness is nothingness, it is the nothingness that man sets over against Being. This may puzzle us if we remember what Hegel says about Being – that it is an 'emptiness', it is what is left when all the essences of an object have been subtracted, while for his French successor it is the *opposite* of 'nothing'. The point is that Hegel's Being is the first (or, if we prefer, last) quality or essence in a hierarchy of such concepts whereas in Sartre Being is *everything* including all qualities, essences and, as we have seen, even dreams, hallucinations and feelings as intangible as boredom. So in Hegel two simultaneous announcements start (or finish) his system – the announcement that Being is and the simultaneous announcement that nothing is. Being is nothing. This includes everything is a general sort of way – there is nothing in heaven or on earth that is not included under these first categories. But this means that nothingness here acquires an existence, it is one of two equiprimordial existents. Meanwhile in Sartre Being and nothingness far from being a pair of vast brackets that *include* everything, respectively *are* everything and nothing. Being is the solid mass of all that is, nothingness is human consciousness set over against Being. They never become merged into one another (in Hegel they join forces in the synthesis of 'Becoming') but are opposites – although if Being vanished we would not be left with nothing, nothing would vanish too, before Being there was not nothing either. This last point is not reversible, Being is not dependent on nothing in the way that nothing is dependent on Being. Being can be completely and satisfactorily described without any recourse to the concept 'nothing'. As Sartre puts it, nothingness merely 'haunts being'. (BN,16)

This anti-Hegelian phase of Sartre's argument has some light to throw on Beckett. Sometimes the word 'nothing' appears in Beckett in a context that seems to need Sartre's stricture on Hegel that 'before Being' there could not have been 'nothing'. For instance in *Watt* the narrator tells us that in Mr Knott's establishment 'nothing changed...because nothing remained'. (W,130) With Sartre on Hegel in mind we can gloss this as: 'We must find a new conception of nothingness if we want to talk about what "remains" when "nothing remains" because, surely, when we say that nothing remains we are thinking about the *remaining* which implies some sort of Being for the entity which remains.' In other words, one aspect of Mr Knott's negativity makes the Hegelian mistake of attributing some sort of Being to nothing and Watt feels an inadequacy in the words and concepts at his disposal for the correction of this mistake.

Similarly in *The End* the narrator says, first, that he can see 'nothing except...the grey light of the shed', and comments, 'To see nothing at all, no, that's too much'. (NK,64) Here is a perfect example of those entirely Beckettian moments of wordplay that so often cry out for a philosophical gloss. Because of the 'grey light' we *can* take 'nothing at all' on a purely physical level. But how can that explain 'no, that's too much'? This forces us to move from questions of vision to the next nearest possible interpretation: perhaps it's 'too much' to hope that oblivion ('nothing at all') will be granted, say after death. But, although 'nothing' here *may* have a visual (i.e. physical) meaning and a post-mortem meaning, we are still troubled by the apparent oxymoron of 'to see nothing at all'. This is where we find ourselves plunging into a philosophical reading whether we will or no. With Sartre on Hegel once again in mind we can bring out the full irony of 'nothing' being 'too much', for, if we cast aside Being and gaze upon the 'nothing at all' as a Hegelian object we will become aware, with Sartre, that it is not 'nothing' that we are looking at, but something. 'Real' nothing is that of which nothing can be affirmed, not even that it 'is' nothing.

Having improved on Hegel, Sartre moves on to improve on Heidegger. He quotes with approval Heidegger's theses about man's *Angst* in the face of nothingness and about the absolute negativity of nothingness, '*Das Nichts nichtet*', nothing 'nihilates' itself, it is not. But he perceives an inconsistency in Heidegger's development of this. When Dasein 'negates' the world it does so by saying what it is that he is negating — 'I am not the world'. Thus for Heidegger nothingness 'carries being in its heart'. (BN,18) Sartre prefers the opposite possibility, that 'Nothingness lies coiled in the heart of being — like a worm'. (BN,21) Apart from the obvious coincidence of the name Worm in *The Unnamable* we can associate this with Beckett by quoting Sartre's own example — that of distance. Put simply, Sartre establishes that even in something with such positive being as the statement that 'the distance from A to B is X' there is a core of negativity. For either we must say that this statement means that A is *not* in proximity to B by X amount, or, if we see the distance as a positive length (X *is* a line a yard long), we must say that the line X extends to A in one direction and to B in the other direction and that beyond A and B there is *not* any more distance. As Spinoza says, *omnis determinatio est negatio*.

In general this principle of negation applies to Beckett in his handling of beginnings and endings. In *Endgame*, for instance, there are numerous ambiguities about what constitutes a start and what a finish. 'The end is in the beginning', says Hamm, 'and yet you go on.' (E,44) And Hamm's story goes on and on and, like the two acts of *Godot*, seems infinitely repeatable. There is a theme in the play of things piling up, the millet-grains of 'that old Greek' and the constituent parts of the 'little heap, the impossible heap.' The point of all this is that until the end is reached nothing is known. Unless the line X has end-points we cannot conceive what distance X is. When will grains of sand, or of millet, get to the point that we can say, 'now there is a heap of sand'?

I would associate this paradoxical element in *Endgame* (which is present *passim* in Beckett as the last words of *Molloy* and of *The Unnamable* show) with Beckett's desire to reach the end, the nothing. Once the end *really* comes, once all has been said, once it has '*mounted up to a life*' (E,45) we have found a negation, and that means a determination, which is to say knowledge and understanding. Here is another recipe for hell in Beckett: only when the end of something comes can we understand it.

After these discussions of Hegelian and Heideggerian nothingness, Sartre poses the question now laid bare, 'where does Nothingness come from?' (BN,22) His answer is that man brings nothingness into the world, that man, as pour-soi, consciousness, finds that he opposes a nothing to the Being of the world. But, once he has established consciousness as the 'origin of negation', Sartre follows Heidegger in discussing the results of this in terms of freedom (a concept which involves a consideration of *Angst*), the Self, man's responsibility and the creation of values by choice.

*   *   *

FREEDOM ANGST THE SELF

Man brings nothingness into the world by being conscious. Man is free, by virtue of his consciousness, but this freedom is not a quality he possesses, it *is* him. 'There is no difference between the being of man and his being-free.' (BN,25) Following Kierkegaard and Heidegger Sartre says that man can 'fear' beings in the world but feels 'anguish', *Angst*, in the face of himself. *Angst* is fear plus 'vertigo' (Sartre uses the same word as Kierkegaard), dizziness at the prospect of my own freedom to will. This is clarified by Sartre's explanation that there are no motives *in* consciousness, only *for* consciousness. Thus I am not 'in anguish' on account of my motives, which are objective to me, not subjective, but on account of the freedom I have, as a conscious being, to disregard even my strongest motives. He gives the example of the man on the cliff path. In spite of all motives towards safety and caution, the man *can* walk too close to the edge, deliberately throw himself off even. The possibility is always open at any rate.

This is important for Beckett, not directly but as it leads into the Existentialist and Beckettian view of the Self. If we say that 'I' choose between 'my' possibilities, even to the extent that I can choose to disregard all motives and act gratuitously, say by jumping off the cliff, then we have a useful way of looking at the idea that 'I' make 'myself'. If the *motive* determined the action I would not be free. (We may presume that this is the situation for at least some animals – the hungry dog will *always* eat the food, in response to his motive of hunger, unless a stronger motive supervenes.) As pour-soi I can choose between my motives, I can decide what I am going to be. If I am offered an alcoholic drink, I can accept it, or ask for a non-alcoholic drink, or have no drink at all. Not only can 'I' choose between these possibilities, I *must* choose between them. This example shows what Sartre means by pour-soi deciding what it is going to be. When I choose between these drinking alternatives I am 'making myself' in that I am defining myself along such possible lines as: being thought a sociable fellow, becoming an alcoholic, being prepared to make a fuss to get what I want, making an ostentatious display of my teetotalism, and so on. Now Sartre, speaking of this process of choice, says that 'Freedom...is characterized by a constantly renewed obligation to remake the *Self* which constitutes the free being.' (BN,34–5). The emphasis on 'Self' is Sartre's, but is just where we need it for Beckett. It emphasises the point that the division in Sartre's dualism (if that term is permissible) is between consciousness on the one hand and the Self on the other. We have seen that this Self is not transcendental, it is me and yet it is an object for me. It is my 'essence' and yet I am always separated from it by a 'nothing', for, given all my motives, there is still an 'I' to choose freely between them. My essence, my Self, is everything of which I can say 'that *is*' about myself (as in: 'fear *is* one of my motives' or 'happiness *is* what "I" am feeling'). My essence explains my action but the *choice* of that action is beyond such explanation. Since my consciousness is nothing, my Self is what constitutes my 'free being', 'I' exist as other than 'me'. My *Angst*, which is my peering into the abyss of my freedom, 'appears as an apprehension of self inasmuch as it exists in the perpetual mode of detachment from what is'. (BN,35)

I have dealt with this point at some length because I think that we are here approaching something like Beckett's view of the Self. His early work is haunted by an absolute dualism of the older, Cartesian, sort. I would suggest that his later work shows evidence that his thinking has moved towards a 'dualism' of the Sartrean type.

Sartre's thesis depends on the notion that consciousness is absolutely subject: 'I' speak out of my absolute subjectivity in such a way that I can never turn round and look at my 'I'. What I would see, were I able to do so, would be consciousness, that is, nothing. This could explain the lack of success of Beckett's quest for the Self – there is any amount of stuff in his narrators' worlds that qualifies as 'mine' but none of it is 'I'; there is plenty of objective Self but it is always 'Not I'. As the Unnamable reaches the climax of his last page his desperation takes a form that bears this out; 'perhaps it is I' he says, 'perhaps somewhere or other it was I', but then, 'it's not I' and then, 'it will be I.' (T,418) However, in principle, he can never say 'I' and thus will never be done.

This analysis generates two points to consider in Beckett: first the freedom that arises from the radical detachment of 'I' from 'me', and then the question of the *content* of the objective Self.

In discussing consciousness, above, we came to the conclusion that Beckett expresses Sartre's insight that man is condemned to freedom. We can now see more exactly why this is so. Man must choose; he can never relinquish responsibility and relax in a determinism where all is done for him. This is the almost constant condition of Beckettian man. 'You must go on' even when you can't; even choosing not to choose is choosing. Beckettian man wants to stop choosing, to stop being free. The narrator of *From an Abandoned Work* expresses well one reason why this is so: 'I have never in my life been on my way anywhere, but simply on my way.' (NK,36–40) This states both of Sartre's points – I am 'on my way' because I must 'go on', I must go on choosing, but there is no guide, no direction to go in, I am free. So what do I choose to do? How do I find out where to go? In *The Expelled* there is one of many possible examples of this. The 'hero' is walking in the streets of what seems to be Dublin. He enters a cab ('of my own free will') and is forced by the driver into saying where it is that he wants to go. The sheer contingency of the world and the hopeless results of total freedom appear in his answer: he must say something, so he says 'To the Zoo' and adds 'It is rare for a capital to be without a Zoo.' (NK,16–17) In other words he chooses because he must but chooses completely at random; he has no desire to go to the Zoo. But even if he had a desire his choosing to fulfil it would be free and unconditioned. Thus when he decides to eat, a little later in this text, it comes as a suprise to us that he expresses a desire, and no details of the meal are given; it surprises us less to realize that perhaps he ate nothing. Similarly, that night, our 'hero' is 'seized, then abandoned, by the desire to set fire to the stable' in which he is sleeping. (NK,23) We notice in these examples that desires seem to come to him from outside, (they 'seize' him) and that he, his conscious 'I', is untouched by them, as in Sartre. The same thing is taking place on another level. Beckett the author, or perhaps the narrator himself, interjects, 'No reason for this to end or go on. Then let it end.' (NK,16) Indeed, there is finally no reason for conscious beings to choose one course of action rather than another. The greatest possible number of motives and desires do not add up to necessity.

Our second point for consideration is the content of the objective Self. In Sartre this can be summed up as being all that 'I' recognizes as 'me', with the rider that 'I' is free to determine what 'me' shall be like, within the limits of the factical. Take the following passage from *The End*:

> To know I had a being, however faint and false, outside of me, had once had the power to stir my heart...(NK,64)

Here the narrator's consciousness recognizes his 'being' as an objective Self. He describes himself 'shitting' in the boat he has turned into his refuge and, when he has criticized himself for this, he comments, as if in answer to an objection, 'The excrements were me too, I know, I know, but all the same.' (NK,65) So his being 'outside of' him includes his excrement. And it includes his body as we can see from the last clauses of that highly physical text, *From An Abandoned Work*:

> You could lie there for weeks and no one hear you, I often thought of that up in the mountains, no, that is a foolish thing to say, just went on, *my body doing its best without me*. (NK,149. My italics)

The body and its products are far from the free, absolute realm within which consciousness is doomed to babble alone, its babble becoming objective even as it is conceived and thus bringing the babbler no closer to himself. But not the body only, even the will is something other than the 'I', as this from *The Calmative* makes clear:

> I said, Stay where you are till day breaks, wait sleeping till the lamps go out and the streets come to life. But I stood up and moved off.

This narrator chooses, as he freely can, to do exactly the opposite of what he has just decided to do – as Sartre says, no amount of past willing can make me act now. 'At each instant we are thrust into the world and engaged there.' (BN,37–8) Beckett continues:

> I hugged the walls, famished for shadow. To think that in a moment all will be said, all to do again. And the city clocks, what was wrong with them, whose great chill clang even in my wood fell on me from the air? What else? Ah yes, my spoils. I tried to think of Pauline, but she eluded me, gleamed an instant and was gone, like the young woman in the street. So I went in the atrocious brightness, bedded in my old flesh, straining towards an issue and passing them by to left and right and my mind panting after this and that and always flung back to where there was nothing. (NK,40–1)

Here again the body is part of the objective Self; 'I', the subjective Self, is 'bedded in my old flesh'. The voice of consciousness, of 'I', interjects the sentence 'To think that in a moment all will be said...', and also the question 'What else?' The burden of these interjections is that the 'I' is coming to the end of his babble (as indeed he is; *The Calmative* finishes a page later) and he is making sure that he has said all he has got to say. So, he has dealt with an incident, told a story, accounted for his body, now what else is there in his objective Self to be mentioned? Ah yes, his 'spoils'. The mention of his 'thought' of 'Pauline' makes it clear that these spoils are memories. Thoughts and memories are like lights that gleam an instant as consciousness 'intends' them and then vanish. My mental life, (for example my memory of Pauline), here as in Sartre, is an object of my perception just as a 'real' young woman whom I see in the street is an object of my perception. And the 'I' in this text is trying to get out of this, to escape from 'this hell of stories' back into his impossible Self, the subjective absolute. He is 'straining towards an issue' in which his 'mind' (objective) will catch up with his Self (subjective) but, as we realize must happen since the 'I' is nothingness, he is always flung back to 'where there is nothing'. The ambiguity here between objective and subjective exactly reflects Sartre's thesis about reflective consciousness. When 'I' has looked at world, at body and at mind and found it*self* lacking from these it tries to look at itself. But in doing so it reduces itself to an object, so it is no longer looking at itself, and even if it were looking at itself it would be looking at nothing.

Only with this sort of an interpretation in mind can we make any sense of the last page of *The Calmative*. The 'hero' falls down but says 'I didn't lose consciousness, when I lose consciousness it will not be to recover it.' When the crowd leaves him, soon after this, the daylight comes back but he states, 'I had no need to raise my head from the ground to know I was back in the same blinding void as before'. (NK,42) Consciousness, in Sartre and Beckett, is the inescapable absolute that is nothing.

*   *   *

FREEDOM CHOICE RESPONSIBILITY

All that we have said so far about freedom is based on the first chapter of *Being and Nothingness*. Before leaving the subject we must look at the substantial section of that work (Part Four, Chapter One) entitled 'Being and Doing: Freedom'. Early in this chapter Sartre offers a resumé of what he has so far said about freedom in his work. This is the point at which his famous dictum 'I am condemned to be free' appears, but there are two other dicta here that are of as much interest to us in our search for light to throw on Beckett.

First, Sartre summarizes a paradox, for Beckett a torment, that we have come across before: freedom is the negative, the 'nihilation', the nothing of consciousness; as such, when I talk about it I am not really talking about it. 'It is through this (negativity) that the for-itself escapes its being as its essence; it is through this that the for-itself is always something other than what can be *said* of it.' (B,439. Sartre's emphasis.) This perhaps explains the difficulty of Beckett's task; in trying to *say* his 'I' he is attempting the impossible. As he says, there is 'nothing to express', the 'nothing' is his consciousness. How is he to express this, which is in principle inexpressible?

Second, Sartre defines the pour-soi, the for-itself, as 'the one which is already beyond the name which is given to it.' (BN,439) He intends this is the sense that conscious 'human reality' has no fixed essence, is forever creating itself anew, cannot be pinned down, cannot be labelled and given a name. Whence, perhaps, Beckett's final abandoning of names in the trilogy, culminating in the 'unnamable' hero of the third volume. This is reinforced by the namelessness of the being who writes *Texts for Nothing* and by the random and empty nomenclature of *How It Is*.

Besides this summary, most of Part Four, Chapter One deals with choice and responsibility. On the matter of choice Sartre offers a solution to the problem of the limits of choice, the problem of whether I have the freedom, for example, to choose the impossible. It is amusing that the test-case that Sartre chooses to employ in this context concerns bicycles. Rather like Molloy or Moran, Sartre proposes to consider the project of arriving 'on my bicycle as quickly as possible at the next town'. (BN,504) This whole discussion reads very like another view of Beckett's world. The projected bicycle ride 'involves my personal ends, the appreciation of my place and of the distance from my place to the town. . . But I have a flat tyre, the sun is too hot, the wind is blowing against me, etc., all phenomena which I had not foreseen: these are the environment.' (BN,504–5) Later, Sartre defines my awareness of the environment as being determined by the latter's 'coefficient of adversity'.

But a puncture does not really reveal the limits of my freedom. After all, again like Molloy and the others, my 'fundamental project' to be myself still holds good, whatever obstacles impede secondary projects. (That is, I still choose to be the sort of person who would make that journey.) And then, it is up to me freely to renounce a task even when its accomplishment has become impossible – I *could* go blindly on trying to achieve it for ever without any hope of success. Then again, 'freedom's very project is in general to *do* in a resisting world by means of a victory over the world's resistances.' (BN,507) These considerations are intended by Sartre to be quite impartial, neutral descriptions of some of the characteristics of choice, and their slightly pessimistic tone must not mislead us. Sartre is describing the world; it is not a fault of the bias of his mind that our world is made up of things that we first encounter as resistances or obstacles. In this he improves on Heidegger. After all, Heidegger's neutral examples of the world as '*Zeug*', for instance that of the clouds 'meaning' rain, also relate back to a situation of adversity. The clouds 'mean' rain to the farmer because the farmer needs to grow crops; he needs to grow crops because, ultimately, some Dasein somewhere feels the uncomfortable sensation of hunger. The world is to be battled with. This is implicit in Heidegger, explicit in Sartre, and a nightmare reality in Beckett.

With choice comes responsibility. 'I am absolutely free and

absolutely responsible for my situation.' (BN,509) Sartre's explanation of this responsibility reads very like a description of the situation of Beckettian man:

> We are taking the word 'responsibility' in its ordinary sense as
> 'consciousness (of) being the incontestable author of an event or of
> an object.' In this sense the responsibility of the for-itself is over-
> whelming since he is the one by whom it happens that *there is* a
> world; since he is also the one he makes himself to be, then what-
> ever may be the situation in which he finds himself, the for-itself
> must wholly assume this situation with its peculiar coefficient of
> adversity, even though it be insupportable...this absolute re-
> sponsibility is not resignation; it is simply the logical requirement
> of the consequences of our freedom. What happens to me
> happens through me, and I can neither affect myself with it nor
> revolt against it nor resign myself to it...(BN,553–4)

We can fit this to Beckett stage by stage. There is no doubt that his
novels and texts are pervaded by 'responsibility' in that there is a
permanent consciousness of authorship, in both senses of the word.
We are not allowed to forget for very long that there is a writer
writing these words that we are reading, but in Sartre's sense, too,
there is a consciousness of authorship. Beckett's characters create
their worlds. Not in the early novels, perhaps, where the 'big' world
has its own ways of bursting in upon and tormenting people. But
from *Molloy* onwards we are aware that the world that rises up
under the pencil of the narrator does so at his bidding. Thus there
are two levels – Malone is in bed and dying because Beckett has put
him there, and we know it, and Saposcat, for instance, comes into
existence because Malone bids him appear. At times the two levels
coincide, as when we come across the interjection 'What tedium'
which could be the view of both Beckett and Malone. This means
that sometimes, although we must attribute authorship either to
novelist or narrator, it is 'contestable' which of the two is actually the
author. But there is never any question that we are seeing a world
being created by a consciousness. '*There is*' a world for Saposcat
because Malone invents it (or 'intends' it), there is a world for
Malone because Beckett does likewise.

But, Sartre goes on, man, pour-soi, does not simply make the
world, he makes himself too. Here we find Beckett at his most
Sartrean. All through the trilogy and the later works the narrators

are engaged on making themselves. Sartre proposes, in the passage quoted, that *because of* this self-construction man is also responsible for his situation: 'the for-itself must wholly assume this situation.' And so it is for Beckett. The Unnamable is really doing nothing other than making himself and his world, revealing his responsibility for it by continuing to talk about it, 'going on', even when it is 'insupportable', even when 'you can't go on'. He says, 'I'm made of words.' (T,360)

It is some slight encouragement to our task of fitting this passage from Sartre to Beckett to realize that the 'resignation' rejected by the former is not present in the latter either. 'This absolute responsibility is not resignation.' Indeed, Beckett's people are never exactly 'resigned'; that is not an epithet that we ever think of applying seriously, even to the tramps in *Godot* who 'do not move' according to the famous stage-direction. Their attitude shows that they see their situation to be inescapable and they are somehow quite determined to go on waiting, but they could hardly be called 'resigned'.

The last sentence of our quotation from Sartre brings us yet closer to Beckett. It provides an explanation for some of the more mysterious inabilities that afflict Beckett's characters. Let me first stress that Sartre is here talking on an ontological level. Thus, when he says that man cannot 'revolt' against what happens to him he does not mean that I cannot choose to object to what I dislike. Of course I can. But I cannot choose that X should happen to me and that X should not happen to me simultaneously. If we bear this in mind we can perhaps answer the following questions that arise in Beckett more clearly: Why does Hamm, at a crucial point in the development of *Endgame*, exclaim 'I was never there...it all happened without me'? (E,47) Why do the tramps in *Godot* not succeed in hanging themselves? Whence the imperatives that force Molloy on to his destination, Moran on in his pursuit of Molloy? Why does Watt go to the house of Mr Knott? Why does Malone keep on writing? Why does Clov obey Hamm?

All these *can* be taken on various non-ontological levels; thus: the tramps just aren't efficient and decisive enough to do anything, Hamm and Clov are Master and Slave, and so on. But I would propose that we are missing an essential element in their meaning if we exclude the possibility of an ontological level at which these questions are partial or complete parables.

Thus, Hamm is isolated from even his own most intimate experience, from 'all' that has 'happened', because he is free. He cannot 'affect' himself with 'what happens' because 'what happens' is what he makes happen, it is him, and yet, as a conscious nothingness, he knows himself to be radically 'other' than the world he creates. What I do is me, but 'I' am nothing, 'I' can never be 'there' where it is happening, 'I' am 'here', in the indefinable silence of the subjective. Because of this, incidentally, it is really all the same whether I have 'real' experiences or whether I invent them. Hamm's story is every bit as 'real' a part of the play as Clov's boots.

The tramps in *Godot* cannot hang themselves. This is a parable to illustrate man's condemnation to freedom. Vladimir and Estragon cannot 'revolt against' the world created by their choices. Death would presumably represent choiceless oblivion – but that is not for man, and these two are 'all mankind', as we know. (WFG,79) We must always choose, even in the emptiness of the world of *Godot*, and we can choose anything except not to choose, because that is a choice too. Of course, this does not work on a natural, non-ontological level. In a 'natural' situation, man can, by making the unique choice of suicide, choose to stop choosing, the significance of which is the burden of that most perfect of Existentialist writings, *The Myth of Sisyphus*, but surely nobody supposes that *Godot* is concerned with literal suicide, it is not a play that can be satisfactorily interpreted with a phrase such as 'Let's kill ourselves' taken at simple face-value. The deaths of Vladimir and Estragon would utterly destroy the play at the ontological level.

The imperatives that drive on Molloy, Moran, Malone and the other narrators are an expression of their inability to 'revolt against', or to 'resign' themselves to, themselves. Again, there is the natural, sociological level on which Youdi is 'the boss', Gaber his factotum and Moran his employee; and there is the psychological level on which Molloy has an Oedipus complex that drives him towards his mother's bed. But there is also the level of the ontological parable. On this level there is a condemnation to responsibility that becomes clearer and clearer as Beckett progressively strips his characters. They are sloughing off the *world* at a fair rate between *More Pricks Than Kicks* and *The Unnamable* but we do not feel that they slough off so much as an ounce of *responsibility*. On the contrary, as the world retreats it becomes more and more apparent that all that they are and have depends upon themselves, and, quite amazingly all things considered, they almost never revolt.

This last point proves a great deal. If Beckett were the 'natural' pessimist he is sometimes taken to be, and if we read him as a prophet of gloom, his hellish universe would be full of flaring revolts against the 'human condition'. There are some, especially in Clov's moments of violence, but not many. The mud-creatures of *How It Is*, for all their horror and violence, hold nothing against the scribes, the 'they', whoever it is that has flung them into the depths. This is because *The Unnamable* and *How It Is* cannot be read (cannot *only* be read, anyway) at a 'natural' level. The absence of revolt makes full sense only when we take their situations as ontological parables and see them as trapped in their own worlds for which, in principle, they can only 'blame' themselves. Clov obeys Hamm because Clov chooses to as much as because Hamm chooses to, a point specifically made in the play in the exchange, incomprehensible without our reading, in which Hamm thanks Clov for his services and the latter turns on him 'sharply' and insists 'Ah pardon, it's I am obliged to you.' (E,51)

Hamm and Clov, by being towards each other, being together, choose that each should be a component of the other's 'coefficient of adversity'. As Sartre puts it, 'our freedom itself creates the obstacles from which we suffer.' (BN,495)

*   *   *

THE SELF

We have said a good deal about the Self, the Ego, consciousness and so on in the course of the preceding sections, but we must conclude this theme by mentioning the highly Beckettian 'circuit of selfness' that is Sartre's summary of his general views as expressed in *The Transcendence of the Ego* and *Being and Nothingness*.

Both in Sartre and in Beckett the pour-soi, man, is chasing his 'lack', his Self. Sartre likens this to the ass which pulls a cart forwards because it has a carrot dangled before it. Because the carrot is attached to the cart it is moved forward by the ass's own motion and can never be caught up with. He explains his simile thus:

We run towards ourselves and we are — due to this very fact — the being which cannot be reunited with itself. In one sense the running is void of meaning since the goal is never given but invented and projected proportionately as we run towards it. In another sense we cannot refuse to it that meaning which it rejects since in spite of everything possibility is the meaning of the for-itself. Thus there is and there is not meaning in the flight. (BN,202–3)

This image, and its gloss, apply directly to Beckett. They explain the impossibility of his narrators' attempts to 'say' themselves, and the hopelessness of the quest for Self. At the same time they give the world just the meaning that it has in Beckett – the meaning that arises from my meaning that there should be meaning. 'The world appears inside the circuit of selfness.' (BN,198) is just exactly what the Unnamable finds. We are separated from ourselves by a world and only 'nothing' could be the result of our attempts to catch up with ourselves.

So, of course, we cannot *be* anything. As we have already seen, Beckett reduces this to the dictum that his narrator has never been on his way *to* anywhere, but always on his way. We are always pursuing, never reaching, always travelling towards that from which we are shut off by consciousness. If we ever arrived, we should become en-soi or, in simpler terms, if we were ever able to define ourselves as '*this*' we would not be free to be other, we would cease to be human, time would stop and the hole in Being that is consciousness would fill up. 'What the for-itself lacks is the self – or itself as in-itself.' (BN,89) This strikes me as being an excellent rendering of the Beckettian pursuit of the Self.

This pursuit, in Sartre explicitly and in Beckett perhaps, gives rise to value. We shall consider value as one Sartrean equivalent of an absolute in the last chapter of this.

*   *   *

BAD FAITH

Sartre adopts Heidegger's thesis about 'inauthentic' existence and develops it into his famous concept of 'bad faith'. In *Being and Time* Heidegger discusses man's flight into the 'they'; man ceases to be what he authentically is and becomes dominated by others; the 'they' start to make his choices for him and his existence becomes inauthentic. In Sartre there is this same flight from oneself, similarly motivated by a desire to escape from the *Angst* engendered by one's own absolute freedom to be oneself. But Sartre takes the matter further than simply positing these two possibilities (being oneself, being one's 'they'-Self) and asks what man must be like if he can both be himself and not himself. 'Bad faith' is the perfect example of this and is selected primarily *as* an example. In bad faith I am simultaneously one thing *and* another; how is this possible?

Bad faith is different from lying. The liar goes through a simple conscious process – he knows one thing to be the case, sees the advantage of concealing this fact and so states the opposite. He deceives you and me, but he does not deceive himself. In bad faith I deceive myself.

It is easy to make the mistake of putting an ethical interpretation on Sartre's discussion of this point. As in the case of Heidegger on inauthentic existence it would be wrong to do so. Bad faith is only an *example* in Sartre, it is not being held up as a bad thing. It is a phenomenon that he investigates and, indeed, he finds it to be a universal, inescapable phenomenon that occurs not by choice or by chance but as the inherent structure of the pour-soi. This is important to us because the bad faith in Beckett is also devoid of ethical content and is also presented in its ontological significance.

The pour-soi *must* be in bad faith because it cannot be what it is. For me to be angry I must know that I am angry, I must be conscious of it. If I am conscious of something I am not it. Therefore for me to be angry I cannot *be* angry. Only the en-soi is what it is and coincides with itself entirely. Thus if I were to be 'sincere' I would have to become what I am, I would have to become en-soi, and of course I can never be en-soi in principle. So I can never *be* 'sincere' or 'angry'; so I am forever in bad faith.

Popularly, Sartre's famous example of the café waiter's bad faith (BN,59ff.) is thought to hold up the waiter as a bad thing because he acts his job and is not sincerely himself. This is quite wrong. There is no way in which the man can cross from being what he is ('I am') to being what he does ('a waiter'). If, then, we remember that the café waiter is an ontological parable, and that bad faith is an example, we can turn our attention to the meaning of this parable and the significance of this example.

This waiter illustrates bad faith, and bad faith illustrates that man's being is such that he is not what he is. This is so because man is conscious and consciousness is a sort of inverting mirror in which everything is stood on its head. When consciousness appears, the principle of identity that works for the en-soi, which is what it is, breaks down and everything becomes for consciousness what it is not.

This brings us to Beckett rather quickly. Here we have a convincing gloss on Beckett's most constant and most mysterious theme, the inability to be.

I have already quoted Beckett's view of Proust that applies here. Direct contact between subject and object, he says, is impossible 'because they are automatically separated by the subject's consciousness of perception.' (PTD,74) This basic idea, developed as necessary, reappears frequently in the later work with an ever-increasingly Sartrean intention. In general, none of the later 'heroes', not even Watt, can be what they are, certainly they are all separated from themselves. We can now see why.

Watt, for instance, makes 'the distressing discovery' that of himself too 'he could no longer affirm anything that did not seem as false as if he had affirmed it of a stone.' (W,79) Indeed, on the Sartrean principle, anything that we say we are, we are not. Thus the 'programme' established at the beginning of *The Unnamable* is to 'proceed' by 'affirmations and negations invalidated as uttered'. (T,293) In *Watt*, too, it is Mr Knott, the principle of negativity, who is the centre of the circle that is the world of his house and garden. He is the nothing of consciousness that, according to Sartre, cannot *be* anything, and indeed he is nothing at all, he is indefinable, ineffable. It is Mr Knott's influence that stands Watt's mind on its head – after contact with that negativity Watt walks and talks backwards, playing 'being' to Knott's 'consciousness'.

Hesla relates this Sartrean point to *Endgame*. He observes first the necessity for language: if I *were* something, say 'suffering', I would not have to express it, to weep and cry out. It is because I am *not* 'suffering' that I need to express it, need to play at it, to act out the experience that is mine but not me. So here we have an explanation of the frequency with which we are reminded that Beckett's actors are acting, the equivalent of the reminders that his narrators are writing. Hamm is a ham actor, as we all know, or Hamlet, or anything but himself. Even when he veils his face at the end of the play the act goes on: 'an act...whose purpose is to keep my suffering alive by exhibiting it to others, including myself as reflecting on myself as suffering.' (Hesla, op. cit., p. 190) And certainly Hamm is incomprehensible unless we see him this way, or at least he is hopelessly ambiguous, for we can see that he 'is suffering' in the usual sense of those words (there is blood on the 'old stancher'; we, too, are horrified by the lack of pain-killers) but we are puzzled by his need to act, to overact, his sufferings, 'can there be misery – *he yawns* – loftier than mine?' I would suggest that this makes sense best if we regard it as an ontological parable along Sartrean lines. Hamm cannot be what he is, he must act, he must be in bad faith; that is the message.

There is perhaps a general explanation to be found in Sartre on bad faith for the inability of Beckett's characters to coincide with themselves. None of them ever achieves the goal of silence, the goal of rendering themselves en-soi, finishing, because it is in principle impossible. The nearest they can get to this dubious Nirvana is expressed in The *Calmative* where the narrator realizes that he can at least objectify himself by talking of the present as though it were past:

> Yesterday indeed is recent, but not enough. For what I tell this evening is passing this evening, at this passing hour...I'll tell my story in the past nonetheless, as though it were a myth, or an old fable, for this evening I need another age, that age to become another age *in which I became what I was*. (NK,26. My italics.)

In their perpetual present Beckett's pour-soi narrators can never become what they are.

*   *   *

OTHERS

One of the most important developments that Sartre makes of a Heideggerian thesis concerns other. Heidegger principally establishes that, insofar as we are, we 'are with' others; Sartre devotes considerable space to explaining *how* we are with others. For him, others are of enormous importance in existence, even more so than for Heidegger. In *Being and Time*, we will remember, there are really only two ontological categories, besides Being itself; there is Dasein's '*existenz*', conditioned by facticity, made of possibility, already in a world, already with others; and there is the Being possessed by what is not Dasein, the '*vorhanden*' and the '*zuhanden*'. Sartre roughly adopts Dasein's '*existenz*' as the pour-soi, and calls objective existents the en-soi, but he adds a third category to these, existence '*pour-autrui*', existence for others. (I shall henceforth use 'pour-autrui' as an English word.)

The category of pour-autrui arises because pour-soi recognizes that some of the objects in his world are not en-soi but are fellow men, pour-soi like himself, and as he can perceive and judge them so they can perceive and judge him. For Sartre, our bodies 'mediate' between our consciousnesses. He makes it clear that he has reached this position by working through and beyond Husserl, Hegel and Heidegger (I give these names in the order that Sartre does).

Husserl, in positing a transcendental Ego, cannot escape solipsism but, by his phenomenological approach, opens the way for Existentialist thinking. Hegel it was who saw that self-conscious being is only real when it recognizes the self-consciousness of others, but he falls into the error of talking of self-consciousnesses as though they were objects, whereas self-consciousness can only be subjective. Heidegger 'cuts the Gordian knot' (Sartre's phrase here, BN,244) by simply defining man's being as being-with others. However: 'Heidegger's being-with is not the clear and distinct position of an individual confronting another individual.' (BN,246) Sartre maintains that even if 'being-with' could be proved to be the ontological structure of man's being-in-the-world this would not help us to explain individual, 'ontic' relationships such as my relationship with 'Pierre' or whoever. *Being and Time*, it appears, does not escape from solipsism, idealism or realism and, according to Sartre, leaves Dasein 'isolated' as always. He now makes his own attempt to establish a satisfactory way of seeing others and offers the following theory. (BN,250ff.)

I have a direct apprehension of others, similar to my direct apprehension of myself. When I see another man I see him as an object, but not only as an object; I also apprehend that, since he is also a subject, he is surrounded by his world as I am by mine. My environment, when he enters it, flees away from me as I know that it is also in relationship with him. His perceptions and projects orientate elements in my world towards himself. For me, he is a kind of 'drain hole' in the middle of being. (BN,256) He, too, presents a nothingness to the solidity of being; objects no longer 'group towards' me as they did, but towards him. He has stolen the world from me. Of course, I then re-group my world so that it includes him, but that only re-affirms how thoroughly I have apprehended the other as other.

Now, however, the other looks at me. When he does so, I do not see his eyes at first, I cannot tell what colour they are, or how attractive, that only comes later. Immediately, I am aware of myself as his object. 'Beyond any knowledge which I can have, I am this self which another knows. And this self which I am – this I am in a world which the Other has made alien to me.' (BN,261) Sartre emphasizes this creation of a Self by the look of the Other. Previously we discussed the Self exclusively in terms of reflective consciousness, as an object my consciousness creates by reflecting on itself, perceiving that it is conscious. Now we see that even on the unreflective level of immediate consciousness a Self can be created, this time by the consciousness of another being turned on to me. If I am concentrating on something, peering through a keyhole for instance, and I hear footsteps behind me I become 'aware of myself' not because of reflective consciousness but in an immediate way.

As a corollary to this we learn the following. The other is unpredictable, (Sartre here refers explicitly to Kafka as the novelist who has explored this fact most thoroughly) and the other makes us 'slaves' when we appear to him. (BN,267) We are possible instruments for the purposes of the other and hence 'in danger'. We cannot know the other because knowledge requires an object and the other is always subject. All my acts imply the existence of others. Consciousness of them reinforces my selfness, not only am I not the en-soi, I am, even more certainly, not the other. When I die I shall no longer have the possibility of revealing myself as subject; others will thenceforth always regard me, that is, my body or their memories of me, as object.

We can relate these points to Beckett in two stages, the two main points first, and then the corollaries.

First, the other 'steals' the world from me. We notice at once the tone of Sartre's imagery here – the other is a 'drain hole' an 'internal haemorrhage' in my world. Is there anything comparable to this Beckettian imagery in Beckett himself? Certainly some of the couples seem to act as owners or destroyers of one another's worlds. Clov's world is stolen by Hamm, Lucky's by Pozzo. In the fiction, the 'I' is often invaded, attacked, at least endangered, by another pour-soi. In *Enough*, for instance, we have a sort of poetry of masochistic submission to a 'he'. 'I did all he desired. I desired it too. For him. Whenever he desired something so did I.' (NK,153) Throughout this text the world of 'I' is stolen by 'him'.

Second, we know from *Murphy, Film* and elsewhere that Beckett has toyed with Berkeleyan idealism – pondered the relationship of *esse* to *percipi*. By the time of the *Texts For Nothing* this interest has taken on a Sartrean flavour; the other 'betrays our presence' and even Beckett's narrator feels that he must sometimes have been 'perceived' by others:

> I can scarcely have gone unperceived all this time, and yet you wouldn't have thought so, that I didn't go unperceived. I don't refer to the spoken salutation, I'd have been the first to be perturbed by that, almost as much as by the bow, kiss or handshake. But the other signs, irrepressible, with which the fellow-creature unwillingly betrays your presence, the shudders and wry faces, nothing of that nature either it would seem, except possibly on the part of certain hearse-horses, in spite of their blinkers and strict funereal training, but perhaps I flatter myself. Truly, I can't recall a single face, proof positive that I was not there, no, proof of nothing. (NK,115)

This narrator knows that he must have been perceived (for he exists and the other is a condition of existence) but his isolation is stressed, correctly, to the point where he can doubt his own existence ('I was not there'). This doubt is based on his inability to conjure up an image of an other *recognizing* him. The open eyes of an unconscious man are not the other. The 'look' that betrays my presence has never betrayed this narrator's presence, so is he present, is he 'there'?

On the one hand, Beckett's characters have their worlds 'stolen' by others and on the other, their 'presence' is 'betrayed' by the other's look. On the first of these points we can agree that the vice-existers steal the world of the ultimate narrator (the Unnamable? Sam? 'I'?) in that we soon learn to give equivalence to all that is said in Beckett's fiction – whoever is telling the story, it is the same to us, Malone's world is metamorphosed into Macmann's and we cannot object. We can only be sure that these others have stolen Beckett's world from him. On the second point we find evidence in the plays that the other's look is important – Hamm needs Nagg to watch him, his dog to look up at him, Clov to listen to him. *Happy Days* needs Willie to give a reality similar to that conferred on the mouth in *Not I* by the Auditor. But, stepping back a stage as we have just done with the fiction, the plays all depend on the collective look of the audience. Perhaps Beckett is Berkeleyan in all this, but he is also Existentialist.

Besides these two features of Sartre's theory of the existence of others, we listed half a dozen corollaries, subsidiary features which we can now apply directly to Beckett. First, the other is unpredictable, we are before him as Joseph K. is confronted by his trial or his castle, we cannot know what the other will do, he too being a free consciousness. Thus, in Beckett, 'the expelled' is flung down some house steps, into the story, for no given reason, and 'for once' 'they' do not beat him in the street, again with no reason given. Similarly, in *Godot*, 'they' beat Estragon, regularly but for no necessary reason, unless we accept Vladimir's reason, which is that Estragon may have been 'not doing anything' in a particular manner that caused the attack. But the matter is as broad as the play itself – Godot is unpredictable in that he says he will come, and he *may* come, but he doesn't, and Pozzo and Lucky are unpredictable in that if you offer them sympathy you may get a kick on the shins, and if you meet them one day they may be all talk, confidence and aggression while the next they are helpless, blind and dumb. If the tramps are everyman, then Pozzo, Lucky and Godot (or his boy) are others, and what are we able to predict of them except unpredictability?

Second, the other makes me a 'slave' when I appear to him. As there are so many obvious parallels to this to be found in Beckett I shall simply say here that we should again remember that Sartre is proposing these points on an ontological level, however immediate and quotidian his discussion of them may appear. His 'slave' here is an ontological metaphor and, if we apply it to Beckett then we are claiming an ontological significance for the master-slave relationship that appears so often in his work. Perhaps, thus, the goad in *Act Without Words II* could be the other.

Third, I am a possible instrument fo the purposes of others and hence 'in danger'. This fits Beckett in two ways. Some of his characters are subordinated to the purposes of others (Moran to Gaber, Gaber to Youdi, Moran Junior to his father, at least for a while) and all of his characters are subordinates to their superiors in the hierarchy of narration (Worm is there for the Unnamable's purposes, the Unnamable for Beckett's.)

Fourth, the other, as subject, is in principle unknowable. This is a point that Beckett makes frequently but nearly always by implication only. Throughout the *Texts For Nothing*, for instance, 'others' appear: 'he', 'they', and so on. We are never allowed them in their full value as others, except for an occasional 'little canter' always demolished by a contradictory aside. The boundary between the 'I' and the others becomes fluid, disintegrates; we do not believe or disbelieve the voice that says 'he' any more than we believe or disbelieve the voice that says 'I'. If pressed to explain this we would say that the voice itself seems dubious as to its certainty or authority on any subject, whether its 'I' or its 'he' or its 'they'. In other words, the subject can only talk as subject, and however much it says 'he' it can only either miss its mark (the other is unknowable) or engulf its objects in subjectivity. As Beckett says, it's the fault of the pronouns, any old pronoun will do. This incorporates our fifth point – all my acts imply the existence of others – for I cannot avoid saying 'he' and 'they' any more than I can simply stop saying. Even the slush of words is churned for somebody, even the Unnamable has an objective existence in the world of others notwithstanding their unknowability.

Sixth, the look of the other gives me an immediate awareness of me as a Self. This, being of course a partial contradiction to our fourth and fifth points, seems to leave Beckett behind, but perhaps we could claim that, when the system of pronouns has broken down, and we are left with the all-devouring babble of the Unnamable, one of the points towards which Beckett tries to move is the point at which his narrator can posit an 'other' to give him back some sort of a self: 'it's not me they're calling, not me they're talking about, it's not yet my turn, it's someone else's turn, that's why I can't stir . . .' (T,416)

Our seventh and last point is that death will finish me as a subject; thenceforth others will treat me only as an object, I will be knowable at last, but only in that I shall be reduced to others' memories of me and my physical components – my body. Beckett's view of the body, like Sartre's, extends beyond the scope of our discussion of others and must be dealt with separately.

*   *   *

THE BODY

Man wants the security of reducing the other to an object and keeping it objective. Sartre extends this to our consideration of death and our way of loving. When another pour-soi is dead he has no more possibilities, no freedom, no subjectivity. We have 'won' over the other when he is dead, reduced him to the captivity of the objective forever. We attempt the same thing in the experience of love – each partner in the affair or the marriage tries to reduce the other to the neutralized, safe state of objectivity. In death always, and in love sometimes, we reduce the other from pour-soi to en-soi.

This makes it sound as though Sartre is resorting to an old-fashioned mind-body dualism, but this is not so. Certainly a dead body is en-soi, but a living body is pour-soi, at least for its possessor. I *can* treat another's body as en-soi, if, say, I am a cannibal, and I can even treat parts of my own body as en-soi if I imitate the man who treasures his pickled appendix after having it removed. But basically for me my own body is all pour-soi; further, I am aware of the bodies of others as being pour-soi for them, and I am aware of my body as it falls beneath the look of the other. (cf. BN,303–59 for all these considerations about the body.)

The most important of these points, and the most Beckettian, is the claim that *my* body is pour-soi not en-soi. Sartre observes that 'there is nothing *behind* the body. But the body is wholly "psychic".' (BN,305) The body is not an en-soi within a pour-soi, it is pour-soi, the pour-soi cannot be 'separated' from the body. 'The body is *lived* and not *known*.' (BN,324) Heidegger's worldly series of instruments and signs stops at the body. Thus an author generates the series: 'book-to-be-written' – paper – writing – pen – hand. The series stops with the hand. Consciousness 'exists' its body – Sartre gives this verb a transitive usage here – the body is a structure of self-consciousness. Finally, the body exists in contingency, it is the consciousness' experience of contingency, because of the body contingency can 'recapture' consciousness. (BN,338) Furthermore the body itself is contingent and, on its account, we 'suffer' hate, love, acts and qualities. There is no way out of this – 'when no pain, no satisfaction or dissatisfaction is "existed" by consciousness, the for-itself does not cease thereby to project itself beyond a contingency which is pure and...unqualified. Consciousness does not cease "to have" a body. Coenesthetic affectivity is then a pure, non-positional apprehension of a contingency without colour, a pure apprehension of the self as a factual existence.' (BN,338) This apparently neutral state turns out not to be neutral at all – instead it is 'nausea.'

We can relate these points to Beckett in turn. First, the body is 'lived', not 'known', is pour-soi, not en-soi. Certainly Beckett is a highly physical novelist and poet, and even in his plays there is enough eating, drinking, urinating and pain to keep our attention on the body. In the novels and texts this physicality operates as a kind of disgusted counterpoint to the mental activities of the narrators, a concrete objection to any fanciful notions about the Self. It is as if the body is evilly insisting on being taken into consideration in the quest for the Self, knowing that it will be just another spanner in the works. But for all the babble and mentation, the narrators are solidly, hideously there, plunged in flesh, themselves inescapably flesh. They talk often enough of their bodies, their infirmities, but no real distance is ever established between themselves and their bodies. In the *Texts For Nothing* the narrator tries to 'will' himself a body, a head, strength and courage and even seems to succeed in this apparently dualistic undertaking:

> There you are now on your feet, I give you my word, I swear they're yours, I swear its mine, get to work with your hands, palp your skull...then the rest, the lower regions...(NK,82)

So far so good, but the project collapses because the narrator is unable to maintain any distance between this physical creation and his 'I'. 'I'll wait for you here' he says to his creation, and follows this with phrases that are most curious without something like a Sartrean gloss: 'I'll wait for you here, no, I'm alone, I alone am, this time it's I must go.' (NK,82) The point is that without a body to 'exist' the 'I' is alone, a nothing, a point of subjectivity without existence. So he goes on: 'I know how I'll do it, I'll be a man, there's nothing else for it' (NK,82) which is to say that he must be a body in order to exist.

Second, the worldly series of instruments stops at the body. The pen 'refers' to my writing and thus to my hand. My hand when writing *is me* writing. We cannot go 'behind' my hand. In Beckett there is a strict division between the characters' bodies and their instruments – crutches, sticks, stones and bicycles are dispensable, objects for fascinated consideration, clearly means to ends. Meanwhile arms and legs are obsessively, preoccupyingly 'me'. Thus Molloy's bicycle is highly doubtful in a way his stiff legs are not:

> So I got up...and went down to the road, where I found my bicycle (I didn't know I had one)...It was a chainless bicycle, with a free wheel, if such a bicycle exists...(T,16)

I shall only add that every hundred yards or so I stopped to rest my legs, the good one as well as the bad, and not only my legs, not only my legs. (T,16–17)

In all of Beckett's work there is remarkably little doubt thrown on the body. The instrumentality of the world, the past, the world itself, others (at least as other versions of himself), all are dismissed by the series of narrators. But the body goes marching, crawling, babbling on. Even in *How It Is* and the latest short texts there are bodies – Pim's body and those of his fellow-creatures have a reality greater than that of their mental activities and the 'little body' of *Lessness* is a sort of inescapable minimum, holding Beckett back from the final plunge into the purely abstract.

Finally we must consider Sartre's point about the body as contingency and nausea. In Beckett the body is frequently addressed by the controlling voice of the narrator as though it were a random possession of his consciousness. We know that this is not true and that Molloy *is* his legs, the Unnamable *is* his head and so on, but pour-soi *can* always see his body as en-soi, and, when he does, its openness to the contingent is at once apparent. Thus Beckettian 'heroes' are subjected to the thousand natural shocks that flesh is heir to, and a few more besides. They never really complain, because their sufferings, being contingent, are inexplicable and somehow distant from them. And, as in Sartre, the body's own emotions, actions and qualities are also contingent, which perhaps explains Beckett's strange tone whereby we are given the impression that there is nothing much to explain his narrators' desires, no way of explaining their actions and a curious indifference to even their own freely-chosen ends. Beckett excludes all necessity, and events in his world are either governed by the fantasy of the person who narrates them or the blind contingency of brute fact.

And nausea – 'contingency sickness' – my apprehension of my body even when it is feeling neither pleasure nor pain – surely this is the *status quo* in all Beckett's work. The great symphony of suffering that makes up *All That Fall* can stand as a prime example. It is not just that people are blind or ill or murdered, worse still is the permanent undercurrent of nausea, directed, in Maddy Rooney's case at least, at her own vast, vile body.

How can I go on, I cannot, Oh let me just flop down flat on the road like a big fat jelly out of a bowl and never move again! A great big slop thick with grit and dust and flies, they would have to scoop me up with a shovel. (ATF,9)

*   *   *

CONCLUSION

There is a lot more in *Being and Nothingness* than the topics we have dealt with here. Some of Sartre's theses are not particularly relevant to Beckett, others we have covered in the chapter on Heidegger. Among these latter, however, are two points that are worth mentioning, temporality and death.

Sartre echoes Heidegger on temporality more or less point-for-point, insisting that time depends on man, that the past is an aspect of facticity, the future the emptiness of possibility and so on. (BN,107ff.) Objects, the en-soi, have no time, and pour-soi becomes en-soi when it has slipped into the past. To this Heideggerian point Sartre adds that what distinguishes pour-soi is that it 'has to be' its own past – I am what I have been. This may sound commonplace enough, but it is in fact an almost uniquely Existentialist view in that it is meant to imply that I am *nothing other than* my past (and my present freedom if you like, but that is a 'nothing'.) I do not have a given essence or nature to which I can cling, or to which I can appeal. If I have behaved with consistent cruelty, for instance, I cannot set against the history of my cruel actions some claim that I am 'really' tender-hearted; I am 'really' what I have been, cruel. And this again is where Beckett is Existentialist. He claims no fixed nature for any of his major characters; how often do we find one of them claiming any character at all? Which of them seriously proposes himself as finally kind, say, or intelligent, or pertinacious, or boring or even erratic? What could we say, laying our hands on our hearts, about the *character* of Vladimir or Clov or Malone or Worm? Certainly Pozzo could be defined, perhaps Nagg, the earlier Moran, Saposcat and other lesser types, but the 'basic' characters, the reduced people, the remnants whose 'story' we are hearing – Molloy, Hamm, the tramps, the Unnamable himself – these defy definition. On the other hand they are clearly made by their pasts, wondering about the connexion between what they were and what they are. But the connexion is Sartre's connexion – they *are* what they were. For Molloy there seems to be a hiatus between his adventures with bicycles and crutches and his position here and now in his mother's room; and so it *seems* to all of us, unable as we are to blend the pour-soi present with the en-soi past; but what does Molloy talk about? What are his concerns? How do we learn to say anything about him at all? The answer to all these lies in his past. What Sartre says of the past applies exactly to the characters who narrate the trilogy and *How It Is*: 'If the past does not determine our actions, at least it is such that we can not take a new decision except *in terms of it.*' (BN,496)

That is Existentialist temporality in Beckett. When Sartre proposes how we can consider time separately, in a non-Existentialist manner, apart from 'human reality', he offers a thesis that is also to be found in Beckett. (This is often the case – Beckett plays with a traditional philosophical problem in a way that reveals it as incomprehensible; this puts him into the same position as the Existentialists at the start of their discussions.) Sartre looks at the conventional approach to time thus:

> If Time is considered by itself, it immediately dissolves into an absolute multiplicity of instants which considered separately lose all temporal nature and are reduced . . . to the total a-temporality of the this. (BN,215)

Here we have another statement of the time problem that appears throughout Beckett from the grains of Millet in *Endgame* to the light which 'gleams an instant' in *Godot*, the 'one enormous second' of the Unnamable and *Breath*. Or, as we have it in the first of the *Texts For Nothing*, 'All mingles, time and tenses, at first I only had been here, now I'm still here, soon I won't be here yet.' (NK,74)

Connected with temporality is death. Here Sartre contradicts Heidegger roundly. Death is not my 'ownmost' possibility, cannot be the only thing that nobody can do for me. After all, every choice I make is uniquely mine, nobody can do anything for me. Of course, somebody can 'stand in' for me, 'take my place', but that is quite different from giving up my freedom to another which is an impossibility. When somebody does something 'for' me he does not annihilate me, I remain. So every choice, in Sartre, is my 'own-most' possibility. What is more, it is very hard to develop any 'being-towards' death since I cannot know the hour or manner of its arrival.

Thus, for Sartre, death, far from being an end that gives a meaning to life, is absurd. We are like the condemned man who is

preparing to give a meaning to his life, to 'close the account' satisfactorily, by making 'a good showing on the scaffold' and who is
then carried off by a 'flu epidemic. (BN,533) What death reveals is
the absurdity of every expectation, even the expectation of death
itself.

We are always expecting, always waiting; our freedom is a
projection towards an end for which we wait, 'our life is only a long
waiting' (BN,537) and thus we are waiting to wait, 'there we have
the very structure of selfness: to be oneself is to come to oneself.'
(BN,538) This waiting implies a final term, death, in which, as in
Heidegger and perhaps Christianity, one will 'come to oneself' and
meaning will arise. Alas, this final term cannot bring with it the
meaningfulness Heidegger supposes unless we posit a God who
chooses the hour of my death. If there is no such chooser how can
meaning arise? One minute more or less of life may perhaps change
everything and who is to say exactly when I shall die? If I try to
'round off' my life by writing some definitive philosophical work and
then committing suicide, I may have a fatal heart attack as I pick up
my pen to write the first sentence. Death is arbitrary, the conclusive
proof of contingency, absurd. 'Death is never that which gives life its
meanings; it is, on the contrary, that which on principle removes all
meaning from life.' (BN,539) Here we can already see a possible
reason why Beckett's characters can't come to the end: the only hope
is to keep going, keep trying the possibilities, because the end will
only bring about an automatic collapse of all meaning. But to
conclude Sartre's exposition.

> Since the for-itself is the being which always lays claim to an
> 'after', there is no place for death in the being which is for-itself.
> (BN,540)

Waiting for death, then, is waiting for what I cannot know or
understand, it is 'waiting for an undetermined event which would
reduce all waiting to the absurd, even including that of death itself.'
(BN,540) Death is not just not my 'ownmost' possibility, it is not
even one of my possibilities at all.

Now this applies so obviously to *Godot* and *Endgame* that I can be
brief. Again we are faced with looking at Beckett's works as ontological parables. Death is impossible for pour-soi, and that in the
literal sense that it is not one of my possibilities. *Godot* shows man
waiting, waiting for what cannot possibly come to him. If Godot

himself is some sort of absolute (God) then he won't come because, as Sartre says, death is not a confrontation with any absolute, it is the opposite, the generator of chaos not of worlds. The tramps fail to kill themselves because death is not one of their possibilities (cf. Sartre on suicide, BN,540). They must be there, they must wait, they wait for further waiting, wait to wait, and meaning never comes, the self never comes. As every theatregoer must at some time have suspected, if Godot came there would not be a joyous revelation of the meaning of the waiting (i.e. of suffering, life). On the contrary, it would only confirm the absurdity of existence.

In *Endgame* we are watching people waiting for death. It comes in random ways to the flea, the rat, Nagg. It implants no meaning in the world. The play opens with the word 'Finished', but it isn't, and it concludes with the word 'remain'.

NOTES AND REFERENCES

1. The en-soi/pour-soi model is not unique to Existentialism, appearing in Hegel and German Idealism generally, but Sartre's version gives it an extra importance. Hegel's version is available in various formulations, among them this:

    > Spiritual life is distinguished from natural, and particularly from animal, life in this, that it does not merely remain *in itself*, but is *for itself*. (*Lesser Logic*, quoted by J.N. Findlay in *Hegel: A Re-examination* (London: Allen and Unwin, 1958), p. 37)

2. *La Transcendence de l'Ego: Esquisse d'une description phénoménologique* (Paris, Vrin, 1965). (1st ed. 1936.)
3. The theses of *The Transcendence of the Ego* reappear in *Being and Nothingness* in a limited form that requires a knowledge of the earlier work. What is particularly clarified in the later work, however, is Sartre's concept of the 'circuit of selfness.'
4. Hesla's consideration of Sartre as an analogue for Beckett is quite extensive (op. cit., pp. 184–92). It consists largely of an exposition of Sartre on consciousness in *The Transcendence of the Ego* and *Being and Nothingness*; it is beautifully done and the Beckettian side of the equation is only lightly touched upon, but most suggestively. The different versions of the self offered by Sartre and Beckett (and by mathematics, phenomenology and other disciplines) are all seen as 'metaphors': Husserl talks of a consciousness examined by a conscious Ego; Sartre of a consciousness reflecting itself, mathematics of 'finding the square root of 2' and Beckett of the character who is an author who is a character.

4 Hegel's *Phenomenology of Mind* and Beckett's *The Unnamable*

I shall now offer, by way of an experiment, an analysis of the first sections of a major work by a philosopher who belongs to a century supposedly unafflicted by Existential *Weltschmerz*. This analysis of Hegel will be principally orientated towards Beckett's *Unnamable* and it is partly based on a view of Hegel as the Universal Philosopher, the thinker who tries to leave nothing untouched. Thus, if Beckettian situations have philosophical analogues there is theoretically every chance that they will be found in Hegel.[1] But this is less important as a reason for considering Hegel than the simple fact of the strong parallels to be found between some of Hegel's ideas and some of Beckett's. These parallels are reinforced in several cases by a similarity of expression and, it must be admitted, a similar obscurity. First, however, I shall briefly consider a central Hegelian thesis.

The insight that makes Hegel's philosophy possible is, on one view, similar to the motive force that makes Beckett's work continue. Hegel developed the dialectical method in an attempt to overcome the problem that had exercised Hume, among others, namely the problem of causation. Because X is always followed by Y are there any good logical grounds for assuming that X is the cause of Y? Can Y legitimately be deduced from X? For example, whenever I put my finger into a flame I feel pain, but can the pain be said to be caused by the flame? The difficulty is that the pain does not seem to be logically 'present' in the flame. To combat this problem Hegel adopted a method the outstanding characteristic of which is that it will only proceed in so far as consequences are contained in causes. Dialectic moves in threes, in triads that

114

approximate to thesis, antithesis and synthesis. If the dialectic works the antithesis is contained in the thesis and the synthesis in them both.

Thus, for example, Hegel avoids the concept 'God' because he sees that an act of faith is, indeed, required, to deduce the world from it. There is no logical necessity for 'God' to give rise to 'world'. When he posits the concept 'being', however, he finds that it *contains* its opposite, 'nothing', and that these two contain their synthesis, 'becoming'. How being can contain nothing is explained thus: the being of an object is what is 'left' after we have subtracted all its qualities and properties such as its size, shape, colour, age and so on; but what are we in fact left with when we have done this subtraction? Nothing. So nothing is already in being. There is no need to deduce one from the other. Thus, at least in the realm of abstract thought, we have an alternative to the traditional way of handling causation.

The dialectic is the motive force behind Hegel. It is not merely a method, it is a self-propelling account of the universe; indeed, it is the logical structure of the universe. As Stace puts it,

> This entire process of categories is a compulsory process forced onwards by the compelling necessity of reason. By rational necessity the thesis gives rise to its opposite and so to a contradiction. Reason *cannot* rest in what is self-contradictory, and is therefore forced onwards to the synthesis. And so throughout. This process cannot stop. It *must* go on until a category is reached which does not give rise to any contradiction. (Stace, *The Philosophy of Hegel*, p. 93)

This could serve as a pretty accurate description of Beckett's endless attempts to 'get it all said'. Hegel refers to consciousness as 'absolute dialectical unrest' in one of many passages of the *Phenomenology* that rehearses elements also found in Fichte. The latter's conception of the self-positing Ego, set forth in his *Groundwork of the Complete Theory of Knowledge* of 1794, regarded as a central influence on Hegel, is summarised thus by the Hegelian Findlay:

> The Ego has . . . another *absolute* activity, which is not reflected from any barrier, but which presses on beyond all barriers towards infinity. This absolute activity is the one with which the Ego posits its own being, unlimited and unlessened by anything

objective. Since it is not an objective activity, it cannot posit itself, the Ego, as anything fixed and definite. It must therefore be for itself no more than the goal of an infinite *endeavour* (J.N. Findlay, *Hegel: A Re-examination*, Allen and Unwin, 1958, p. 50–1)

It is this endlessness of the consciousness that appears in Hegel as the Dialectic and in Beckett is exemplified by the narrators, particularly the narrator of *The Unnamable*.

The inexorable march of reason, as described by Stace, is the basis of man's inability to fall silent, although silence would so obviously be an immense relief to Beckett's narrators. As the Unnamable says, 'you must go on'. Beckett, too, employs the dialectic or, better, the dialectical nature of the mind and the world is what confronts him and his narrators. They proceed, as he does, by 'affirmations and negations invalidated as uttered' (T,293) just as Hegel's logic works by cancelling its previous moments as it moves from thesis to antithesis and thence to synthesis. It is doubtful whether Beckett ever reaches a synthesis; this will be our problem in the next chapter.

Hegel's world-picture, then, is triple. It rests on such triads as 'Being-nothing-becoming'. The world is adequately described for him under three main heads, Logic, Nature and Spirit, the three divisions of the *Encyclopaedia*. The things of 'Nature' include physical objects and the laws that govern them; the things of 'Spirit' include all mental and psychical phenomena and are clearly to be distinguished from Nature in that my conception of, say, a table is a different sort of thing from the table itself. The category 'Logic' presents more difficulty: Hegel, here at his most Platonic, wants to be able to account for such phenomena as Appearance, Cause, Relation, Reason and so on. Of these he says that they have being (you can't very well admit the world without admitting Relation, say) but no 'existence'. Logical abstractions such as these are clearly not physical objects. They are not mental things either. When I stop feeling angry my anger is simply not there, but Hegel cannot suppose that Cause is 'not there' when isolated from human perception. So we have three categories of being, Nature, Spirit and Logic, of which one, Logic, presents some difficulties, notably as to 'where' its components are to be found.

Beckett is also aware of a triplicity in the world.[2] For instance, in the section of *The Unnamable* where the narrator is 'confusing himself with Worm' and where the prose becomes disjointed, leaping from topic to topic and switching pronouns at will, we find him asking, 'I wonder if I couldn't sneak out by the fundament, one morning, with the French breakfast.' He answers his own query with 'No, I can't move, not yet.' This creates a rich and tormenting Beckettian confusion while repelling the understanding. Obviously the 'I' here is ambiguously placed and must be read as both a physical 'I' that, for example, 'can't move' and a mental one that can be isolated from its body. Perhaps it is a foetus, waiting to make the first movements of life; we have, after all, just been treated to the gnomic sentence 'Worm will I ever get born?' The sentence that follows makes it clear that Beckett too is tormented by confusion: 'One minute in a skull and the next in a belly, strange, and the next nowhere in particular.' Brain, belly and bowels. But not just that.

To repeat, the whole passage runs: 'I wonder if I couldn't sneak out by the fundament, one morning, with the French breakfast. No, I can't move, not yet. One minute in a skull and the next in a belly, strange, and the next nowhere in particular.' (T,355)

This sort of passage is conventionally, and correctly, read as a puzzle about the Self. Is the Self mental or physical? However, the Hegelian parallel may be able to take us further than this. It is not just a matter of where 'I' am, it is a matter of where and what the world is. But to start with the Self: the digestive element and the worm-foetus element must be taken largely as metaphors. Their strength may lie in their heavy physicality but their sense must be elsewhere; there are strong indications that this passage, and many like it, should be read as abstract speculation. The narrator considers moving, tries to move perhaps, realizes that he can't move and resorts to generalization instead. He says in effect, 'It's funny how I locate my Self first in my skull, then in my belly and then nowhere' thus abstracting from his earlier pondering about the chance of sneaking out by the fundament. Here we have the Hegelian triad. In the skull are psychic things, the things of the Spirit; but is the Self there? The belly is the archetypal physical entity; is the Self there? And 'nowhere in particular' is the best we can do to imagine where the Self might be.

But we said we could go beyond this with Hegel's help. He is talking about the *world* not about the self and I would suggest that we try to see Beckett's speculations also as being potentially about the world. When the Unnamable moves from thinking about his own chances of escape to thinking in more general terms he is surely thinking about the world too. *All reality* is one minute in a skull, then in a belly, then nowhere: all reality is mental (Spirit) physical (Nature) or abstract (Nowhere in particular; Logic).

A little later the Unnamable is again talking about 'they' who seem to control him and he says 'They want me to have a pain in the neck, irrefragable proof of animation, while listening to talk of the heavens. They want me to have a mind where it is known once and for all that I have a pain in the neck, that flies are devouring me and that the heavens can do nothing to help.' (T,356) 'They' seem to propose the triad, the three levels of being: physical, the pain in the neck, mental, the mind that knows it has a pain in the neck, and our abstract plane (the heavens). Examples like this could be multiplied.

The interpretation of Beckett which emerges from this sort of analogy-drawing with Hegel has repercussions for other interpretations and it certainly amplifies them. The view, for instance, that the reference to 'the heavens' in the above passage is simply a bitter pointing to the irony of the non-existence of the heavens is perhaps not enough – we can go beyond it with Hegel's help. Beckett *is* being ironical, of course, but the irony is made more than just another antitheistical jibe by our Hegelian approach. The dialectic has the effect of cutting us off from the cosy personal relationship with God in which He is presented as the antidote for despair. Hegel's God is Absolute Reality, that is He is the structure of the world. In other words God does ordain 'how it is' but is unavailable for later modifications. 'Talk of the heavens' is useless blather. There is not much 'help' to be found in a Nowhere land of logical abstractions.

The above remarks have already brought Beckett closely in touch with Hegel, more so perhaps than has yet been done by any of his critics except possibly Schulz and Hesla. But all that has been said has been very general and the examples taken at random. The purpose of this study is to show that systematic, detailed comparison of works of philosophy and works of literature will produce interesting results, so I have chosen to use one novel of Beckett's, the one most in need of illumination in my opinion, and to compare it with one work of Hegel's – the first sections of the *Phenomenology of Mind* are laid alongside *The Unnamable*.[3]

SUBJECTIVITY (THE PREFACE)

In the Preface to the *Phenomenology* Hegel, insisting on the importance of a scientific philosophy, observes that the religious man shrouds his consciousness in 'sheer emotion' and sleeps. The painfulness of consciousness is a demon with which Beckett will wrestle long and hard. Hegel lays down the foundations for a language in which to discuss consciousness (in Baillie's translation the three main divisions of the *Phenomenology* are 'A. Consciousness. B. Self-consciousness. C. Free Concrete Mind'). Already in the Preface he justifies this stress on consciousness, the subject; I offer a section of this Preface together with glosses from the early pages of *The Unnamable*:

> The living substance, further, is that being which is truly subject, or, which is the same thing, is truly realized and actual (*wirklich*) solely in the process of positing itself ('I, say I' says the Unnamable), or in mediating with its own self its transitions from one state or position to the opposite ('I seem to speak, it is not I, about me, it is not me'). As subject it is pure and simple negativity ('Impassive, still and mute, Malone revolves, a stranger forever to my infirmities, one who is not as I can never not be'), and just on that account a process of splitting up what is simple and undifferentiated, a process of duplicating and setting factors in opposition ('Malone is there')...True reality is merely this process of reinstating self-identity...It is the process of its own becoming, the circle which presupposes its end as its purpose, and has its end for its beginning ('And indeed I greatly fear, since my speech can only be of me and here, that I am once more engaged in putting an end to both. Which would not matter, far from it, but for the obligation, once rid of them, to begin again, to start again from nowhere, from no one and from nothing and win to me again, to me here again, by fresh ways to be sure, or by the ancient ways, unrecognisable at each fresh faring'). (PM,80–1. T,293–304)

This section of the Preface to the *Phenomenology* comes under the subtitle 'The Absolute as Subject'. We shall have more to say about this. Beckett works out the subjectivity of his characters to the point where it too appears to be described as absolute:

> What I say, what I may say, on this subject, the subject of me and my abode, has already been said since, *having, always been here, I am here still.* (T,304. My italics.)

The confusion as to what is him and what is not him that the Unnamable feels echoes Hegel's paradox that 'substance is essentially subject'. With this we are introduced to an idealism and to a sort of Deism – 'the Absolute as Spirit' – which are not more realistic or comprehensible than the Unnamable's wandering speculations.

This marriage of substance and subject is 'the truth'. The Absolute is the combination of substance (the 'an-sich', the objects of consciousness) and subject (the 'für-sich', consciousness itself). Now, although Hegel leaves the door open for God[4] as Absolute Subject, what he is concerned with in the *Phenomenology* is man's mind – human self-consciousness; of this he admits that 'consciousness' for itself 'is a state quite outside of science'. (PM,88) This hint is important – it allows of an indefinable area at the heart of the self that is useful for Beckett.

Subjectivity, then, is uniquely human – the attribute of developed human minds:

> While the embryo is certainly, in itself, implicitly a human being, it is not so explicitly, it is not by itself a human being (*für sich*); man is explicitly man only in the form of developed and cultivated reason, which has made itself to be what it is implicitly. (PM,83)

The German words in brackets in the above lead me to prefer 'for itself' to 'by itself' earlier in the sentence. We then have a conformity between Hegel and Sartre on the distinction between things (including embryos), which are 'an-sich', 'en-soi', 'in themselves', and human minds, which are 'für-sich', 'pour-soi', 'for themselves'. What a double-headed monster this is for Beckett's heroes. Not only are they human, with the thousand natural shocks that flesh is heir to, but they are 'human for themselves', 'für-sich'; conscious, that is, of being; of being themselves; of being human.

Hegel, however, does not pursue his analysis of the subjective with Sartre's vigour.[5] He certainly insists in several places that subjectivity is 'being-for-itself' and is 'pure negativity', concepts to be much clarified and developed by Sartre; but his self is not quite the 'empty' entity that this might lead us to suppose. For example, Purpose is 'the unmoved which is self-moving; as such it is subject'. This leads Hegel into his idealist thesis in which he claims that the actual has an identity with our mental pictures of it; but 'what is actual and concrete is the same as its inner principle or notion simply because the immediate *qua* purpose contains within it the self or pure actuality. The realized purpose, or concrete actuality, is movement and development unfolded but this very unrest is the self'. (PM,83) It is worth considering here this 'aside' of Hegel's to the effect that purpose is 'in' the self, or vice-versa. Malone, for instance, in proposing to tell his stories, is really after the 'pure actuality in himself'. The offensiveness of this suggestion that 'purpose, contains the self' and that 'pure actuality' is in the self, which is also 'pure negativity', gives us some insight into Malone's problem. He spins out his words and stories in an attempt to create an existence; after all, if the actual is the same as its 'notion' then if we manage to get the notion right we should also be getting the actual right. He is in search of meaning – of himself – and our reading of Hegel would seem to suggest that Malone's 'executed purpose' (in this case his scribbling) is 'the actual as existent' or, better, is an 'unrest' which, precisely, 'is the self', 'Unrest' describes the condition of Beckett's 'narrators' very well. But there is something inadequate in the assertion that Malone's self is *constituted* by his babblings. It would not help Malone to know himself, or Beckett to understand Malone, if the theory were adopted that the very pain of his unfulfilled quest for the self *was* his self. At least, it would be the last and worst joke.

*   *   *

CONSCIOUSNESS (THE INTRODUCTION)

Altogether, Hegel establishes a vocabulary with which to discuss the self. That this is important follows naturally from his view of the centrality of the self. What the Hegelian analysis also offers, however, is a spotlight on a new and peculiarly ruthless kind of despair. Equipped with this new vocabulary, fluent in the intensely abstract and confusing language of consciousness, what are we going to say? Some clarification of what is sayable is made in the Introduction that follows the Preface to the *Phenomenology* and we want to know now what Hegel has made possible.

In the Introduction we come across this ominous tag, 'consciousness. . .suffers this violence at its own hands; it destroys its own limited satisfaction'. (PM,138) What is this consciousness, then? Things, we have seen, exist 'an sich', per se, in themselves; this is their 'Truth'. They give themselves to me, however, in another form of being – 'being-for-my-consciousness'. This is my knowledge of an object. But what, then, is the 'Truth' of knowledge? the table's 'Truth' is its existence 'an-sich'; what is the 'Truth' of my knowledge of the table? Hegel answers that 'consciousness furnishes its own criterion in itself', this criterion being our immediate apprehension, 'inside' consciousness, of what is true. (PM,140) Knowledge has 'being-for-my-consciousness' and the 'being-an-sich' of the object simultaneously in consciousness. 'For consciousness is, on the one hand, consciousness of the object, on the other, consciousness of itself.' (PM,141) In other words, I am conscious of the table and conscious of being conscious of the table. Three things are thus in play – the table, my consciousness of it and my consciousness of that consciousness. The table is self-substantiating, it is 'True' in its existence 'an-sich'; my consciousness also furnishes its own 'Truth' in that it observes itself as well as observing the object and automatically irons out any discrepancy between them. Here Hegel makes another of his disturbing asides – this 'ironing out' process *changes the object per se.* If this is not Mr Watt's problem, I don't know what is.

Consciousness, thus, has two objects – the object per se and the existence for consciousness of that object. We have so far spoken of this latter as though it were merely reflective consciousness (consciousness conscious of itself) but it is in fact our 'experience' of the object. To make this clear: when I am conscious of a table I can also become conscious that I am conscious of the table; I cannot simply become conscious that I am conscious. I cannot say that I am conscious that I know; I must say that I am conscious that I know X. (Naturally there are objections to this rather dogmatic elucidation of Hegel.) Our 'knowledge' of an object per se is our consciousness of it, our 'experience' of it is our consciousness of our knowledge of it. The mind is not content to rest here however, it wishes to 'press forward' to its true form of existence. This involves the abolition of the discrepancy between the object 'an-sich' and our knowledge of it. We are sickeningly aware of the distinction between the two objects of our consciousness, viz. the object and our knowledge of it. And we feel that our mind's true form of existence is one in which it 'will reach a position where appearance becomes identified with essence'. (PM,145) This 'essence', presumably, is the object's existence 'an-sich', and this 'appearance' is how it appears to my consciousness.[6] In other words, Hegel is proposing a *terminus ad quem* for consciousness, a point towards which the mind tends. At this point a marriage will take place between the essential existence-per-se of objects and our consciousness of them. But this implies that here our consciousness of objects will come to share their 'an-sich' 'Truth'. In other words, when consciousness effects the marriage between objects and our knowledge of them, by embracing both, it is grasping its *own* essence and will 'connote the nature of absolute knowledge itself'. (PM, 145)

This is the thesis of Hegel's Introduction to the *Phenomenology*. (PM,131–45) What must be borne in mind for our understanding of Beckett is how destructive it is of the old stable Ego and how freely it moves into absolute, mystical and religious language. It is not trivial to add that it also demonstrates the maddening complexity and inclusiveness required for any serious discussion of the fundamental issues of subjectivity. This complexity itself throws considerable doubt on the value of the results achieved and here perhaps one can obtain an insight into that peculiarly Beckettian torment of having 'to speak of things of which I cannot speak'. (T,294) Hegel, having posed the question of the nature of the mind, is forced on up an ever-more-tortuous path towards an unobtainable 'atomic' paradise – a paradise, that is, where *all* the possibilities have been explored, *all* the exceptions given. The connection between this unapproachable peace and Wittgenstein's 'atomic language' will be obvious; the connection between both these and Beckett's need to 'get it all said' is also evident.

A comparison between Hegel's Preface and Introduction and parts of *The Unnamable* on stylistic grounds would be revealing. We are concerned here, however, not to establish a stylistic analogy but to find out whether Beckett and Hegel are talking about the same subject, if that pun is allowed. The Unnamable says:...all sounds, there's only one, continuous, day and night, what is it, it's steps coming and going, it's voices speaking for a moment, it's bodies groping their way, it's the air, it's things, it's the air among the things, that's enough....'. (T,390, 391) The lack of conventional punctuation is deceptive, the monotony can hypnotise. But if we remain alert we can feel the weight of a sort of epistemological fury here. We could paraphrase this passage: 'Our heads are always full of sound – there is no rest and silence in the mind, but what is it that so constantly impinges on our consciousness? It is the events of life reduced, as a philosopher always reduces them, to their simplest – all human action is steps, voices, bodies...perhaps that's not enough, perhaps we are not allowing for the invisible, the air...well, the air and all it contains, air filled with things, things surrounded by air'. This is the Unnamable battling on with his 'pensum'. Like Hegel, he is simply trying to say something, some simple something about the simplest fact – himself, his existence. He goes on:

> . . . that's enough, that I seek, like it, no, not like it, like me, in my own way, what am I saying, after my fashion, that I seek, what do I seek now, what it is, it must be that, it can only be that, what it is, what it can be, what what can be, what I seek, no, what I hear, now it comes back to me, all back to me, they say I seek what it is I hear, I hear them, now it comes back to me, what it can possibly be, and where it can possibly come from, since all is silent here, and the walls thick, and how I manage, without feeling an ear on me, or a head, or a body, or a soul, how I manage, to do what, how I manage, it's not clear, dear dear, you say it's not clear, something is wanting to make it clear, I'll seek, what is wanting, to make everything clear, I'm always seeking something . . . (T,391)

The opening phrases of this quotation refer to the sound mentioned in the passage quoted immediately above (the sound is an external object, an object of perception) and state that the reciter 'seeks' the sound. Does he do this in the same way as the sound does ('like it')? That is, do I comport myself towards objects as they comport themselves towards me? No. I comport myself 'like me' ('für-mich'). So, do we agree that I comport myself like me as I seek the external object, the sound? No, I seek 'what it is', I seek what the sound *is* (it's essence, in Hegel's terms, but it's existence in the terms of Sartre). 'It can only be that; that it is'. That what is? The sound, 'what I hear'. But how can the Unnamable 'possibly' discover what anything is? He is not aware of having an ear, a head, a body, a soul. Now this, of course is precisely how perception works. We hear sounds without hearing our ears. We receive the sense-data in our heads without feeling (Beckett's word) our brains. We experience physical and mental phenomena without being aware that it is our body that is doing so. And where, in any of this, is the soul to be found?

This is precisely the 'mess' on which Hegel has turned the spotlight of his analysis. We *are* aware of sounds. And we are aware that we are aware of sounds. The 'Truth' of the sound is its existence 'an-sich'. The 'Truth' of my awareness of it lies in my awareness of that awareness. Any mind aspires to a marriage between these truths in order to arrive at 'absolute knowledge itself'. If Hegel's analysis is inaccurate it deserves to become the chief torment of the intellectual damned. If it is accurate, if, that is, it reflects a real situation in our commerce with the world, it has really only made matters worse. We are 'always seeking something', we cannot stop; but 'all is silent here' and there is no way out of the echoing prison of subjectivity – I am me, perceiving sounds. How do I know? Because I am aware that I am perceiving sounds as well as being aware of the sounds. And how do I know *that*? Hegel, after all, has made matters worse; quite literally it becomes 'folly to be wise', the Unnamable goes mad under the burden of the incomprehensibility of consciousness as set out by Hegel.

*   *   *

SENSE-CERTAINTY

The lengthy sections of Hegel's *Phenomenology* which deal with morality, culture, world religions and so on have much less light to throw on Beckett than the early sections on consciousness, the Self and the Absolute and it is with these last that I shall be concerned.

Section A, the first of the three main sections, is entitled 'Consciousness'. It begins with a chapter called 'Sense-Certainty', that is with the simplest situation, that of consciousness confronted with an object: this is the situation beyond which we have felt nervous to move since the Cartesian *cogito*; certainly it is the first situation of the Unnamable.

> The knowledge, which is at the start or immediately our object, can be nothing else than just that which is immediate knowledge, knowledge of the immediate, of what *is*.
> We have, in dealing with it, to proceed, too, in an immediate way, to accept what is given, not altering anything in it as it is presented before us, and keeping mere apprehension free from conceptual comprehension. (PM,149)

which is at least no clearer than:

> And things, what is the correct attitude to adopt towards things? And, to begin with, are they necessary? What a question. But I

have few illusions, things are to be expected. The best is not to decide anything, in this connexion, in advance. If a thing turns up, for some reason or another, take it into consideration. (T,294)

This is where Beckett must be seen as genuinely philosophical. He begins this novel at precisely the point at which modern philosophy starts. The first three sentences are 'Where now? Who now? When now?' and these have their equivalents in Hegel who proposes two 'universal' forms of the 'this' – 'Now' and 'Here'. 'Now' and 'Here' are forms which do not alter according to the actual When or Where they apply to. 'This' is therefore universal, but it depends on another 'universal' – 'I', 'pure Ego'. These three universals (Now, Here and Ego) are established by posing the questions Where? When? Who? Where *now*? Who *now*? When *now*? For it is always *now*. So the Unnamable's consciousness, like Hegel's, starts with 'what *is*'; here, now, with me.[7]

'How proceed?' is the question the Unnamable asks next, 'By affirmations and negations invalidated as offered, or sooner or later'. (T,293) And indeed this seems to be the valid way in Hegel's view:

> The truth for consciousness of a 'This' of sense is said to be universal experience. Every consciousness of itself cancels again, as soon as made, such a truth as e.g. the Here is a tree, or the Now is noon, and expresses the very opposite: the Here is not a tree but a house. (PM,158)

As Moran says, by way of bringing *Molloy* to a close, 'Then I went back into the house and wrote. It is midnight. The rain is beating on the windows. It was not midnight. It was not raining.' (T,176)

Hegel and Beckett, so far, are parallel; immediate knowledge is followed by immediate negation. The negation, of course, depends on a previous affirmation. 'Here is a tree.' The paradox of the negation stems from the affirmation. It is in trying to 'say' the tree that we go wrong.

> Those who. . .speak of the 'existence' of external objects, which can be more precisely characterized as actual, absolutely particular, wholly personal, individual things, each of them not like anything or anyone else (say that) this is the existence which. . . has absolute certainty and truth. They 'mean' this bit of paper I

am writing on... but they do not say what they 'mean'. If they really wanted to *say* this bit of paper which they 'mean', and they wanted to *say* so, that is impossible, because the This of sense, which is 'meant', cannot be reached by language, which belongs to consciousness, i.e. to what is inherently universal. In the very attempt to say it, it would, therefore, crumble in their hands; those who have begun to describe it would not be able to finish doing so: they would have to hand it over to others, who would themselves in the last resort have to confess to speaking about a thing that has no being. (PM,159–60)

This is exactly what happens to the Unnamable. All that he says 'crumbles in his hands', he cannot finish 'describing', he admits at last that he is talking about nothing.

What we have learned from Hegel on immediate knowledge is that objects, simply contemplated, do not yield us up their here-and-nowness; on the contrary, they are evanescent and elude us as we grasp at them. We have now learnt that one cannot *say* an object; there is a difference in kind between words and objects that makes this forever impossible. Hegel goes so far as to suggest Beckett's own solution (the employment of 'vice-existers') when he talks of 'handing it over to others' who, eventually, will learn that they are talking about nothing. Mr Watt learns this lesson of the inherent falseness of all propositions; 'He made the distressing discovery that of himself too he could no longer affirm anything that did not seem as false as if he had affirmed it of a stone'. (W,79) What is so illuminating about these parallels is the fact that Hegel's version establishes the point (in this case the point that one cannot grasp the Here and Now, cannot say the This) as philosophically necessary. No longer can we think, 'Yes, poor old Malone seems to have lost his grip on reality; I have felt that way myself sometimes, but after all there *is* a graspable reality which other people – philosophers for instance, or I myself when I am feeling up to it – can discuss, clarify and explain'. We now have to consider the possibility that when Beckett produces his paradoxes, seemingly self-contradictory asides and so on, he is not merely attempting to find objective correlatives for the psychological state of his characters. He is telling the philosophical truth. He is not dealing with madmen and their warped views of reality; he is dealing with reality itself, exactly as conceived by the sane, prosaic reason of a 'normal' academic philosopher.

One is faced with a choice, after all. One can do one of two things when confronted, for example, with this from *The End*: 'Strictly speaking I wasn't there. Strictly speaking I believe I've never been anywhere' (NK,61). One can either let one's mind skate over it, relishing it as a paradox, a crazy aside, a meaningless pair of sentences interesting only in that they are a grammatical joke (because they sound all right and exist as legitimate sentences); or one can decide that they are serious, that they have a meaning. 'Strictly speaking I believe I've never been anywhere' says Beckett's narrator, and Hegel's philosophical rigour happens to lead him to make similar statements when he, too, is speaking 'strictly'. This should encourage us to choose our second possibility and try to read Beckett as meaningful. Even without Hegel, Beckett's tormented battle with expression seems to deserve serious consideration. 'Strictly speaking'. Why 'strictly' if there is not a 'strict' fundamental, true, non-everyday way of speaking? And if there is such a way of speaking, who speaks in it? In this case, it so happens, Hegel for whom, strictly, the Self is nowhere.

*   *   *

PERCEPTION

The second chapter of 'Consciousness' is 'Perception', alternatively titled 'Things and their deceptiveness', which promises some light on the Unnamable, and others. It is Malone in fact who has most to say about 'things'; but first, Hegel.

Perception 'has negation, distinction, multiplicity in its very nature'. (PM,163) Hegel is trying to establish the point at which perception moves from sense to intellect, for example the point at which my sensory apprehension of an object becomes an intellectual understanding of what I am looking at. 'Negation' comes at the very beginning of this process, as we saw in the last section.

> The This. . .is established as *not* This, or as superseded, and yet not nothing (*simpliciter*), but a determinate nothing, a nothing with a certain content, viz. *the This*. The sense-element is in this way itself still present. (PM,163)

Which is to say, among other things, that when we consider a state of awareness just slightly higher than immediate sense-certainty, when we consider 'Perception', there at once enters a destructive agent. Before even considering self-consciousness we have arrived at a 'contradictory' point in the nature of the world – the This established as *not* This. The reason for this contradiction would appear to be that 'This' should refer to the immediate existence of a thing but can in fact only refer to the properties of the thing apprehended by the senses; thus, to take Hegel's example of salt, if I enquire of myself what I mean by 'This' salt I can only reply that I mean this white, powdered, sharp-tasting entity; but these things are not, of course, 'This' salt; the whiteness is different from the 'thisness'. So 'This' brings a 'not-This' with it, a situation which it is hard to conceive but without which the deceptiveness of things in Beckett's world is hard to understand.

The properties of the salt that give themselves to our perception are quite distinct from one another (PM,164–5). Its whiteness does not at all affect its sharp taste for example. But they all share the same Here-and-Now and Hegel hits on a happy way of expressing this relationship by saying that the 'also' required in a description of an object (the salt is white and *also* tastes sharp) can be promoted to an 'Also' which is 'the pure universal itself...the "Thinghood" keeping them together'. (PM,165) But we do not perceive universal 'whiteness' or 'sharp-tastingness', we perceive *this* whiteness and also *this* sharp taste. The salt is 'One'; we exclude from our perception all *other* things, all the properties which the salt does *not* have. Thus there is an inherent contradiction between the fact that I identify the salt by perceiving its properties and the fact that these properties are universals. Hegel deals with this contradiction quite specifically (PM,167–8) and develops it further. Properties may be universals, he says, 'but the particular quality is a property only when attached to a "one", and determinate only by relation to others'. (PM,168) It is this step that takes us from sense-impressions to consciousness. The contradictions breed a higher consciousness which is concerned with itself and not with the sense-object. To express it crudely, when we start to think about our perception of an object we actually think about ourselves, *our* perception, and we cease to think about the object. Hegel describes what happens in this process in language that echoes the Trilogy;

I am thrown back on the beginning, and once more dragged into the same circuit, that supersedes itself in every moment...Consciousness, then, has to go over this cycle again (PM,168)

Life in the Beckett world tends to be cyclical (Moran recapitulates

Molloy's decomposition, Malone comes back again and again to his point of departure, the Unnamable sees Malone pass before him 'at doubtless regular intervals'). But here in Hegel we are dealing with a very short-term cycle, the cycle of sense-certainly-perception-consciousness. This feels rather like the churning and whirling of the Unnamable's 'mind' but the points of connexion that I think worth establishing are (a) the *compulsory* aspect of Hegel's and Beckett's descriptions of the thinking process and (b) the incomprehensibility of some parts of the Trilogy, especially *The Unnamable* in any other light than this. I need hardly quote passages to establish the compulsory nature of the 'pensum' undergone by Beckett's 'heroes', the 'you must go on' in the last line of *The Unnamable* can stand for them all. Point of connexion (a) is between this compulsion and the compulsion expressed in the careful choice of words in the passage from Hegel quoted above – 'dragged' and 'Consciousness. . . has to'. The thinking mind must go on, it cannot stop. Point (b) is really the thesis I am propounding – viz. that Beckett is not really comprehensible without some philosophical illumination. Again the point to be stressed is that the hypnotic music of Beckett's prose is only a part of the journey – there *is* further to go. Thus: Hegel proposes a sleight-of-mind whereby consciousness, when engaged in perception, is found, as explained above, to have 'gone back into itself'. (PM,168) Only such a philosophical proposal can make sense of the following.

> Perhaps its the door, perhaps I'm at the door, that would surprise me, perhaps its I, perhaps somewhere or other it was I, I can depart, all this time I've journeyed without knowing it, it's I now at the door, what door, what's a door doing here, . . . (T,418)

The tension in this passage between perceiver and perceived is quite clear. From the dialectic of the door (object) and the 'I' (subject) arises what the Unnamable cannot help having – the Hegelian experience of 'going over' the cycle of sense-impressions, perceptions and consciousness.

*   *   *

THE UNITY OF OBJECTS

So far, under 'Perception', we have looked at properties, the 'Also' (existence?) that connects them, their distinction, their union, their contradictory universality. The difficulties Hegel has encountered have really arisen as he has tried to move from simple sense-certainty (the sort of 'consciousness' we share with animals, I would hazard) to a 'perception' which includes a measure of understanding. This latter, as we have seen, is a mixed blessing to say the least.

In considering understanding we can start from properties again: 'The entire diversity of these aspects comes not from the thing but from us; and we find them falling apart... from one another, because the organs they affect are quite distinct *inter se*, the eye is entirely distinct from the tongue and so on.' (PM,170) Thus it is *we*, ourselves, some self 'behind' our organs of perception, who constitute the unity of an object, '*We* preserve and maintain the self-sameness and truth of the thing, its being a "one".' (PM,170) Consciousness thus makes an object 'one' at the same time as distinguishing its properties, and

> Consciousness is at the same time aware that it reflects itself also into itself, and that, in perceiving, the opposite moment to the 'also' crops up. This moment, however, is the unity of the thing with itself, a unity which excludes distinction from itself. It is consequently this unity which consciousness has to take upon itself. (PM,171)

Which is as much as to say that an object's real *esse* is its *percipi*. This burden that consciousness carries is the burden of the existence of the world – only man perceives, so all that is perceived is man's. Beckett's Berkeleyan background is well known and instantly available in *Film*, the plot of which involves Buster Keaton in ridding his environment of all perceivers to be confronted at last by himself.

To formulate Hegel's position here we can say: Perception and understanding create the unity of objects (a unity jeopardized by perception's inevitable fragmenting of objects into properties.) However, among these objects must be numbered the empirical self – the personality and properties of the individual; 'consciousness... reflects itself also into itself'. Thus consciousness creates the unity of the human being himself. In *Proust* Beckett makes an oblique approach towards this conception when he attributes to Proust the idea that the world is 'a projection of the individual's consciousness'. (PTD,19) This world projected by consciousness does not have an innate unity – it depends on voluntary memory for its unity: 'The creation of the world did not take place once and for all time, but takes place every day'. (PTD,19) It is Habit that insists on this daily re-creation of the world, the Habit that is bred of (and breeds) familiarity. We must notice carefully what Beckett says of this: 'Habit then is the generic term for the countless treaties concluded between the countless subjects that constitute the individual and their countless correlative objects.' (PTD,19) I would lay a stress on the 'countless subjects' of Proustian man which relate to the 'countless objects' of the world. Here we have an empirical self confronting the phenomena of existence on an *ad hoc* basis; the Habit which holds these selves together is the *ersatz* Self, it imitates and performs the function of the Self. Habit, supported by voluntary memory, assures us each morning that we are still the same person that we were yesterday, 'It insists on that most necessary, wholesome and monotonous plagiarism – the plagiarism of oneself.' (PTD,33) Only by self-plagiarism can we be assured of continued identity.

To sum up: perception creates the unity of objects, but perception also perceives itself; thus it creates the unity of itself. This unity is described in *Proust* as the work of a particular organ of perception, the voluntary memory.

*   *   *

CONSCIOUSNESS THE 'INNER WORLD'

The third section of 'Consciousness' is entitled 'Force and understanding – the world of appearance and the supersensible world.' Here Hegel makes his first approach to a mystical/existential view of the world and comes yet closer to Beckett country. In 'perception' he discussed objects first as groups of properties and then as unities. He now points out further that we apprehend objects as universals, but also in their singleness, in other words that when I look at a table I know it belongs to a universal category 'Table' but also that it is 'this' single, unique, table. This leads Hegel into a discussion of the 'true being' of things, the 'inner world' of the object. He establishes the lines of force of his picture of perception by proposing four areas between which perception takes place: there is consciousness (1) which perceives the object (2) and creates its unity (Hegel insists here that these two are, in a sense, only one 'moment'; we can talk as though there are two objects, 'my con-

sciousness' and 'the table', but what we are concerned with is one
unified entity, viz. 'my consciousness of the table'). Beyond (1) and
(2) there are: (3) the 'inner world' of the perceived object and (4) a
further consciousness to correspond to this. We can expect that this
duality, (3) and (4), will also be subject to the rule that in consciousness of an object there are not two objects but only one unified
entity — in this case 'my consciousness of the inner world' of the
object.

> The inner world is so far for consciousness a bare and simple
> beyond, because consciousness does not as yet find itself in it. It is
> empty, for it is merely the nothingness of appearance, and
> positively the naked universal. This type of inwardness suits those
> who say that the inner being of things cannot be known (Hegel
> here refers to Goethe); but the reason for the position would have
> to be taken in some other sense. Certainly there is no knowledge to
> be had of this inner world, as we have it here; not, however, owing
> to reason being too shortsighted, or limited, or whatever you care
> to call it...but on account simply of the nature of the case,
> because in the void there is nothing known, or, putting it from the
> point of view of the other side, because its very characteristic lies
> in being *beyond* consciousness. (PM,191–2)

It is time to relate this to *The Unnamable*, but first I think we
should stress that when Hegel says that the 'inner world' is 'merely
the nothingness of appearance' he is not contradicting himself; he
means what he says. He goes go to explain this point by telling us
that the incomprehensible 'inner world', called 'the holy of holies,
the inner sanctuary', must be 'filled' with *something* and that we try
to fill it with 'dreamings, *appearances*, produced by consciousness
itself.' This, however, is unnecessary; the 'inner world' of an object is
not a sanctuary nor need consciousness implant anything in it — it is
something that arises naturally out of our perception and it is filled
with '*appearance qua appearance*'. Hegel says he realizes that an
'inner world' is usually taken to be the opposite of 'appearance' (i.e.
'inner-world' = 'reality') but he points out that 'Understanding'
(which is the sort of consciousness that relates to the inner world, the
No. 4 that relates to the No. 3 in our description of lines of force
above) is related to 'inner world' only through the 'mediation' of the
'play of forces' of sense-certainty and perception (i.e. of No. 1 and
No. 2). (PM,193) In short, the 'inner world' of an object appears at

first as 'the implicit, inherent being, universal and still without a filling' and then, in truth, as appearance qua appearance. (PM,193)

Assuming here, as elsewhere, that Beckett's descriptions may be taken metaphorically, an assumption justified by the fact that if we only take them literally we are bound to dismiss them as impossible, we find that the Unnamable's surroundings read remarkably like Hegel's paradoxical theorising. The Unnamable is motionless, staring straight ahead into the grey air, 'close to me it is grey, dimly transparent, and beyond that charmed circle deepens and spreads its fine impenetrable veils'. (T,302) The 'charmed circle' seems to be the immediate area of Perception in which the narrator perceives Objects and beyond which the light of certainty, such as it is, cannot penetrate. 'There is no night so deep', however, 'that it may not be pierced in the end, with the help of no other light than that of the blackened sky, or of the earth itself'. (T,302) The unexpected conclusion of this sentence parallels Hegel's paradox about appearance – both preclude the possibility of some light being thrown on 'reality' from *outside*, both propose man's perception, consciousness, understanding as a closed system within which all possible explanations are, or can be, given; both exclude divine or supernatural help from the process of understanding the world. The Unnamable now suggests that the grey he perceives may in fact be 'the enclosure wall, as compact as lead' (T,302), a suggestion that he accepts (there being no possibility of going *beyond* for explanations). At least he proposes that, if it were possible, he could throw a 'javelin' into the grey to tell 'whether that which hems me round, and blots out my world, is the old void, or a plenum'. (T,302) This is exactly how Hegel proceeds – observing that the 'inner world' of objects is a void and then showing how it is a 'plenum' in fact, a space entirely filled, filled by 'appearance'. Quite how satisfying Hegel's process is may be questioned. After all, has one advanced much beyond 'void' when one has rejected it and come up triumphantly with a 'plenum' called *appearance qua appearance*? Beckett, as so often, expresses in strong metaphorical terms the dissatisfaction we feel with this sort of philosophical 'solution' – not the dissatisfaction created by disagreement but the agony created by agreement.

In this situation where the solution is no less painful than the problem and the correct solution no more help than a false one, the Unnamable is doomed to his babble. Hegel calls his 'inner world' the 'supersensible'. It is beyond the reach of sense-perception, it is 'the changeless kingdom of laws, the immediate ectype and copy of the world of perception'. (PM,203) The 'inner world', for under-standing, is the *'appearance qua appearance'* of these laws; but when we try to explain this we run up against a tautology. If we perceive lightning we 'explain' it by referring to the changeless laws of electricity – the lightning is the 'appearance' of, an example of, electricity; its 'inner world', its 'true being', is just this appearance itself. But this is an explanation which explains nothing – the laws of electricity are identical to the laws of lightning, they *are* the laws of lightning. It is like trying to explain the growth of a puppy by saying that all puppies grow. Consequently, to say that the inner world of an object of perception is its appearance, and specifically its appearance *qua* the appearance of a changeless law, and then to say that this changeless law exists in its appearances, such as the appearance of the object, is as much as to say nothing at all. To quote Hegel, 'It is explanation that not only explains nothing, but is so plain that, while it makes as if it would say something different from what is already said, it really says nothing at all, but merely repeats the same thing over again.' (PM,201)

This puts the Unnamable's babble into perspective. We started by calling the 'inner world' a void; then 'filled' it with the formula *'appearance qua appearance'*; now we learn that it is inexplicable and that all rational discussion of it 'says nothing at all'. In the section which starts 'All these Murphys, Molloys and Malones do not fool me' the Unnamable goes through a similar process. (T,305) Having dismissed the superficial (perceived objects) he claims 'only I and this black void have ever been'. (T,306) Is he certain? He asks 'And the sounds?' but replies 'No, all is silent'. Then 'And the lights...must they too go out?' and answers 'Yes, out with them, there is no light here.' So the world of sense-certainty and perception has indeed been transcended. What is left? 'Nothing then but me, of which I know nothing, except that I have never uttered, and this black of which I know nothing either, except that it is black, and empty'. (T,306) Thus far the 'inner world' is void. He will try to 'speak of it, of its appearance'. He then makes a move that is incom-prehensible without something like our Hegelian reading. He returns to 'Basil and his gang' (why, if he has not been 'fooled' by the Murphys and Molloys?) and dismisses them with 'Inexistent, in-vented to explain I forget what', just as if they had been made to fill the void like Hegel's 'changeless laws' – explaining nothing. 'Ah yes, all lies, God and man, nature and the light of day, the heart's

outpourings and the means of understanding, all invented...'
(T,306)

Of course, Hegel does not leave us here. He proposes an 'inverted' world to replace the tautological world he has dismissed. The 'first super-sensible world' was the world of changeless laws conceived in Platonic terms. Now a 'second supersensible world' emerges which admits change as an inherent part of its reality. So much is change part of this 'inverted' world that, indeed, everything within it is in a permanent state of tension with its opposite. Hegel expresses this in an almost mystical passage in which all that is in 'the first super-sensible world' is contradicted in the second; black becomes white. But the meaning of this emerges as Hegel moves on to a discussion of opposites in a true dialectical process. The point is that black is 'the inherent nature of white'. (PM,208) The marriage of opposites is obscurely but emphatically established here – a necessary thesis in view of the way the dialectic works.

*   *   *

CONSCIOUSNESS THE 'SUPERSENSIBLE' WORLDS

We are now approaching the end of the first main section of the *Phenomenology*, 'Consciousness'. Hegel is moving upwards, from the lowest form of awareness to the highest. His aim is to give an adequate account of man's comprehension of the world. This account starts from the premiss that understanding is first a matter of universalization.[8] The tendency to universalize produces the 'first supersensible world'. But when we want to explain the world this first level is not enough. We may start to understand, say, white things because we associate them with one another and learn in the end to posit the universal 'whiteness', but we cannot explain this without resorting to the 'second supersensible world', the world in which whiteness is defined by its opposite, blackness, and *vice versa*. Once this stage is reached man has, without noticing it as it were, moved from consciousness to self-consciousness, (PM,210) and therein lies the burden of this whole dialectical process. 'Explanation' requires, produces, self-consciousness.

There is so much satisfaction in explanation, because consciousness being there, if we may use such an expression, in direct communion with itself, enjoys itself only. No doubt it there seems to be occupied with something else, but in point of fact it is busied all the while merely with itself. (PM,210)

Is this true of Beckett? That is, is 'explanation' a path towards self-consciousness for the vice-existers? We might remember here that Hegel's *Phenomenology* is not really chronological on any large scale. More important than the possible 'real-time' chronologies (man's development from the animal, for instance, or the growth of perception in the child) is the *logical* time or *logical* space within which his categories are related to one another. This same distinction could profitably be made in the case of Beckett; it is a neglected point, but if the simple rule is observed that we cannot take the trilogy, for instance, literally (except on one of many levels) it becomes probable that its non-literal meanings do not necessarily inhabit 'real' time and space. In which case the *apparent* development from, say, *Molloy* to *The Unnamable* can parallel the development, also only apparent, that we find in Hegel. The dialectical process may take time but its significance lies in its logical, not in its chronological, order. This distinction leaves us freer to move about within Beckett in our search for explanations.

In a sense all Beckett's work is an attempt at explanation of the inexplicable. It appears often that explanation is a substitute for a real confrontation with the issue of existence. The Unnamable tries to explain why he stopped believing Mahood at a certain point; 'I'll explain why', he says, 'that will permit me to think of something else and in the first place of how to get back to me'. (T,324) Explanation enables the mind to start moving 'back' towards the Self, while the explanation is irrelevant because 'in point of fact', as we know very well, the Unnamable is 'busied all the while merely with himself'. There is a strong underlying assumption, especially in *Malone Dies*, that explanation is a duty owed to 'them', or to someone, a 'pensum' intimately connected with discussion of, or attempts on, the Self. Malone, after a few preliminaries, starts on the elegant tale of the impossible Saposcats, breaking off with the reflection, highly reminiscent of Hegel, 'I wonder if I am not talking yet again about myself'. He asks himself, 'Shall I be incapable, to the end, of lying on any other subject?' (T,189)

So, 'explanation', for Hegel and for Beckett, is a dawning of self-consciousness. And we saw that for Hegel explanation is only possible once the mind has risen to an appreciation of the 'second supersensible world', the world in which white is defined by black to the extent that he can claim that black is 'the inherent nature of white'. The evident self-contradiction of this sort of juggling with opposites is again familiar to us from Beckett; to give only one of many examples, in *Endgame* Hamm narrates a story which is punctuated at close intervals by 'It was an extra-ordinarily bitter day', 'It was a glorious bright day', 'It was a howling wild day' and so on.

Struggling to include as much as possible of the world in his explanation, before moving on to the section directly concerned with Self-consciousness, Hegel raises his eyes, as it were, from the details of the mind's perception, understanding and explanation of objects and lets into the picture 'infinitude' and the mind's perception of itself. Life *is* every distinction and every unity (and perception is concerned with these.) 'Explanation' brought self-consciousness out of mere perception and this new, self-conscious view of life must include an 'apprehension of infinitude' that is, of the infinite number of distinctions inherent in objects. This is tantamount to an 'apprehension' of the ineffability of the objective world. Hegel puts it thus: 'In that this notion of infinitude is its object, it (consciousness as self-consciousness) is thus a consciousness of the distinction as one which at the same time is at once cancelled.' (PM,211) This is obscure, but it seems to me to involve the (Beckettian) ungraspability of the world. There is implied an infinite distance between perceiver and perceived brought out by the simultaneous self-perception of the perceiver. For example, I perceive the whiteness of an object; I 'explain' it by resorting not merely to the 'first supersensible world', the world in which the white object participates in the Platonic Form of Whiteness, but also to the 'second supersensible world' the world in which I understand white by knowing black. In this world there is already an infinitude of self-reflections between white and black and the situation is exacerbated by the introduction of the self-reflections of self-consciousness. In mere consciousness I 'am' the perceived object; in self-consciousness I am both the perceived object and aware of myself as perceiver. But being aware of myself as perceiver means that I am also aware of myself as a perceived object in which case I am aware of myself as aware of myself as a perceived object. This is the 'infinite regress' of self-consciousness objected to by Sartre.

To substantiate this as being Hegel's meaning it is only necessary to quote the passage immediately following the sentence cited above.

Consciousness is for itself and on its own account, it is a distinguishing of what is undistinguished, it is Self-consciousness. I distinguish myself from myself; and therein I am immediately aware that this factor distinguished from me is not distinguished. I, the self-same being, thrust myself away from myself; but this which is distinguished, which is set up as unlike me, is immediately on its being distinguished no distinction for me. Consciousness of an other, of an object in general, is indeed itself necessarily self-consciousness, reflectedness into self, consciousness of self in its otherness. (PM,211)

Beneath the complexity of this concluding section of 'Consciousness' lies an immediately recognizable account of what happens between man and his world. In the final page of this section Hegel ties up the threads of his argument and crowns the mountain he has built with a disarming trick of the dialectic whereby all the terms of the process-so-far are dismissed. He is clearing the ground before moving on to Self-consciousness, and his summary of the position reached at this point, besides its remarkable coherence and clarity, also reads like an exact description of what *The Unnamable* is about. Hegel's thesis, in the discussion that follows, is summarized in the scheme of perception involving poles numbered 1 to 4, as on pages 132 and 133.

Raised above perception, consciousness reveals itself united and bound up with the supersensible world through the mediating agency of the realm of appearance, through which it gazes into this background that lies behind appearance. The two extremes, the one that of the pure inner region, the other that of the inner being gazing into this pure inner region, are now merged together; and as they have disappeared *qua* extremes, the middle term, the mediating agency, *qua* something other than these extremes, has also vanished. This curtain [of appearance], therefore, hanging before the inner world is withdrawn, and we have here the inner being [the ego] gazing into the inner realm – the vision of the undistinguished selfsame reality, which repels itself from itself, affirms itself as a divided and distinguished inner reality, but as one for which at the same time the two factors have immediately no distinction; what we have here is Self-consciousness. (PM,212. The square brackets are Baillie's.)

To clarify this passage we can rely on Mure's gloss on it: 'The curtain hides only a void until the understanding penetrates and finds – only itself.'[9] This sense of looking through appearance to see oneself is prevalent in Beckett one of whose greatest achievements is his ability to objectify the horrific and sterile self-communion that constitutes all consciousness of all objects. (I perceive the table because I am conscious of perceiving the table; there is no exit from this closed and self-depending system.) As so often Beckett reveals the painfulness of the philosophic intuition.

> Do they consider me so plastered with their rubbish that I can never extricate myself, never make a gesture but their cast must come to life? But within, motionless, I can live, and utter me, for no ears but my own. They loaded me down with their trappings and stoned me through the carnival. I'll sham dead now, whom they couldn't bring to life, and my monster's carapace will rot off me'. (T,327)

This is one anguished cry among many in Beckett that parallels Hegel's theory of consciousness as the constituent of a union with a world, not the world of 'trappings' and appearances, but that of a 'within'. As Hegel puts it, in a passage reminiscent of Beckett's style, 'It is manifest that behind the so-called curtain, which is to hide the inner world, there is nothing to be seen unless we ourselves go behind there, as much in order that we may thereby see, as that there may be something behind there which can be seen.' (PM,212–13)

*   *   *

SELF-CONSCIOUSNESS

In 'Consciousness' Hegel has established that there is a unity between consciousness and its objects. This indissoluble marriage appears to torment Beckett in various guises, among them the Unnamable's 'It's of me now I must speak, even if I have to do it with their language', (T,326) where the silence of 'me' is only attainable through an involvement in the trappings of the world; that is, where consciousness is doomed to an objective babble.

The unity between consciousness and its objects gives rise to self-consciousness which, compared with 'sense-certainty' and 'per-

ception' is a 'return out of otherness'. (PM,219) This is the first point
made in section B of the *Phenomenology*, 'Self-Consciousness'. It
appears that there are two possibilities, or that there must be two
'moments'. There is self-conscious apprehension of the otherness of
objects (referred to as 'negative' and involving the thought 'I am *not*
X') and there is pure self-awareness ('I am I'). This latter is
described as 'only motionless tautology, Ego is Ego'. (PM,219) This
is remarkably similar to the Unnamable's 'but within, motionless, I
can live, and utter me, for no ears but my own' quoted above. Of
course, no Beckettian character does remain 'within' or 'utter me'
because of the opposite urge, the desire for life. As Mure expresses
Hegel, 'Desire is the subject's urge to live through filling the empty
"I = I" with an element of the sensible world' (op. cit., p. 74) which
is exactly why the 'vice-existers' are needed. And indeed both of the
'moments' of experience described by Hegel seem to be equivalent to
Beckett's often-stated dichotomy. In the present example, the
'objective' world of Hegel is the 'rubbish', the 'trappings', the
'carnival' of Beckett. I would suggest that the crude mind-body split
celebrated in *Murphy* relates, as Chapter 6 of that novel makes
explicitly clear, to the relative simplicity of Cartesian dualism while
the voices, words and rubbish surrounding the Unnamable's elusive
Self relate, as we might well expect, to a more sophisticated
epistemology and metaphysic. In other words if *Murphy* is
Cartesian, *The Unnamable* is Hegelian.

Hegel elaborates further on this relationship between self-
consciousness and the world. Self-conciousness becomes 'convinced
of the nothingness of the other', and by 'negating' the 'other' thus, it
'acquires the certainty of its own self'. (PM,225) This does not have
the despair in it that Beckett's version has, but in a sense that is the
foundation of Beckett's uniqueness – he offers a creative, emotional
reaction to a precise, philosophical reality in place of the
commoner, and easier, reaction to the generalized conditions of
'life'. Beckett's 'version' of this negation of the other and affirmation
of Self by Self-consciousness is present more or less *passim* in the
trilogy as one of the 'profounder' modes of narration adopted when
the games no longer serve. The 'moment of truth' early in *The
Unnamable* illustrates this:

Ah yes, all lies, God and man, nature and the light of day, the
heart's outpourings and the means of understanding, all
invented, basely, by me alone, with the help of no one, since there

is no one, to put off the hour when I must speak of me. (T,306)

And the references to the negativity, indeed the non-existence, of the objective world appear on nearly every page: either it is suddenly made apparent that all the objective details of the monologue are fictions of the Unnamable's ('That's a good continuation' (T,398) 'But let us close this parenthesis and, with a light heart, open the next' (T,357) etc.) or the objects mentioned are simply and violently denied, ('Mahood, he was called Mahood, I don't see him any more, I don't known how he lived any more, he isn't there any more, he was never there, in his jar, I never saw him...' (T,399))

We can follow this parallel between the novelist and the philosopher right up to the conclusion of this passage on negation and self-affirmation. Hegel crowns his argument with the following sentences:

> ...self-consciousness is thus only assured of itself through sublating this other, which is presented to self-consciousness as an independent life...Convinced of the nothingness of this other, it definitely affirms this nothingness to be for itself the truth of this other, negates the independent object, and thereby acquires the certainty of its own self. (PM,225)

Except for the last clause, this quotation is a philosophical equivalent of 'Nothing then but me, of which I know nothing, except that I have never uttered, and this black, of which I know nothing either, except that it is black, and empty.' (T,306)

The last clause of the Hegel quotation marks one radical difference between the two writers that is everywhere apparent. In Beckett there is no certainty. But one might do well to ask whether 'certainty' is really the inevitable outcome of Hegel's dialectic.

*   *   *

MASTER AND SLAVE

Having considered the relationship of self-consciousness to the un-self-conscious world of objects, Hegel naturally moves on to the relationship between different self-consciousnesses. 'Self-consciousness attains its satisfaction only in another self-consciousness'. (PM,226)

This is leading in to the famous discussion of master and slave ('Lordship and Bondage' in Baillie's translation) of which much has been made. For our purpose the two features of this discussion that throw light on Beckett are, first, the necessity of the master-slave relationship for continued self-consciousness ('Servitude is not only a phase of human history, it is in principle a condition of the development and maintenance of the consciousness of self as a fact of experience' – Baillie's note (PM,228)) and, second, the violence inherent in the master-slave 'struggle' and *its* necessity.

The first of these points is based on the fact that self-consciousness needs another self-consciousness to achieve 'satisfaction' – in simple terms, a man totally isolated from other men since birth would never appreciate his self-consciousness on the level of a pure abstraction, he would not be conscious of being self-conscious. Two self-consciousnesses, then, brought into contact, realize their own self-consciousness and immediately assert it by acting so as to show that they are not mere objects and 'the relation of both self-consciousness is in this way so constituted that they prove themselves and each other through a life-and-death struggle.' (PM,232) The winner of this struggle is master, the loser slave. The winner shows that he is not a mere object and both parties can assent to his full self-consciousness: 'the master is the consciousness that exists *for itself*'. (Here, incidentally, we find Hegel's usage, 'für sich', coming close to Sartre's usage 'pour-soi'. But the important thing for us here is that Sartre attributes 'pour-soi' existence *ex hypothesi* to all human beings and not merely to 'masters'. There is much of the Hegelian version in Beckett, as we shall see.) So the master establishes and nourishes his self-consciousness at the expense of the slave. But the slave reaches the same point by another route; through 'labour' and working to effect what the master desires the slave enters into a creative relationship with the objects on which he works and through 'this activity giving shape and form' he attains 'the direct apprehension of his independent being as its self'. (PM,238) Thus servitude is necessary to the maintenance of consciousness, which is our first point, and the condition of servitude is that of violent struggle, which is our second point. How do these relate to Beckett?

The answer to this will involve an assessment in Hegelian terms of the significance of the couples and 'pseudo-couples' in Beckett. If there is one thing in his work that is almost as definite as the agony of being alone it is the agony of being with another. Murphy and Mr

Endon, the pairs of servants in Mr Knott's household, Mr Knott himself and Watt, Mercier and Camier, Didi and Gogo, Pozzo and Lucky, Nagg and Nell, Hamm and Clov, Winnie and Willie, A and B, Moran Senior and Moran Junior, and then, passing lightly but not insignificantly over the second two parts of the trilogy, the endless pairs of *How It Is*; this is only a list of the more important examples. Not all of these, of course, are master-and-slave couples; indeed, only Pozzo-Lucky and Hamm-Clov fall into that category exactly.

Certainly the mutual dependence of Hegel's master and slave is faithfully reproduced in these two pairs. Pozzo, having treated Lucky like the lowest sort of slave (and he refers to him as a slave by implication in Act One, 'As if I were short of slaves!') reveals that it was Lucky who taught him 'all these beautiful things' ('I can't bear it...any longer...the way he goes on.' (WFG,34) In the second act of *Waiting for Godot* Pozzo's dependence on his slave is even more marked as they come in together with Lucky leading Pozzo because the latter has gone blind.

Hamm and Clov are equally mutually dependent, although here, too, the initial impression given is that Hamm is master and Clov slave. But Hamm is blind and needs his slave for all sorts of tasks. On the other hand only Hamm knows the combination of the larder lock. In the case of both these pairs it seems that consciousness, including self-consciousness, is one of the products of their union, as in Hegel. They literally keep each other conscious in that they keep each other alive, and they develop self-consciousness by reassuring themselves that the other is paying attention. The masters (Pozzo and Hamm) are prepared to go to great lengths to achieve any sort of an audience; Nagg, Nell, Didi, Gogo will do very well, but obviously Lucky and Clov are the usual recipients of their masters' voices. Didi and Gogo need one another as witnesses of the Hegelian sort ('So there you are again'; 'Am I?') as do Mercier and Camier who, when they are reunited, begin once again to look at one another 'with something of the old look' and Camier says 'I all but gave myself up.' (MC,114) Even Mr Knott needs a witness to his not needing. The consciousness of self is in some degree dependent on other self-consciousness in these examples; the most extreme version of this, of course, is the Berkeleyan *esse est percipi* which is the thesis of Beckett's *Film*.

The necessary involvement of violence in these relationships is made quite clear by Beckett. Pozzo whips Lucky who kicks

Estragon. The assaults range from the trivial (the tramps cannot bear to embrace on account of the stink of garlic) through the comically violent (the stoning of Watt by Lady McCann) to the grotesquely cruel (the means of communication adopted in *How It Is*). In both Hegel and Beckett the violence appears gratuitous, but in both cases the reason for it is the same. Hegel puts it that master and slave 'must enter into this struggle, for they must bring their certainty of themselves, the certainty of being for themselves, to the level of objective truth'. (PM,232) Beckett is naturally not as explicit as this, but even in the obscurity of *How It Is* where we find Pim and Bom communicating by violent nauseating means the result is that the narrator can say of their meeting and first exchange 'me too great benefit too I have that impression great benefit especially at first hard to say why less anonymous somehow or other less obscure'. (H,66) Later, throwing confusion as ever on the issue of whether there really are many consciousnesses in the world or only the one, the narrator puts in: 'With someone else to keep me company I would have been a different man more universal.' (H,74)

Thus far we have been covering fairly well-trodden ground. It will be noticed that *Malone Dies* and *The Unnamable* were omitted from the list of works given above in which Beckett employs the device of the couple. In these two works, though not exclusively there, Beckett develops a more sophisticated version of the two consciousnesses. We do not really find couples as such but we do become aware of a tension between an 'I' and a 'You' that replaces the tension between couples. The 'I' is characteristically the narrator; the 'You' is characteristically a 'Them' an 'other', 'voices' or, in *How It Is*, 'scribes'. This tension appears also in *Watt* in the complex relationship between Watt and Sam, and it can be extended perhaps to include the relationships between Watt and Beckett, Sam and Beckett, Watt and Knott, Knott and Sam and Knott and Beckett. I do not propose a lengthy analysis of these 'moments' in the novel which are, besides, not altogether *in* the novel; suffice it to observe that these relationships are obviously different in kind from, say, that between Didi and Gogo, and yet mutually-dependent consciousness is clearly an issue with all of them. For example, is Sam creating Watt, If so, who is creating Sam? Beckett? But Sam *is* Beckett, isn't he? And who is creating whom between Watt and Knott, And so on.

Now this second type of 'I-You' 'couple' relationship in Beckett, as found particularly in *Malone Dies* and *The Unnamable*, has not been analysed in Hegelian terms as the Hamm-Clov and Didi-Gogo type has been. But it seems crucial that the transparently fictional couples set up in the trilogy (Narrator and Narrated) be considered in these terms. The clue dropped by Beckett in naming his sub-narrator in *Watt* 'Sam' cannot be ignored. The most important twosome in Beckett's *oeuvre* is Beckett and the blank page; as an objective correlative of this there is Malone and his stories or the Unnamable and his babble. Early in his monologue Malone, describing his 'present state', says 'all my senses are trained full on me, me,' (T,186) which sets up the position of Beckett poised over his paper, waiting. Of course, in spite of, or because of, this concentration on himself, he does not penetrate through to himself; mind and body, ego and experience, remain apart; 'It is there I die, unbeknown to my stupid flesh.' (T,187) Meanwhile Malone/Beckett yet again resorts to the establishing of a fictional couple, himself and his creature, in this case Saposcat. Before plunging into the Saposcat story he concludes his account of his 'present state' with 'Somewhere in this turmoil thought struggles on, it too wide of the mark. It too seeks me, as it always has, where I am not to be found. It too cannot be quiet. On others let it wreak its dying rage, and leave me in peace.' (T,187) All that Beckett can do is tell stories about Malone: all that Malone can do is tell stories about Saposcat. They cannot talk of themselves so they talk of others; but, in the end, we find we can talk about them by talking about their creations. This is exactly the mirror situation between self-consciousnesses that Hegel describes.

In *The Unnamable* this process is tidied up. The 'Malone' stage is jettisoned. The self, Beckett's self, babbles on in search of itself, casting aside 'All these Murphys, Molloys and Malones' (T,305) and making the relationship between himself and his 'vice-existers' quite explicit:

> It is now I shall speak of me, for the first time. I thought I was right in enlisting these sufferers of my pains. I was wrong. They never suffered my pains, their pains are nothing, compared to mine, a mere tittle of mine, the tittle I thought I could put from me, in order to witness it. (T,305)

The created 'other' is there for the 'one' to witness it and it is now being rejected as a waste of time, as an impediment preventing the Unnamable from speaking of himself. Here, we might think,

Beckett has risen above Hegel's formula whereby self-consciousnesses are mutually-determining; now we are going to get some
direct action. But no, there are two further road-blocks, one contingent and one necessary. The contingent impediment is the
appearance of Basil, Mahood and Worm. The central section of
The Unnamable does not in fact talk directly about 'me' so much as
about these three. The necessary impediment to talking about 'me'
is of course the simple fact that the 'I' who inhabits the pages of the
novel is *not* Beckett. Even here there is a dialectic to be perceived,
this time between author and character. In other words the process
of self-consciousness in Beckett is necessarily dual, as Hegel says.

*   *   *

STOICISM SCEPTICISM UNHAPPY CONSCIOUSNESS CONCLUSION

We have now reached the end of the section of the *Phenomenology*
most useful for the elucidation of Beckett. Section B, 'self-consciousness', continues with a discussion of Stoicism, Scepticism and the
'Unhappy Consciousness'. Stoicism is seen in somewhat Beckettian
terms in that it is found to confine itself to the realm of thought
where consciousness is 'free' (rather in the way the Unnamable is
'free') whether in prison or on the throne. 'Thought is free.'
Unfortunately this is precisely the source of Beckett's anguish –
although no attack can penetrate the citadel of my thought, I
cannot get in there either; alternatively I cannot get out. Murphy
and the Stoics have 'body tight' minds.

Scepticism finds itself to be the only reality in the flux of uncer-
tain life. The sceptic can take nothing as certain but behaves as
though, at least, he exists. In fact this is almost identical to the
Stoical position: Scepticism 'is aware of being this stoical *ataraxia* of
self-thinking thought, the unalterable and genuine certainty of itself'
(PM,248) which leads us beyond Beckett. However, Hegel develops
a point here that will, in the end, enable us to make a final
confrontation between him and Beckett in Chapter 5 below. He
relates the stoical consciousness to the Master and Slave discussion,
as his example of prison and throne should make reasonable. In
scepticism Hegel proposes that the Master-consciousness and the
Slave-consciousness are contracted into one. This produces the

'unglückliches Bewusstsein', the 'Unhappy Consciousness' which is 'the Alienated Soul which is conscious of self as a divided nature, a doubled and merely contradictory being' (PM,251) that thirsts for unity. This thirst for unity is regarded as a thirst for unity with the 'unchangeable', with 'immutability'. (PM,252–3) This 'unchangeable' is at first defined as 'the alien, external Being', glossed as 'God as judge' by Baillie. The second 'moment' of the unchangeable is Christ (who is a 'particular' like conscious man and not only universal). The third 'moment' is the self-discovery of consciousness in spirit ('Geist') through which consciousness 'becomes aware' within itself that its particularity has been reconciled with the universal'. (PM,253)

Clearly we are in no position to push Beckett, protesting, through these sudden Christian hoops. It will perhaps become slightly less ludicrous to suggest doing so when we have looked at a later Beckett text with a later part of Hegel's *Phenomenology* in mind: the two concluding sections of Hegel's work being entitled 'Religion' and 'Absolute Knowledge'.

As with Heidegger it proves that it is the earlier sections of the philosophical work in question that are most useful for our purpose. There is no implication here, however, that the later sections are not important *for Hegel* or are in some way secondary. It is simply that Beckettian man, stark and curiously simple, offers an embodiment of such fundamentals as Consciousness, Perception and Others and has less relevance to some of the philosophical developments that follow from these. The exception here is when we come to such concepts as 'Absolute Knowledge' which will once again challenge Beckett's capacity as a creator of ontological parables.

NOTES AND REFERENCES

1. The most substantial Hegelian study of Beckett is that by Hans-Joachim Schulz in his short work entitled *This Hell of Stories: A Hegelian approach to the novels of Samuel Beckett*. This opens with an explanation of its purpose, which is to draw an illuminating parallel between Beckett's way of writing and Hegel's way of thinking:

    Why do the Beckett artist-bums want silence, why do they not achieve it, why do they not die? To show the importance of these questions to the Beckett novels, to show that they enter us (*sic*) into a dialogue with Hegel which will expose their timeless nature, this is the purpose of the following chapters. (p. 30)

This German critic has seen that any explanation of Beckett's unwillingness to fall silent, and of similar paradoxes, is going to require philosophical aid.

2. David Hesla has recourse to Hegel in the closing pages of his *Shape of Chaos*. He suggests that the trilogy may be patterned according to the dialectical impetus. Molloy is the thesis, Moran the antithesis and Malone the synthesis; the Unnamable, in the next stage, negates Malone. Hesla then offers to push this interpretation to the limit: Molloy, following Hegel, could be not only dialectical but also 'Spirit in its manifestation as the Greek world...' (pp. 219–20) Hesla has his tongue in his cheek I think.

3. I have used the Baillie translation of Hegel's *Phenomenology* but I am also indebted to the translation by A.V. Miller, *Hegel's Phenomenology of Spirit* (London: OUP, 1977).

4. Hegel prefers to avoid the 'meaningless' word, 'God'. This is not logical Positivism but an attempt at clarity: in a specific context which gives it meaning the word is admissible.

5. For a discussion of the foreshadowing of Sartrean ideas in Hegel cf. W. Kaufmann's *Hegel* (London: Weidenfeld and Nicolson, 1966), e.g. p. 379.

6. Hegel, evidently, is using 'essence' without its Existentialist meaning.

7. Beckett's problem seems to be echoed in this formulation of Hegel by J.N. Findlay: 'What we feel to be unrepeatable and particular in the given, is also vanishing and unseizable, opaque to thought and unsayable in words. It is a point greatly stressed by Hegel that words like 'This', 'Now', 'Here' and 'I' are implicitly universal: one may seek by their means to pick out what is unrepeatable and individual, but they remain instruments of general use, applicable by their nature to ever different contexts'. (J.N. Findlay, op. cit., p. 44).

8. This is Hegel's Platonic inheritance. Cf., for example, the *Parmenides*.

9. G.R.G. Mure, *The Philosophy of Hegel* (London: OUP, 1965), p. 73.

5 Towards the Wellhead

SURFACES AND DEPTHS

What has been offered so far amounts to a case for a philosophical reading of Beckett; what remains is to undertake that reading. Three philosophers have been dealt with at length and in detail with the aim of exposing their worlds, their languages and their methods. In each case, at each turning point in the philosophical argument, I have tried to show how a particular formulation or view fitted into a Beckettian pattern. This has demonstrated that Beckett can be read alongside certain philosophers and that they can throw light into his darker corners. I have tried to establish this unselectively. That is, it has not been simply a question of applying a few individual moments of philosophical insight to Beckett but of applying to him the main body of three interrelated philosophies, three world-views as expounded in three immense and systematic works.

I have not pursued Hegel, Heidegger or Sartre to their conclusions, even in the three main works discussed. Thus I did not follow Hegel into his historical theses, Heidegger into his time-and-historicality section or Sartre into all of his concepts. However, I have tried to present the central picture of man's being and existence as it is to be found in these three. In each case the edges of the canvas may have been left dark but the view of the man himself (Hegel's man, Heidegger's, Sartre's) has been reasonably clear and complete. We have accounted, in all three cases, for what Heidegger would have called the 'equiprimordial existentialia' of man: consciousness, the objects of consciousness, the world, others, and so on.

Beckett can be best understood, and at times only understood, if we see his work as a literary expression or realization of something that resembles these pictures of man. He shows us what it is like to live in a world which bears a striking resemblance to the world of these philosophers. He shows us how it is if their views of man and his world are lived through, carried through into consciousness and not merely considered as appropriate to the study or the library. Beckett's work offers us a horrific world, but it is the world as it exists for philosophy rather than as it exists in 'average everydayness'. If this is not the case, where does the trouble lie? Beckett seems to be in violent revolt against the nature of this world and it is clearly not something political or psychological that he is revolting against. It is something ontological. In general terms it is *la condition humaine* that is wrong, there is something wrong at the *root* of the human situation, something wrong that no amount of love or donations to relief agencies will cure, something wrong ontologically.

In other words I would suggest that Beckett's works are, in one central aspect, ontological parables. A demonstration of this can be found in the self-destructive nature of his fiction. We always know that the narrators' stories are only stories, we have the arbitrary act of invention thrust under our noses at every turn. This forces us to search for stable ground in the quicksands and to give only provisional value to the unstable areas, which is as much as to say that we are thrust back to an ontological level in the end, however much we may have enjoyed the fiction while it was in progress. In principle, once this process of destroying himself or giving himself away has started in an author, all his statements become suspect; but there is an analogy to be drawn, nonetheless, between our going back into Beckett's fundamental concerns (searching for a stable area) and the narrators' emerging from their fictions to talk about themselves. Thus we have one way of getting closer to the meaning of Beckett's parables if we extrapolate back in the direction: fictions (eg. Macmann) — narrators (eg. Malone) — author (Beckett?). This process leads us towards the concerns of philosophy, as can be shown if we follow up the example of Macmann and Malone.

Although Macmann is so obviously a creation, we can respond to him in a variety of serious ways. We must, after all, be able to suspend our disbelief or fiction would be altogether impossible, and I think that, for example, we are likely to feel pity for him, but in the end Beckett forces us back away from him and we have to realize that we are being asked to respond to something other than his adventures. These adventures, anyway, are inclined to be trivial and inconclusive. Here is an example from the end of *Malone Dies*.

So. . .a little later Macmann, having brought back from his walk a hyacinth he had torn up bulb and roots in the hope of being able to keep it a little longer thus than if he had simply plucked it, was fiercely reprimanded by Lemuel who wrenched the pretty flower from his hands and threatened to hand him over to Jack again, no, to Pat again, Jack is a different one. (T,277)

As the conclusion of this passage shows, we are not allowed to forget the fictional nature of the episode for very long. The episode itself, although pathetic, is trivial, meaningless, absurd, unless, perhaps, we take it as an indicator of the general nature of Beckett's world (if the surface is like this we cannot expect the depths to be particularly pleasant.) The mad Macmann makes a sad figure, picking flowers for comfort, flowers which do not last long anyway and which he paradoxically destroys to make them last a little longer; his rather pathetic gesture earns him a fierce rebuke. This is the surface of a world that is perhaps not organized for man's happiness, a fact so obvious in every painful line of the trilogy that we are forced to interrogate the narrators about this world. They are, in any case, responsible for creating the world which their creations inhabit.

Malone, the dying narrator of the Macmann episodes, gives us some relief by turning back to himself from time to time and discussing his fictions. But his world, the next stratum of literary creation, is as bad as Macmann's. He dismisses his story-telling with 'But that is all beside the point, like so many things.' He continues:

All is pretext, Sapo and the birds, Moll, the peasants, those who in the towns seek one another out and fly from one another, my doubts which do not interest me, my situation, my possessions, pretext for not coming to the point...(T,278)

This sort of aside tells us not only that we should read the stories, such as Macmann's, as a special sort of rubbish, but also that we should question Malone's own babble about himself. His 'doubts', his 'situation', his 'possessions' are mere pretexts. Once again we are being forced on: just as Macmann is not 'the point' Malone is not the point either. But his stratum of words, although it too is a fiction, is closer to the reality that underlies the novel and drives it on. Thus we are being directed towards that which *is* 'the point', that which is 'reality'. We are once again given a strong indication that it will not be pleasant, that there is something amiss in the ontological structure of the world; Malone, after all, is dying in stinking confusion, his 'horror-worn eyes linger abject on all they have beseeched so long'. (T,278)

What next? Macmann has passed us on to Malone and Malone seems to be passing us on to someone or somewhere else where we can read or discover 'the point'. He says that his eyes have 'beseeched so long' in a 'last prayer, the true prayer at last, the one that asks for nothing'. (T,278) We might agree to stop here and abandon ouselves to oblivion or to mysticism but someone will not let us (it is still Malone, nominally at least):

> And it is then a little breath of fulfilment revives the dead longings and a murmur is born in the silent world...(T,278)

With that 'murmur' we are off again:

> The last word in the way of viaticum. Let us try it another way. The pure plateau.
>   Try and go on. The pure plateau air. Yes, it was a plateau, Moll had not lied...(T,278)

This takes us back in the direction we have come from, back to the stories about Moll and Macmann. In the matter of getting through to reality we want to go beyond Malone rather than back to the surface of transparent invention. Malone may hint that the way to reality (to the 'true prayer at last') is through further fictional invention, but there is no sign of it in Macmann's story which, anyway, is also explicitly intended as a time-filler.

I have chosen this example from the end of *Malone Dies* because here, more clearly than elsewhere, we are actually given another stratum 'beyond' Malone, the stratum of *The Unnamable*. In the opening pages of *The Unnamable* the 'I' speaks of Malone objectively and is clearly further down, further away from the surface, than his previous narrators. 'Is Malone the culprit?' he can ask. (T,298) Then, in the same way as Malone discussed himself after talking about Macmann, 'I' now talks about himself after mentioning Malone. What he says about himself takes us deeper into the real concerns that we feel to be underlying the trilogy, the concerns that are apparent in its very first lines where Molloy asks how he has got to where he is. The Unnamable comments:

> It would help me, since to me too I must attribute a beginning, if I could relate it to that of my abode. Did I wait somewhere for this place to be ready to receive me? Or did it wait for me to come and people it? By far the better of these hypotheses, from the point of

view of usefulness, is the former, and I shall often have occasion to fall back on it. But both are distasteful. I shall say therefore that our beginnings coincide, that this place was made for me, and I for it, at the same instant. (T,298)

Here, having sloughed off the surface fantasies of Macmann and the 'vice-existence' of Malone, an unnamable 'I' turns to himself, poses a question and suggests an answer, that are rendered intelligible only if we take them ontologically. Beckett is a creative artist and as such is speaking to our emotions as well as our intellects but surely it is not enough to say of this passage that it offers us the generalized sense of anguish of a being lost in an incomprehensible world without going on and specifying what that anguish is, why that being feels it and how he can conceive of the world as incomprehensible? If we are thrust from the surface to the depths, if we feel we are being taken closer to the fundamental vision, the basic quest, of the author then our wits need to be sharper not duller as we descend. The surface level offers us pain, farce and doubt; although self-consciously a mere creation, it is, *ipso facto*, a vision of the world, but if that is true of the random creations such as Sapo or Macmann it is surely at least as true of the deeper levels.

Our idea of surface and depth is, of course, metaphorical. I have adopted it here for clarity and because Beckett employs it both within the trilogy and in his *oeuvre* as a whole. Our reading of this *oeuvre* now needs to take an overall view which will make some sense, in a large scale, of the claim that we need to see Beckett as a creator of ontological parables in order fully to understand him.

*   *   *

BECKETT'S DEVELOPMENT

I would offer two premises for the discussion of Beckett's development. First, he starts on the surface and moves towards the depths, and, second, his work is a whole, a unified and self-consistent statement about existence which explores the same vision of the world from increasingly profound viewpoints.

The first of these is intended only as a diagrammatic and summary aid to understanding, a metaphor to show where Beckett takes us. In general the amount of naturalistic description of the quotidian world decreases between *More Pricks Than Kicks* and, say, *Lessness*. Earlier Beckett characters tend to be individualized, human, treated as odd examples of normal people; later Beckett characters tend to be nameless, inhuman and extraordinary. You might meet and recognize Murphy in Hyde Park, you will not meet one of the 'Lost Ones'. What is wrong with the earlier characters could conceivably be alleviated by sociological or psychological attentions: Belacqua Shua and Murphy want things within the world, attainment of which brings or could bring some satisfaction; what is wrong later in Beckett is incurable. He moves from an agonized playing on the naturalistic surface of life to an agonized grasping of its ontological foundations. He himself suggests the metaphor of depth when he casts his creatures in *How It Is* into the mud and has them remember life 'up there' in the normal daylight world. As an alternative he employs deserts, cylinders, darkness and other forms of isolation to emphasize the distance that exists, in his later work, between his settings and the normal surface of reality.

Our second premiss, that Beckett's work is a self-consistent whole, can hardly be summarized in the same way. Beckett's vision of the world remains steady but its perceptiveness increases so that the world is laid ever more bare under his gaze and we are shown the depths, the ontological realities that underpin the surface realities with which he was at first concerned. Perhaps we can see Beckett as a sort of bird circling his prey; the prey remains the same and is the centre of each circle he describes, each circle being equally necessary. As the bird comes closer and closer the prey is more and more clearly described. The analogy with Dante that might spring to mind here is not accidental, the descent is certainly into the depths of a kind of hell.

Naturally Beckett does not fit either of these schemes exactly. In the early work there are moments as profound, and as much in need of philosophical explanation, as anything in *How It Is* and the later texts. Furthermore, in the later work there are moments that call for a psychological response rather than a philosophical one – in *Not I*, for instance, where the mouth seems to belong to a paranoiac personality as well as to an ontologically representative entity. But the general scheme is helpful and it shows us where to apply our philosophical exegesis at the same time as hinting that the series of ontological parables we read into Beckett may in the end resolve themselves into one unified statement.

Beckett's work falls roughly into three periods: the pre-war, the post-war and the 'residual' (to borrow a word of Beckett's own.) In terms of our philosophical parallels the first period (the period of *More Pricks Than Kicks* and *Murphy*) is the one best illuminated by the conventional critical technique of glossing and discussing Beckett's references to philosophers. This is his Cartesian period, the period in which he plays with early modern philosophy and is inclined to wear his learning on his sleeve. Here, where conventional criticism is most fruitful, the need for ontological interpretation is least evident.

The second period (the period of *Godot, Endgame* and the trilogy) plumbs greater depths. Where Belacqua, for instance, appears in the first period (in *More Pricks Than Kicks*) a gloss on his name is more or less an adequate explanation of its adoption. But where 'Belacqua or Sordello' appear early in the trilogy the same gloss seems inadequate – for a start, Beckett can no longer remember which of them it is he wishes to refer to and he soon abandons them. I have concentrated on his second period in selecting examples in the three previous chapters, above. In this chapter I shall deal with the later work as well.

Watt acts as a sort of turning-point between these first two periods. It starts in the style of *Murphy* with the hilarious Mr Hackett who lives in the 'big' world of policemen and billiard tables and friends but, once Watt himself comes on the scene, the novel moves rapidly into a world that is at once more obscure and more profound. Dialogue and policemen disappear from the novel (although Watt emerges into the surface-world again at the end) and all certainties, including the reader's, crumble in the house of Mr Knott. The turning-point within the novel, the arrival of Watt at Mr Knott's house, is marked by one of Beckett's most sustained excursions into the profounder reality underlying his work, Arsene's speech at the end of Part one. This speech will be discussed in the final section of this chapter.

To illustrate the development in Beckett between his first and second periods there are plenty of examples. Here are two. In *Murphy* the Occasionalist philosopher Geulincx appears in order to be complimented on his 'beautiful Belgo-Latin' (M,124) and one or two parallels can be drawn between elements in the novel and the solution adopted by Geulincx to the Cartesian mind-body problem; notably this solution appears funny to us and is wryly treated by Beckett at least in implication. In *Molloy*, however, from the second period under discussion, we find Geulincx treated differently. There is still a touch of humour but we feel he is being used more seriously, more passionately and less cerebrally:

> I who had loved the image of old Geulincx, dead young, who left me free, on the black boat of Ulysses, to crawl towards the East, along the deck. That is a great measure of freedom, for him who has not the pioneering spirit. And from the poop, poring upon the wave, a sadly rejoicing slave, I follow with my eyes the proud and futile wake. (T,51)

The reference to Geulincx's theory of freedom, which amounts to the claim that we have very little, is closer to Beckett's own range of serious problems than the solution to the mind-body problem referred to in *Murphy*. The narrator of this passage identifies himself with the slave of Geulincx's example and rises to poetic heights in the process. We are out of the realm of the learned joke and into a more serious confrontation with the issues of philosophy. It is worth noting here, too, that Beckett and his narrator employ the past tense, 'I who *had* loved'. He is leaving behind him the dubious consolations of academic philosophy.

Another example concerns two presocratic philosophers. In *Murphy* we are asked to consider the undignified end of 'Hippasos the Akousmatic' who drowned in a puddle. Here there is nothing to be gained beyond the immediate reference and the response it conjures up: laughter perhaps and a certain pleasant puzzlement. In *Endgame*, however, from Beckett's second period, the philosopher Zeno appears for the sake of his paradox and here we are asked to take him seriously just as Geulincx became serious in *Molloy*. Hamm, towards the end of one of his more terrifying monologues, considers time:

> Moment upon moment, pattering down, like the millet grains of...(*he hesitates*)...that old Greek, and all life long you wait for that to mount up to a life. (*Pause. He opens his mouth to continue, renounces.*) Ah let's get it over! (E,45)

The puzzlement engendered by Zeno's paradox is not really a laughing matter at all, there is a deadly earnestness about Hamm's agonized fight with time and about Clov's 'nearly finished'.

Conventional interpretation, then, is still of some use in the second period of Beckett's writing (we still have to know who Geulincx and Zeno were) but we feel that we are being taken further and that we are going to be obliged to take seriously the issues raised and not merely to regard them as an intellectual game. When we get to the third period it seems to me that conventional interpretation breaks down altogether and that, unless one has squarely faced the philosophical issues inherent in the second period and is prepared to look at Beckett's later work in an ontological light, one is in danger of finding it unnecessarily incomprehensible.

This third period extends from *How It Is* (1960) to Beckett's most recent work. It includes the texts *Enough*, *The Lost Ones*, *Ping*, *Lessness* and *Imagination Dead Imagine* as well as the plays *Come and Go*, *Eh Joe*, *Breath*, *Not I* and *Footfalls*, to mention only these. The plays, generally, lag behind the fiction in the history of Beckett's development. Thus, *Krapp's Last Tape*, although composed in 1958 is clearly akin to *Malone Dies*, composed in French as early as 1948. With this as a precedent it seems reasonable to exclude from our third period some of the plays written after 1960 which belong rather obviously to the earlier period, notably *Happy Days* and *Play* (1961 and 1962 respectively).[1]

Beckett himself has described his work of this period, the 'shorts' since *How It is*, as 'residua' (in the Preface to *No's Knife*.) He glossed this, in reply to a query by Brian Finney, 'they are residual...in relation to whole body of previous work' (*sic* Finney, 1, 10). This would seem to support the contention that Beckett's work is in some way a unified whole – it is as if he has been quarrying his work from the same rock-face and these are the chippings. Certainly it is hard to imagine what these 'residua' would seem like if they had appeared without the earlier work behind them.

Just as *Watt* acts as a turning-point between the first period and the second, *How It Is* acts as the connexion between the end of the trilogy and *Texts for Nothing* on the one hand and the exiguous productions of Beckett's later years on the other.

How It Is comes as something of a shock after the trilogy – one wonders how there can be any more to say and one is surprised by the sudden indulgence in such experimental prose. But the quarry of being is infinite. Beckett in his attempts to 'get it all said', having taken one prose style to its limits, is bound to adopt another method and press on rather than relapse into the impossible silence. 'I'll go on'.

How It Is inaugurates our third period in that it has the

characteristics of coldness, inhumanity and a certain abstraction that are going to become more pronounced in the later 'residua'.[2] But Beckett's work is a whole, *How It Is* is working the same, the same inevitable ground, as the trilogy. These sections, for instance, rehearse themes familiar to us from *Malone Dies* and elsewhere:

> then on my elbow I quote I see me prop me up thrust in my arm in the sack we're talking of the sack thrust it in count the tins impossible with one hand keep trying one day it will be possible (H.8)

> something wrong there (H.9)

Here we find the usual 'I' and 'me', the one seeing the other as in Malone's 'All my senses are trained full on me, me'. (T,186) This narrator, too, is encumbered by and obsessed with his possessions, here his sack, and he makes asides ('something wrong there') that parallel Malone's 'This is awful'. As Beckett goes deeper into the 'mess' of existence he has new methods but no new matter: consciousness and its ambivalent relationship with its world are still the core of the problem, still the monolith he must quarry from. His work is an attempt to find an objective correlative for being – a parable that will somehow manage to 'say' the ontological nature of the world.

Although *How It Is* develops (in my view, inevitably) the same concerns as are manifested in the trilogy, it begins to show the sort of dehumanizing schematism that is the characteristic of Beckett's third period. The creatures crawling about in the mud have a few touches of 'reality' in the shape of tin-openers and memories, but their present existence is in many ways as unrealistic as possible. If we apply realist or naturalist criteria we come up with such obviously banal questions as 'How do these people breathe with their faces in the mud?' and 'How do they know which direction to go in?' and 'Where are they?' and 'What happens when the sardines run out?' and 'Where do the sardines come from?' Clearly we are in a non-naturalistic world here, a world in which such questions do not matter. Beckett has excluded the possibility of realistic interpretation as far as he can by, for instance, employing meaningless, dehumanized names, 'Bom', 'Pim' and so on.

This can be seen as the next stage in the process that has taken Beckett from names such as Celia and Lady Pedal to such brutalized appellations as Saposcat and Worm. What names are possible after *The Unnamable*? Now, in his third period, Beckett is going to dispense with names altogether and with all naturalistic conventions as he moves closer to the core of his concerns, the heart of the problem which is seen at last to be inherent not in the surface mess of everyday life (Ibsen and Dickens faced *that* problem) but in the basic structure of the world, beyond or behind mere names or the suffering of individuals. That this is the case, that these are Beckett's 'real' concerns and that we are not forcing an interpretation arbitrarily upon him can, I think, be established from those pregnant snippets of criticism, the *Three Dialogues with Georges Duthuit* which appeared in *transition* no.5 in 1949.³ In a way it would be appropriate to quote the whole of the second of these dialogues, the dialogue on Masson. I shall attempt a summary, however. What we shall find is Beckett's statement that Masson, for all his talk about the void, is not really attempting to paint some sort of ultimate reality and that Beckett *is* searching for such an art, impossible though it may be. The relevance of this to my thesis about Beckett himself is obvious: he is in quest of an art that will express an ultimate depth – an absolute. 'B' speaks first and he makes this gnomic utterance:

In search of the difficulty rather than in its clutch. The disquiet of him who lacks an adversary.

'D' replies:

That is perhaps why he speaks so often nowadays of painting the void, 'in fear and trembling'.

Masson has no 'adversary', nothing to paint, no problem to solve within the realms of normal painting. As 'D' says, it is not a matter of not being able to paint something, it is a matter of painting nothing – 'the void'. Once, 'D' continues, Masson wanted to paint a mythology, then he wanted to paint man in society, now he wants to paint 'inner emptiness'. He suffers from 'the need to come to rest, i.e. to establish the data of the problem to be solved, the Problem at last'. The capital letter on the second 'Problem' here is revealing. Of the earlier 'problems' (man is society for instance) 'B' says that they have 'by the mere fact of their solubility...lost for him their legitimacy'. Now Masson wants to 'reduce their maladies...to nothing' but he still wants to paint something and, 'D' points out, if 'B' is going to object to all painting in which 'the object remains sovereign' how can Masson 'be expected to paint the void?'

'B' replies that this is a mistake. Wanting to paint the void is 'on the same plane' as wanting to paint *something*, the void of Masson is 'perhaps simply the obliteration of an unbearable presence' and this is not really the void at all. The trouble is that even Masson suffers from 'possessiveness'. Although he tries to avoid the sort of painting that is the mere 'capture of objects' he is still, according to Beckett, doing what others have done in the way of painting things. 'B' finishes by asking 'D' to forgive him for relapsing 'into my dream of an art unresentful of its insuperable indigence and too proud for the farce of giving and receiving'. When 'D' tries to make an emotional appeal on behalf of painting that paints things ('the things and creatures of spring, resplendent with desire and affirmation') it is too much for 'B', whose thinking is moving in so exactly the opposite direction, and the dialogue concludes 'B – (Exit weeping)'.

I think the key point here is that Masson goes some way towards Beckett's ideal, he rejects the surface questions as illegitimate because of their 'solubility', but in trying to go further he goes wrong because he will not admit the 'insuperable indigence' of art and goes on trying to approach the depths as if they were on the same plane as the surface.

If we apply this to Beckett we can easily see that 'the farce of giving and receiving', the surface element in art, is still uncomfortably present in his earlier work where his naturalistic method does the literary equivalent of capturing objects. In his later work he is too 'proud' for this, he becomes cold, aloof, inhuman, and his writing approaches an equivalence with that totally abstract art that confesses its 'insuperable indigence'. The overall impression gained is that Beckett is asking here for an art that will confront ultimate reality, an art that will correspond not to the sociological or 'natural' structure of the world, but to its ultimate structure, its ontology.

This demand is not colourless and unbiased. Inherent in it there is already a statement as to the nature of this ultimate reality. 'D' offers what might be called a positive, optimistic version; defending Masson's inability to move on to another plane he asks two questions to both of which 'B's' implied answer is 'Yes'. They are these:

> But must we really deplore the painting that admits 'the things and creatures of spring, resplendent with desire and affirmation,

ephemeral no doubt, but immortally reiterant', not in order to benefit by them, not in order to enjoy them, but in order that what is tolerable and radiant in the world may continue? Are we really to deplore the painting that is a rallying, among the things of time that pass and hurry us away, towards a time that endures and gives increase?

It is this that drives 'B' out, weeping. Here we have an encapsulation of a misty, sub-religious attitude that affects a confrontation with the nature of the world of a sort that 'B' finds even more appalling than failure to come to terms with 'the void'. 'D' employs a language that is highly revealing. There are biblical echoes in 'creatures', 'the things of time that pass' and 'gives increase', and a general tone of pulpit-like exhortation and encouragement in the two long rhetorical questions with their repetitions ('not in order...not in order...in order') and in the optimistic vocabulary: 'resplendent', 'immortally reiterant', 'radiant', 'rallying', 'endures' and 'gives increase'.

It is quite clear that this is not 'B's' conception of the world; it drives him out weeping. More significantly, this cannot be his conception of the world *on principle*. Masson, the dialogue claims, cannot get off the plane of the 'feasible' (to borrow a term from the third of these dialogues) and on to a plane where he could face 'the Problem at last'. Stuck on the plane of mere 'problems' the only defence for him, in spite of his promising moves towards 'inner emptiness' and so on, is along the lines of the normal defence of normal art: it is good for us. All this, all daily religion, all 'possessive' art, all positive views of man's world belong to the plane of the feasible and Beckett here will have none of it.

To conclude this discussion it seems appropriate to quote, once again, 'B's' view as expressed in the third of these dialogues, that concerning Bram Van Velde. Here it is quite clear how thorough Beckett's rejection of the plane of the normal is: on this plane there are mere 'predicaments' but Beckett wants an art that will face an absolute beyond these, a 'Problem' beyond mere 'problems':

But let us, for once, be foolish enough not to turn tail. All have turned wisely tail, before the ultimate penury, back to the mere misery where destitute virtuous mothers may steal bread for their starving brats. There is more than a difference of degree between being short, short of the world, short of self, and being without these esteemed commodities. The one is a predicament, the other not. (PTD,122)

Thus, in mid-career, Beckett states clearly enough that he is looking for an art that will be able to work on the absolute plane and not 'turn tail' back to the relative plane of the everyday. In Heidegger's terms we can think of an art that, not content with the merely ontical, is able to work with the ontological.

If we look at the development in Beckett's drama we find a general pattern that is the same as that to be found in the prose. *Le Kid* is an early satirical sketch of 1931; thereafter it seems that Beckett considered a play about Dr Johnson and Mrs Thrale whose interest lay, for him, in Johnson's physical sufferings and hypochondria and in the (unconsummated) sexual aspect of their relationship.[4] These are the themes of *More Pricks Than Kicks* and are very much themes belonging to the surface world, everyday reality and the ontical: Corneille, Johnson, historical periods, specific diseases, this is the stuff of the normal world of a disease-prone intellectual. *Eleuthéria* of 1947, as we have seen,[5] floats profounder concerns but still in a sociological and psychological matrix: Victor is recognizably an angry young man, a rebel against parents and their values and against certain social norms as represented, for instance, by his fiancée. With *Godot* the 'surface' reality of Beckett's drama is drastically and famously reduced. 'A country road. A tree. Evening' is all we are given by way of information. Already we are faced with an art which is finding a way of making ontological statements without resorting to the lecture. *Endgame* is another step in the same direction: we have come to the end of the normal world, the end of the surface realities; there are no more people, no more sugar-plums, no more pain-killers, no more bicycle-wheels. *All that Fall*, also written in 1956, may seem a step backwards but it was written in English as a radio play, two factors which quite reasonably encouraged Beckett to attempt a more naturalistic surface (whence all the different noises in the play, from cows mooing to the arrival of a train) and to write with rather more 'style' than he does in French (whence Maddy's rather extraordinary use of the English language.) *Krapp's Last Tape* works in something of the same way – although here again we find the *Endgame* motif of jettisoning the past, the surface, and coming to an end, giving up 'all that'.

Happy Days, written in 1961, brings us up to the date of *How It Is* and the parallels between the play and the novel are inescapable. The 'surface', ontical world is reduced to the contents of Winnie's bag, and Willie's newspaper, and she is stuck, increasingly stuck, in a mound of sand that is equivalent to the mud of *How It Is*. She too exists according to a pattern, the pattern of her days is the equivalent of the patterns of movement in the novel. Here is a play that may still have a 'surface' element in, say, Winnie's psychology, but whose main thrust is clearly elsewhere: Winnie's problem can only be our problem if we take it on a philosophical level. *Play* works in something of the same way; people are trapped in a post-mortal limbo chewing the dry bones of a mutual memory, unable to communicate directly, forced to utter, unable to be silent. To take *Play* only as being concerned with marriage, personal relationships, the eternal triangle, is surely to be unable to see the wood for the trees. The whole play, with its significant title, is about what all plays and fiction tend to be about, a man, a woman, another person. That is normal enough, banal enough, but to imagine that this normal level is the only level on which the creator of *Godot* and *The Unnamable* is working must be based on a mistaken perspective. This is not to deny that *Play* exists on the level of the everyday – all literature does that, there is no alternative, and indeed this is Beckett's problem, how to find a way of saying the ontological with such preeminently ontical tools as fiction and drama. Thus, as we watch *Play* we are busy working out the relationships between the characters, thinking about affairs and marriages, but we cannot stay at this level. Who, after all, is the 'eye' of the spotlight, why is it 'playing' with them? Again we must ask why the first woman opens with, and frequently echoes, the lines,

> Yes, strange, darkness best, and the darker the worse, till all dark, then all well, for the time, but it will come, the time will come the thing is there, you'll see it (PL,9)

The point here is that *Play* is a picture of a sort of Limbo where all is over and consigned to the past and to memory, but the darkness has not taken over completely, that darkness in which, paradoxically, you will be able to see 'the thing' that is 'there'. We tend to try to make this pattern fit on the naturalistic level by associating it with the end of the love-affairs of the play: after they are over all is suffering, and darkness seems desirable although it is not a darkness of total despair; perhaps he will come back, perhaps next time the paradise of real love will be offered. But the end of the affair is a parable just as my reference to Limbo is a metaphor.

*   *   *

I have proposed a tripartite division of Beckett's work and I have offered some account of its first two periods. These periods terminate in *How It Is* (written in 1960) in the fiction, which seems to represent a turning point, a plunge further into the depths, or in *Happy Days* and *Play* (1961, 1962) which in some ways offer a dramatic quivalent to *How It Is*.

In discussing the third period (which, borrowing the title of Finney's book, we might call 'Since How It Is') the position reached so far in this chapter must be related to the chapters on Heidegger on Sartre and on Hegel that precede it and we must consider a synthesis that will constitute an overall reading of Beckett.

*   *   *

ONTOLOGICAL PARABLES 1.SARTRE

Altogether, Beckett's work represents an attempt to escape from the toils of mere facticity and to take possession of the freedom of the now. The factical is the given, what is, how we find ourselves placed, and it appears in Beckett as the surface world, the given situation. It is not only painful and unpleasant, as witness the uncomfortable world of *More Pricks Than Kicks* and *Murphy*, but it is unsatisfactory in principle. Man exists in time and is always projecting forward into the empty future and he can never rest content in the factical even if he should wish to do so. The future, however, is the *Angst*-engendering abyss of freedom – man can choose anything.

Belacqua Shua is well and truly entramelled in the factical but he struggles for ways out, preferring voyeurism to participation in sex, attempting suicide and so on. Victor in *Eleuthéria* wants to be 'nothing'. Murphy seeks escape through trances, mind-deadening work, and takes other routes towards Nirvana. Watt seeks for Nirvana in the negativity of Mr Knott's house. All of these are trying to escape from the commotion and 'hugger-mugger' of the worlds into which they are thrown and to find release in the bosom of some absolute.

That Beckett is himself moving in the same direction is demonstrated by his progressive abandonment of interest in the personality of his heroes and his reduction of their factical environments. Thus we can say that just as Murphy goes from London to a lunatic asylum and from a lunatic asylum to the isolated room in which he finds peace in his rocking-chair, and from there to the big silence of death, Beckett goes from the bustle of his Dublin stories into the increasingly isolated and interior world of his later work. This movement, as the vocabulary I have chosen indicates, reflects the position of Sartrean man and it can be fairly claimed that Beckett's work is a parable encapsulating in literary terms Sartre's theory of the factical and man's freedom. This has been discussed in some detail in Chapter 3 and the task now is to impose some general pattern on the relationship between the philosopher and Beckett, especially in terms of Beckett's third period. The problem for both of them can be stated in the same way: if man is free, if man can be defined as an entity that is always projecting into the future from a present swamped with the inert data of the past (this applies as much to the narrators of the trilogy as to Sartrean man) why is he so profoundly dissatisfied? What, in broad terms, is wrong with man's position?

For Sartre, as we saw, objects exist 'in themselves' (*en-soi*) and man's consciousness exists 'for itself' (*pour soi*); the known, the object, is a being and the knower, consciousness, is a nothing. At its heart, then, human reality is a nothingness 'apprehending itself as excluded from being and perpetually beyond being, in commerce with nothing.' (BN,181) Sartre argues that consciousness is a 'lack', it wants the fulfilment of being, of being in the manner that factical objects are, but it wants to remain conscious, of course; it wants to remain free. Man's project, then, is to become an 'en-soi-pour-soi' whereby, without losing the freedom of consciousness, he can lay claim to objective being: 'I *am* this and this.' His project is impossible, freedom is precisely the freedom to project anew, to choose to be otherwise than one has been, to deny *being* 'this and this'. Only God would be an 'en-soi-pour-soi', and man's 'fundamental value' is to become God, it is

the ideal of a consciousness which would be the foundation of its own being-in-itself by the pure consciousness which it would have of itself. It is this ideal which can be called God. (BN,566)

Man is a 'lack' that yearns for a totality that will be no lack, this is why he is inevitably dissatisfied. Man, condemned to be free, condemned to bad faith, lives by acting a role for the benefit of his own consciousness in an unendable quest for permanence. Man is always trying to catch up with being and always failing. The last sentences of the main section of *Being and Nothingness* run:

> The passion of man is the reverse of that of Christ, for man loses himself as man in order that God may be born. But the idea of God is contradictory and we lose ourselves in vain. Man is a useless passion. (BN,615)

In an *addendum* entitled 'Metaphysical Implications' Sartre stresses that the root of all this lies in the absolute disjunction between pour-soi and en-soi, between consciousness and its objects, between man and his world. Total reality, made up of both pour-soi and en-soi, is an 'ideal' that is never attained, it is 'an abortive effort to attain to the dignity of a self-cause.' (BN,623) Objects are brought into being, made a world for man, by man's consciousness. Man's consciousness is made possible by the existence of things for him to be conscious of. The two sides are mutually dependent but radically separated. Sartre's summary of this is perfectly applicable to Beckett:

> Everything happens therefore as if the in-itself and the for-itself were presented in a state of disintegration in relation to an ideal synthesis. Not that the integration has ever *taken place* but on the contrary precisely because it is always indicated and always impossible (BN,623)

'Always indicated and always impossible' sounds like a formal version of Beckett's constant paradox: 'You must go on, I can't go on.' (T,418)

Here, perhaps, is one of the versions of reality for which Beckett's work is a parable. His narrators (and he himself) are consciousnesses, radically separated from their worlds, hopelessly trying to catch up with them so that they can attain some sort of being and 'find me...say me.' (T,418) Beckett strives constantly for a reduction in the en-soi component in his work, and constantly fails. He gets rid of great heaps of factical environment, cutting out surface realities as he goes, trying to 'say' the being of consciousness, which is, by definition, not among them. But consciousness is 'nothing' and as the only way it can be spoken of is in terms of being, the speaking is never accurate. The passion is useless and, as the etymology of 'passion' indicates, this is, in itself, a process of suffering for which disease and pain are Beckettian metaphors.

This offer of an ontological basis for Beckett as a whole can be applied specifically to his third period with illuminating results. If my picture of his development is accurate we should find that in this period Beckett is least involved with surface reality, most clearly looking for objective correlatives for philosophical insights, with least regard for naturalist criteria and at his most abstract. This indeed seems to be the case. First, by way of an introduction to a discussion of some texts, there is a metaphor that seems appropriate.

Life in *More Pricks Than Kicks* and *Murphy* is purgatory, thoroughly unsatisfactory in every aspect, including the intellectual. It generates a strong desire for escape into some kind of heaven, and man employs to this end, though we may doubt their efficacy, the revolver, the bicycle and the rocking-chair. In the early stages of the trilogy life is still purgatorial and death still seems a possible relief. But Malone dies and the voices go on. The Unnamable finds that, having escaped from purgatory, he is in hell. *How It Is* and most of the subsequent work explore this hell. Now Beckett is influenced here by Dante, mentioned by name in *The Lost Ones* (LO,14) and a well-known influence from undergraduate days. Dante conceived the tortures of the damned with horrific clarity and captured marvellously the most significant aspect of hell (and the one which separates it most radically from purgatory) namely that there is no exit from hell and no end to its tortures. These tortures, furthermore, are repetitive and, necessarily, futile.

The purgatory of early Beckett, then, is 'mere' suffering. The hell of the later work is interminable futile suffering. This corresponds to our view of the later work as being more directly concerned with the ontological. There is no escape from the radical dissatisfaction diagnosed by Sartre as man's condition. Man is perpetually 'condemned to be free' in the famous phrase, it is *in principle* that man's approach to being is a Sisyphean task. For Murphy, as for the soul in purgatory, there is a way out. For the Unnamable and, *a fortiori* for the creatures of *How It Is* and the later texts, there is no exit.[6]

The twin texts *Imagination Dead Imagine* (completed 1965) and *The Lost Ones* (completed 1966) gain considerably if they are viewed as experiments in the depiction of a Sartrean hell. Both are post-mortem visions in which we are aware of a narrator looking in on an abstract world distantly taken from Dante. The first sentence of *Imagination* runs:

> No trace anywhere of life, you say, pah no difficulty there, imagination not dead yet, yes, dead, good, imagination dead imagine. (IM,7)

Sartrean consciousness is set against being, responsible for the creation of its world. Merely by being conscious man inescapably creates his world, there is no alternative. So it is with the narrator here. He starts with the hypothesis of emptiness, the blank page perhaps, where there is 'no trace...of life.' The narrator is consciousness aware equally, as in Sartre, of objective facts outside himself ('life') and of objective facts inside himself ('imagination'). With a disgusted eye ('pah') he watches the latter at work inventing the former. He has been tempted, perhaps, to think that he has coincided with the void already. If there is no life and no imagination perhaps he is free at last. But the very act of becoming conscious generates a world, either outside or inside the head. Although imagination is 'dead', consciousness, condemned to freedom, must invent more imagination: 'imagination dead imagine.'

Anything perceived, as we have seen in our discussion of bad faith, is immediately alienated from us by our consciousness of the perception. Hence the text continues

> Islands, water, azure, verdure, one glimpse and vanished, endlessly, omit. (IM,7)

Both in the case of real vision and in the case of an imagined scene, after the first glimpse what is perceived vanishes as we try to grasp it by grasping ourselves, so that the object of consciousness is no longer the island but my perception of it. This elusiveness of the object is the permanent condition of perception, hence the 'endlessly', but it compromises the status of objects which must then be 'omitted' as the conscious mind moves on, as minds always must, to another round of perception and disillusion. The narrator recapitulates Beckett's entire development here. All through his *oeuvre* he is attempting to 'omit', to 'discard' and to 'have done', in the words of Hamm. So here, having 'omitted' a vision, an imagining, the narrator makes a bid for the void, 'Till all white'. Can he stop here? 'White' would seem as blank a place as any other, but imagination, driven by consciousness, cannot stop and it goes on with a movement of thought something like 'Where is the white? Like all imagined objects it is in my head.' So the sentence runs 'Till all white in the whiteness the rotunda.' (IM,7) We may feel that the rotunda is a skull, into which we are being taken by the narrator as he tries to home in on himself; like Murphy's mind it is a hollow sphere. Equally it could be the world. The usefulness of a Sartrean interpretation here is that it makes little difference whether we choose one of these possibilities or whether we insist that Beckett is simply talking about a rotunda of certain colour and dimensions. Here is a way to cut the Gordian knot of Beckett's ambiguity. The narrator is certainly at least a consciousness, a subject; all the other elements in the text are objects which depend on this consciousness and it hardly matters whether they are aspects of his empirical self (his imagination for example), physical objects or imaginary objects. There is no real way of identifying the status of much of the material of a Beckett text, but the ontological statement remains the same: the hell is the hell of consciousness, the hell of being conscious; the problem is not in the construction of rotundas or in the *literal* plight of their inhabitants, it lies in the nature of the pour-soi.

To summarize this in terms of our discussion of man as a useless passion trying to catch up with being: whatever the status of the rotunda it has being over against the nothingness of the narrator's consciousness. It 'fills' him with words but never becomes him.

The main part of *Imagination Dead Imagine* consists of a description of what is inside the rotunda. It is a glimpse of hell and it is an analogue of the human condition for, needless to say, all this talk of purgatory and hell is mere metaphor, the Sartrean sufferer is always, precisely, in the here and now.

In the rotunda the rhythms of life are reduced to an almost abstract pattern: the temperature rises as the light does and falls as darkness sets in. These patterns follow varying but definite rhythms paralleling the differing passage of the days and the years. In the rotunda the rhythm works in seconds rather than hours or months but the parallel holds, I think, if we consider Beckett's extraordinary difficulties with the apprehension of time exemplified in Pozzo's outburst in the second act of *Godot* where 'they give birth astride of a grave.' In *Imagination Dead Imagine* there are two bodies in the whiteness with their eyes sometimes open and sometimes closed. Man is almost abstractly portrayed, in a minimal version of his world.

The text concludes:

> Leave them there, sweating and icy, there is better elsewhere. No, life ends and no, there is nothing elsewhere, and no question now of ever finding again that white speck lost in whiteness, to see if they still lie still in the stress of the storm, or of a worse storm, or in the black dark for good, or the great whiteness unchanging, and if not what they are doing. (IM,14)

Here we find that the narrator, as consciousness aspiring to being, realizes that there is nothing besides being, here represented by the rotunda, and no chance ever again of catching up with his creation. Besides this, we find that 'life ends' and then there is nothing, 'nothing elsewhere'. Man's aspiration to be God, to be being, would be satisfied by heaven, at least in that definition whereby the soul (pour-soi) becomes one with God, that is, absorbed into the reality of the en-soi, while retaining its identity. But this heaven, the en-soi-pour-soi, is the impossible ideal, the unattainable. Finally, the interest in the last sentence is as much in the 'human realities' inhabiting the rotunda as in the narrator and his enterprise. Here it is significant that although they seem completely trapped in their horrific facticity they are in fact offered a hint of freedom in that they could now be either in the storm or in the dark or in the light, or, possibly, doing something else. Night and day may come and go, but mankind is free and, so, unpredictable.

The Lost Ones is a simpler text to deal with. Most of its sixty-three pages are devoted to a description of the existence of some two-hundred people existing in a 'cylinder'. Most of them spend most of their time seeking a way out, climbing ladders, exploring the 'niches' in the walls of the cylinder, wondering if the way out may not be above them, in just that part of the cylinder they cannot reach.

That this text is metaphorical, a parable, can hardly be in doubt. It certainly attacks the imagination on a literal level in its claustrophobia and in the horror of its physical detail, but that is the way parables work. And this parable works at a number of levels. Here is a circle of Dante's hell again, here is man seeking meaning and creating futile patterns, here is consciousness imprisoned once more in a skull or a world. Dante, as we have seen, is mentioned by name: the 'non-searchers' in the cylinder, sitting in the Belacqua position presumably, are 'in the attitude which wrung from Dante one of his rare wan smiles.' (LO,14) Later we learn of two schools of thought among the searchers, one which swears by the niches in the wall of the cylinder as the means of escape and another which 'dreams of a trap-door hidden in the hub of the ceiling giving access to a flue at the end of which the sun and other stars would still be shining.' (LO,18) This mention of 'the sun and other stars' is again Dantean echoing as it does the line at the end of the *Paradiso*. 'L'amor che muove il sole e l'altre stelle (*Paradiso* xxxiii, 145) There is perhaps also a hint in this context of the line that ends the *Inferno* where Dante and Virgil emerge from hell to see the stars again.

Inside this hell, with its 'sensation of yellow...not to say of sulphur in view of the associations' (LO,36) which is described in terms suitable for a present or past experience, humanity seeks for a way out until it gives up hope and collapses into immobility, 'vanquished'. This will be the 'last state' of all the dwellers in the cylinder and any faint hint of hope is specifically contradicted by the narrator.

> And far from being able to imagine their last state when every body will be still and every eye vacant they will come to it unwitting and be so unawares. Then light and climate will be changed in a way impossible to foretell. But the former may be imagined extinguished as purposeless and the latter fixed not far from freezing point. (LO,15)

There is a hint of hope here in the word 'changed', with its connotations of the end of the world and the last trumpet, and in the rather sonorous words 'in a way impossible to foretell', but Beckett does foretell what the 'last state' of the cylinder will be both here and at the end of the text. The seekers will not find any way out and the situation in the cylinder will not change until they are all 'vacant' and 'unwitting'; especially, the light will not stop until it is 'purposeless'. Here we learn that this world, a world of perpetually hopeless ambition and futile search, is dependent on its inhabitants. Without them the light and warmth vanish. This 'last state' is the 'unthinkable end' towards which existence in the cylinder proceeds 'infinitely'. The whole business started 'in some unthinkable past'. Altogether the suggestion that this is a parable about human existence seems inescapable here; the hint is that *The Lost Ones* are the whole race, trapped in a finite world, overcrowded, suffering, going from an uncomprehended beginning to an incomprehensible end. But the process is identical for the individual consciousness too, going from a birth of which he knows nothing, through the ontological horror of his impossible quest to a death that will annihilate the world. Beckett's hell, like Sartre's, is here and now.

Beckett's work, I am suggesting, can be read as a metaphor for a Sartrean universe, not exclusively but with some profitable results. In the metaphor the voice goes on talking, projecting, feeling itself obliged to fill the void before it and creating worlds that reflect the world in which it exists. In the Sartrean reality to which this corresponds consciousness is confronted with the freedom of the future into which it must project and it creates its world as it goes, always dissatisfied with the past and always aspiring to a future in which it can catch up with itself and come to rest. Without something very like this Sartrean parallel what can we make of a passage such as the following from the *Texts for Nothing*?

> I know it's not me, but it's too late now, too late to deny it . . . what matter how you describe yourself, here or elsewhere, fixed or mobile, without form or oblong like a man, in the dark or the light of heavens, I don't know . . . and if I went back to where all went out and on from there, no, that would lead nowhere . . . (NK,82–3)

What the narrator has said is him is not him (it cannot be him, it can only be an element in his factical past) but it seems hopeless to try to get to him. He mentions two possibilities, however, which are: 'describing' himself and going 'back to where all went out'. The first of these is clearly the kind of project undertaken in texts such as *Imagination Dead Imagine* and *The Lost Ones* where sometimes people are 'fixed' (*Imagination*) and sometimes they are 'mobile' (*Lost Ones*), where there is a tension between the formlessness of abstraction and the forms of representation ('oblong like a man') and where the light and the dark alternate endlessly. The second possibility is to go back 'to where all went out', which is the position of return to the narrator, of Beckett again before the blank page, back to the blank point of the consciousness, the nothing into which all vanishes, Sartre's 'drain-hole in the solidity of being'.

*   *   *

ONTOLOGICAL PARABLES 2.HEIDEGGER

For Heidegger, too, Beckett's work acts as a parable. In Chapter 2 this was looked at in some detail, here it can be examined first in terms of Beckett's overall direction and then in terms of the third period of his work.

Taken as a whole, Beckett's work is making much the same attempt as that of his narrators. He moves toward a method for dealing with ontological reality in art, looking for an objective correlative for the way things are on the most fundamental level. There is a strong parallel between this undertaking and Heidegger's own development. *Being and Time* is an assault on Being (the object of any ontological effort) that fails; similarly Beckett's trilogy is an assault on the way things are. In both cases the writer, having failed in the grand attempt, has gone on to offer further pieces from the same quarry, more ways of approaching the same fundamental problem.

Being and Time opens with the statement that man has forgotten Being and offers to go on the trail of Being in what follows. Much is revealed in the published chapters, especially about the difficulty of confronting Being, but the great work is never finished. Subsequently a number of much shorter works by Heidegger have appeared, increasingly oracular in nature, in which the approach to Being is rehearsed, redirected and made, for example, through the poetry of Hölderlin and the fragments of the presocratic philosophers.

Beckett's trilogy opens with the problem expressed more mundanely. How did Molloy 'get there'? How did he come to be where he is? The question, which in a sense generates the whole word-mountain, is never answered. Indeed it becomes reaffirmed as the central question in, for instance, the opening line of *The Unnamable*. By the end of the trilogy we are aware of a certain relief, that the art-work in our hands is finished, but the parable it contains states clearly enough that the quest is not over: 'I'll go on' are the final words. Subsequently a number of shorter works by

Beckett have appeared, increasingly gnomic in nature, in which the fundamental question is rehearsed and redirected but never answered.

This comparison may appear to be largely formal, based on the publishing-history of two writers, but I do not think it is mere coincidence. The 'going on' of Heidegger and Beckett is not chosen for superficial or aesthetic reasons, it is inherent in the nature of their undertaking. To catch up with Being is going to take until death (Heidegger on *Sein-zum-Tode*) or even further (Beckett's parables set in hell.) The project of each writer is the same and it is doomed to the same failure.

In summarizing Heidegger's equiprimordial aspects of man's existence towards the end of Chapter 2 we found facticity and 'existence' defined in terms that were later taken over by Sartre and which were discussed at the end of the last section. 'Resolute Dasein', for Heidegger, calls itself back from the factical 'they', from inauthentic existence, to the 'being-there' of the present. This call is the call of 'care' that brings Dasein's self back to the authentic now. All this is made possible by time: only Dasein has temporality and thus is the 'between' of the phrase 'between birth and death'. (BT,426)

This 'between' is strongly present in Beckett, incidentally, in his tendency to keep in mind beginnings and ends. The trilogy moves from Molloy's mother to Malone's death, *The Lost Ones* offers the full life-span of the creatures in the cylinder, *Breath* offers a cry to be taken as a life between the poles offered by the words 'birth' and 'death', conflated into 'breath'. In Chapter 2 I discussed Heidegger's other equiprimordial concepts in some detail and in every case found Beckett to have offered some literary equivalent. Now we are working on a more basic level. Care, time and so on are the equiprimordial existentialia of Dasein, but Heidegger's fundamental project, having 'interrogated' Dasein much as Beckett has put his 'vice-existers' through their paces, is to approach Being. We feel that 'behind' or 'beyond' Heidegger's discussion there is an unresolved question and I would propose that the same applies to Beckett: what will remain when he has got it all said?

One of Heidegger's exiguous steps in the direction of Being is the essay *The Way Back into the Ground of Metaphysics* of 1949.[7] This claims that 'metaphysics' is like the roots of a tree. It is a science that deals with beings (*Seinden*). But what of the ground in which those roots are planted? That must be Being (*Sein*). The approach to

Being is behind or beyond or above all the considerations of meta-physics. Not only this; Heidegger cuts the ground from under his own feet by observing that the approach to Being is beyond ontology and theology as well (Kaufmann, p. 219). These 'sciences' also deal with beings, he says, and not with Being.

Once more the parallel with Beckett appears. There is a self-destructive element in both our writers, they both deny themselves the only available tools for the pursuit of their goals. Yet the goals remain and the pursuit must go on and here Heidegger has light to shed on Beckett for he explains *why* it must go on. The explanation is not the sort that would satisfy a court of law, but at this level of 'fundamental ontology', or whatever we are still permitted to call it, the criteria governing the value of statements change so that the radical denial of the existence of the problem, for instance, can be an acceptable solution. Thus in *The Way Back* Heidegger answers the question as to why Dasein should pursue the goal of Being by defining Dasein itself as 'the location of the truth of Being'. (p. 213) This, of course, is just the burden of some of the opening remarks of *Being and Time*. Discussing the question of 'the meaning of Being' Heidegger states that Dasein is

> that entity which already comports itself, in its Being, towards what we are asking about when we ask this question (the question of the meaning of Being). But in that case the question of Being is nothing other than the radicalization of an essential tendency-of-Being which belongs to Dasein itself – the pre-ontological under-standing of Being. (BT,35)

This should assist us with Beckett. His project, and that of his narrators, is not a wilful plunging into difficult terrain in a place where mankind has a perfectly good road to go along, it is a con-frontation of what is already and inescapably there. Thus the Unnamable says

> I'll recognise it, in the end I'll recognise it, the story of the silence that he never left, that I should never have left, that I may never find again, that I may find again...(T,417)

This is one among many examples of narrators in the trilogy referring to some absolute which, while beyond them, is their own. The Unnamable will 'recognize' the absolute ('the story of the silence'), it was once his, otherwise how could he talk about leaving it or finding it again? Now it is not present to him, but its absence is his agony. Clearly the problem is within him, he is already the problem, he already has an understanding of Being that is not enough of an understanding to yield Being itself up to him but which will not let him rest content without it.

Heidegger's view of Dasein as being an entity which *already* comports itself towards Being is an excellent way of seeing why Beckett's characters, 'thrown' on to the page or on to the stage, seem to have *some* understanding of their ontological environment, seem already to be orientated towards an inescapable but mysterious basis for existence. Thus the tramps in *Godot* are orientated towards (waiting for) Godot. 'Waiting' seems an appropriate metaphor for Dasein's comportment towards Being. Waiting is a condition which does not necessarily affect one's daily projects but which underlies all of them. While performing one's job or gardening or even while asleep one could be described as 'waiting', for instance, waiting to get married or waiting to die.

Waiting can underlie or mingle with all one's consciousnesses or conditions.

Paul Tillich has an exalted view of waiting that may perhaps make this parallel seem less far-fetched. In a sermon actually entitled 'Waiting' he has this to say:

> Both the Old and the New Testaments describe our existence in relation to God as one of waiting...Waiting means *not* having and having at the same time. For we have *not* what we wait for...The condition of man's relation to God is first of all one of *not* having, *not* seeing, *not* knowing and not grasping. (Tillich, p. 151)

The tramps, explicitly, do not have Godot, do not grasp his intentions, do not know him, and yet they are conditioned by him and orientated towards him. The parable seems obviously to work if Godot is taken as God but it can operate with any absolute and it is hardly a great step from this to Heidegger's Being which calls to man and towards which he is already orientated but which he fails finally to apprehend.

Tillich emphasizes the 'nots' in his sermon. Waiting is '*not* having' and so on. This negative aspect of waiting relates to Heidegger's further discussion, in *The Way Back into the Ground of*

Metaphysics, concerning Being and Nothing. If Being is not a being, he asks, is it then Nothing? This sort of question is based on a misconception, he claims; only a metaphysics (in his acceptation of the term) which deals with mere beings can see non-being as either Being or Nothing indifferently. A more fundamental ontology must hold these separate.

In *An Introduction to Metaphysics* of 1935, reworked in 1953, Heidegger takes these questions further. He claims that Western man has forgotten Being and that our philosophical language has become devalued. He therefore approaches Being linguistically, analysing the etymology and grammar of the word to see what it will yield. (*Introduction*, p. 43–61) The result of this is that we are left with the Aristotelian-Hegelian position that Being is merely an emptiness. But if Being is empty and indeterminate we are easily able to distinguish it from non-being, so Being becomes a paradoxical entity entitled the 'determinate indeterminate'. We are thrust back to language once again, for Being is essential to language: if we were to subtract the verb 'to be' there could be no language at all.[8]

In *What is Philosophy?* of 1955 Heidegger reiterates that man, as Dasein, is always already in correspondence with Being, that this is man's very nature, but that man does not always listen to 'the appeal of being'. (*What is Philosophy?*, p. 75) Philosophy has an inherent direction, it is always pointed towards Being, and 'astonishment' is the condition of philosophizing. 'Astonishment is disposition in and for which the Being of being unfolds'. (ibid., p. 85) This astonishment is the astonishment of the poet; the poet and the philosopher are linked in that both are at the service of language, they work at extracting the truth of Being from words, they do not seek words to express the truth. Language is the house of Being.

I have summarized these central points from Heidegger's later essays to give an impression of the general drift of his thought after *Being and Time*. The point of this is that it puts us in a position to see the deep similarities between his thinking and Beckett's.

First of all, Beckett chooses to continue; he responds, through his characters and narrators, to the 'appeal of Being'. It is as if he were constantly trying to clear away the debris that separates man from Being, and certainly he is using the tools Heidegger recommends – words. His words are a house for Being, an attempt to 'get it all said' and to confront the silence of Being.

Then, the relationship between language and Being is taken

further by both Heidegger and Beckett, and in the same direction. Language is the house of Being but it is not Being as such. Dasein's capacity for language is identical with Dasein's orientation towards Being. Olga Bernal has said that, for Beckett *'le langage est la condition nécessaire du Je'* (*Langage et fiction dans le roman de Samuel Beckett*, p. 15) and if this 'Je' is taken as Dasein the parallel is very close: 'Je', or Dasein, only arises through language (Beckett's narrators create themselves by narrating) and through language it confronts Being, but Being cannot come to be by being *said*. To quote Bernal again, Beckett's work is *'une oeuvre qui cherche une autre lumière que celle du Verbe, la lumière de l'indit'*. (Bernal, op. cit., p. 15)

This idea of working through words towards the silence of Being, manifested appropriately by Heidegger himself who, after the word-mountain of *Being and Time* contracts towards a silent or poetic 'astonishment' in the face of the ontological, is clearly applicable to Beckett whose early creations, such as *More Pricks Than Kicks* or *Proust* abound in the extravagantly verbal and whose development is towards silence. (Cf. Ihab Hassan's, *The Literature of Silence*.)

At the conclusion of Chapter 2 above, I suggested that the Heideggerian call to 'exist in the nameless' finds its echo in Beckett, that Beckett's world is striving to be the 'nameless' world. This is, of course, a metaphor just as the notion of silence is a metaphor, and here we have, I think, the answer to the facile suggestion that if Beckett wants silence all he has to do is to stop writing. Beckett is not seeking silence *as such*, he is seeking the Being beyond words for which silence is a metaphor or of which it could become an epithet. His continued creation of worlds is a continuing attempt to find the metaphor, the parable, the objective correlative, for Being. A 'nameless' world would be a silent openness to Being and this is what Beckett has been attempting, at least since *The Unnamable*.

A world full of 'names' or 'beings' is the world of 'mere misery' of the *Three Dialogues* (PTD, 122), and in this world there is something for the artist (Masson, Beckett) to express. In the silent astonishment that is man's disposition towards Being there is 'nothing to express'. What metaphors and correlatives does Beckett employ in his self-defeating project of expressing nothing?

Beckett's parables for the Heideggerian approach to Being seem to belong to two types. One is the type that abstracts from beings to Being, that reduces towards the silence. *Breath* represents this development at its last gasp. Somehow this type seems logical and comprehensible, an obvious step towards the end proposed. Far more difficult, and therefore more in need of our attention, is the type of parable, such as *Not I*, that recreates another fearful world out of the ruins of this one and thus seems to contradict Beckett's fundamental project. This type can perhaps be understood more easily in the light of a comment of Robbe-Grillet (he is discussing the world of conventional fiction and suggesting an alternative):

> A la place de cet univers des 'significations' (psychologiques, sociales, fonctionelles), il faudrait donc essayer de construire un monde plus solide, plus immédiat. (*Pour Un Nouveau Roman*, p. 20)

This appeal for a new novel is a call towards namelessness, towards the construction of solid, immediate and 'meaningless' worlds. Is this not precisely what Beckett has achieved in *The Lost Ones*? In this text we are presented with a world that pulsates before us, solid and immediate enough, but from which all meaning has been excluded. Nowhere in the cylinder can a way out be found.

Lessness (1969) creates another little world, another parable for the ontological position of man. Its first sentence makes explicit that here we have man come home at last, that this is his 'true refuge'.

> Ruins true refuge long last towards which so many false time out of mind. (LE,7)

By these ruins stands a recognizable human being.

> Grey face two pale blue little body heart beating only upright. (LE,7)

On all sides of the ruin lies 'endlessness'.

> All sides endlessness earth sky as one no sound no stir. (LE,7)

The ruins are 'the same grey' as the ash or grey sand that makes up the environment of the text; the sky and the body that stands by the ruins are grey, too. All other colours have 'gone from mind' or are dismissed as 'figments' (for instance the white light or the blue sky) with the exception of the often-repeated 'two pale blue' (eyes, presumably). And then, the 'four-square' walls are flattened ('over backwards') and the body is the 'only upright'. So, there *were* colours, things *were* once 'four-square' although they have now collapsed into ruins, the body ('he') in the ruin dreams of 'day and nights made of dreams of other nights better days'. (LE,17) The only thing that stands out from the world in the last analysis is human reality. Heidegger has given a place of special importance to this idea, as we have seen in connexion with *Being and Time* (p. 14, above), and it is summarised succinctly in *The Way Back* in a manner that reads like an ontological paraphrase of a number of Beckett texts.

> The being that exists is man. Man alone exists. Rocks are, but they do not exist. Trees are, but they do not exist. Horses are, but they do not exist. Angels are, but they do not exist. God is, but he does not exist. . . The proposition 'man exists' means: man is that being whose Being is distinguished by the open-standing standing-in in the unconcealedness of Being. . .(Kaufmann, p. 214)

Heidegger is making play with the etymology of 'exist' as being from 'ex-sistere' – 'to stand out from'. Another pointer in this direction involves man's 'ec-stasis' – his position 'out' of Being, conscious of Being.

At the final, abstract level of *Lessness*, metaphorically re-presented by monochrome surroundings, man alone exists, alone coloured (blue) at least in his eyes. But this is his 'true refuge' to which 'so many' have been 'false time out of mind'. Here I would suggest that if we take the 'true refuge' as being offered to man at the ontological level, it shows him confronted by Being. No longer confronted by beings (all of which are perhaps only figments – 'Never but imagined the blue in a wild imagining the blue celeste of poesy'. LE,13) and far out in the wastes of silence and namelessness, man, only residually alive and barely recognizable, has an inevitable orientation towards Being and can perhaps take the miraculous 'one step' into the absolute:

> One step in the ruins in the sand on his back in the endless he will make it. LE,17)

The man, the 'only upright', for whom things *were* better, happier, for whom things *can* be all right, need take only one step into the 'ruins', the indistinguishable and endless nothingness of his 'true refuge' (the Being towards which he is orientated) and things *will be* real and bright and active as in the old days. Here Beckett offers us the clue to the colour blue. The man's eyes are blue but so was (and will be) the sky:

> On him will rain again as in the blessed days of blue the passing cloud. (LE,15)

Now he is in the greyness, the 'flatness', the 'endlessness', timelessness and all the other lessnesses. But he is Dasein, the vehicle of Being, the user of the language that is the house of Being and for him (*a fortiori* for his imagination as for Beckett's imagination or Malone's) there is a world of beings in his past and the possibility of catching up with Being in his future. *Lessness* offers us man in a world reduced to zero (as the title of the text implies; the French title is *Sans*) and shows us two perspectives on him: he can only be discussed in terms of past beings (the ruins he faces are only ruins because they *were* 'four square', the grey is only possible because of previous colour) and his return to them (his return, it seems, to himself) lies beyond a step into the absolute (Being) beyond which all will be restored to him ('true refuge long last').

In reading *Lessness* we are affected by the imagery, the associations of Beckett's carefully-selected vocabulary, for this is literature and not a scientific report. There is an overall impression of desolation, of man lost in the waste but paradoxically close to his true home, and of other subtler impressions that can be demonstrated by critical analysis. At Beckett's level of abstraction, however, it cannot be adequate to stop at this point, it cannot be enough to say that the reader is given such-and-such an impression. These obviously metaphorical objects (and the text is packed with solid and immediate things) cry out for interpretation. The text itself defies the more superficial interpretations, for instance of psychology, and demands at least the sort of treatment it receives in Brian Finney's *Since How It Is*. Finney at once assumes that a text of this sort is microcosmic and parabolic:

> In *Lessness*, then, the white box (of *Ping*) has fallen open, the consciousness has been released from its enclosed state of isolation to confront on 'all sides endlessness earth sky as one.' Man is left

confronting infinity, yet still unable to prevent himself from
making one more finite gesture. (Finney, p. 21)

This is not uncharacteristic of the criticism of later Beckett, by
Finney and others, and it shows that a metaphysical reading of
Beckett seems essential. However, my thesis is that after two minutes
at this sort of level we start to feel uncomfortable and that our dis-
comfort is founded on the absence of a philosophical matrix within
which to understand some of the propositions. *Why* does Beckett see
man's consciousness as being 'released from its enclosed state of
isolation'? *Why* is man 'unable to prevent himself from making
one more finite gesture'? Strictly speaking these questions are
unanswerable, unless by Beckett himself, but we can certainly come
closer to finding a convincing interpretation for ourselves if we apply
ontological pictures to Beckett's picture and take them as far as we
can. Heidegger's analysis of Dasein in one such picture.

On thing that emerges from the parallel between Heidegger and
Beckett is a narrowing of the gap between the tendency towards
silence represented by *Breath* and the meticulous construction of
alternative worlds such as those of *Lessness* and *The Lost Ones*. In
both cases the aim is to create metaphors. *Breath* creates a
metaphor for an ontological insight by a careful selection of sights
and sounds, it is a dramatic literary structure just as real and substantial as *King Lear*. *Lessness* selects other materials which,
because there can be no sights or sounds on a printed page, consist
of a greater number of words, but it too, is an artificial,
metaphorical construct which illustrates an ontological view. In
both cases the metaphor is formally self-defeating; in *Breath* it is at
once apparent that the fastest blink of an eye (or, strictly, the most
infinitestimal moment of time) would have been formally more
correct if dramatically less effective. In *Lessness* it is essential to the
subject exposed by the metaphor that the environment of the text is
actually invisible, although described, and that in spite of the
phrase 'he will make it', referring to the 'one step', there is 'no hold'
in the sand. The point is that, given the inadequacy of all metaphors
(the impossibility of 'expressing') for Beckett's subject-matter, all his
failures are failures in the same medium: the ontological parable.
That is, they may be beautiful or impressive parables but the
ontological reality to which they refer defies successful transposition
into art. Thus we have the paradox of complete and satisfying
artistic creations for which there is no satisfactory interpretation *on*

principle. To understand this we need the aid of philosophers faced with the same impasse.[9]

*   *   *

ONTOLOGICAL PARABLES 3.HEGEL

Beckett moves from the surfaces to the depths. He progressively excludes the human, the quotidian and the satiric to produce colder and more abstract pieces whose significance is increasingly to be found at an ontological level. One of the ways in which this happens is that, by the exclusion of surface reality, the existence of the narrator and the presence of the author are brought into sharper relief. While there are kites and cars, pubs and prostitutes to think about we think about them, but where there is nothing but mud or greyness or breath to think about we are rapidly thrown back to the conceiving mind, the creator.

We have had warning of this, of course, in the constant authorial intrusions into the earlier work such as the opening and closing sentences of Chapter 6 of *Murphy* where the narrator reveals himself as both present and impatient. Then, more forcefully, we have seen the self-conscious narrator at work in the trilogy where the process of composition is laid bare and the narratives are as much about the narration of narrative as they are about any of the stories narrated. 'What tedium', comments Malone, or perhaps Beckett, in *Malone Dies*. This tendency is radicalized in *How It Is* with its constant repetition of 'I quote' and 'I say them as I hear them' where the narrator is obtruding his presence even if only to disclaim responsibility for what he is narrating. This element remains in spite of everything that is thrown away. It appears in different guises; thus in the *Texts For Nothing* there is a continuing dialectic between 'I' and 'He' that suggests a breakdown in distinctions which at once raises the question of the status of the narrator. The assumption tends to be that the narrator is 'outside' his story, objectifying it just as the reader does, but in the first *Text* this is disarmingly challenged:

Eye ravening patient in the haggard vulture face, perhaps its carrion time. I'm up there and I'm down here, under my gaze, foundered, eyes closed, ear cupped against the sucking peat, we're of one mind, all of one mind, always were, deep down, we're fond of one another, but there it is, there's nothing we can do for one another. (NK,73)

Here, as often in *The Unnamable*, Beckett offers us a direct paradox, an oxymoron in fact: 'I'm up there and I'm down here.' 'Up there' is the author's position, the writer is 'above' his material, controlling it, the 'scribe' of *How It Is*. 'Down here' is where the action of fiction takes place, the arena, and the narrator is in both places, he is narrator and narrated, under his own gaze.

In the texts and shorts that make up the third period of Beckett's work, where surface reality is at its least significant, the confusion of identities, the mixing of pronouns and the interest we are consequently forced to take in the narrating self amount to a central issue. *Not I* offers an emblem of this. On the stage are an illuminated mouth, talking, and a silent auditor, listening. They represent an 'I' and a 'He' but in no simple manner. The mouth talks, babbling on in a stream of consciousness, interrupted and stimulated by some unheard questioner, but Mouth never utters the word 'I'. In sharp contrast to so many other Beckett texts, *Not I* in fact never uses the first person and, indeed, insists that everything narrated happened to 'she' not to 'I'. But the auditor listens, a silent witness, a consciousness too. The 'I' is both Mouth and Auditor, both the looker on and the performer, both 'up there' and 'down here'. The Auditor is sorry for Mouth, his gestures being gestures of 'helpless compassion'. As we saw in the first *Text for Nothing* 'we're sorry for one another, but there it is, there's nothing we can do for one another.' *Not I* is about itself.

In a text such as *Imagination Dead Imagine* (1965) the narrator is 'inside' the fictional world and explores it with us, proposing ideas and rejecting them like an archaeologist on a dig and even including in the text the 'you' whom he is addressing. 'No trace anywhere of life, you say, pah, no difficulty there. . .'(IM,7)

In *For To End Yet Again* (1976) the first phrase, which is the same as the title, throws us into consideration of the narrator and of the author. It is Beckett who has ended so often, ended only to recommence; it is the narrating of stories (= living) that seems to go on to an end beyond which, instead of silence, there is the need to end again.

In this text we are once more in the endless lost whiteness of *Lessness* or *Imagination* and once more there is the sense of the narrator, again conceived as an eye, looking in on his own creation: 'Eagle the eye that shall discern him now' he says of the reduced figure at the centre of this vanishing picture.

What is being offered here is another level of parable. On this level these texts can be read in the light of an approach to the Hegelian Absolute. For Hegel, Being is merely a Scholastic universal rather than the endless and mysterious quarry it is in Heidegger. The Hegelian system has Being at one extreme and Absolute Idea at the other, and there is a different sort of priority to be given to the concept Absolute Spirit. Absolute Spirit (or Mind, the German is the ambiguous *Geist*) represents the highest and purest activity of the human spirit, but it is beyond any individual human, an absolute and, as such, identical with Absolute Idea. This is not the place to explain in any detail the logic behind these largest of Hegel's concepts but some glimpse of their mutual structure may be caught in a sentence of Hegel's that orientates us in the right direction for Beckett. It is the last sentence of the last section of the *Encyclopaedia*.

> The eternal Idea, in full fruition of its essence, eternally sets itself to work, engenders and enjoys itself as absolute Mind. (*Encyclopaedia* Third Part — trans. W. Wallace p. 197)

This describes *either* God *or* man. It also describes the process of literary creation so self-consciously engaged in by Beckett and his narrators. Stace's gloss on this part of Hegel is as follows.

> To use metaphorical, i.e. religious language, one may say that absolute spirit is nothing less than the spirit of God...and the assertion that absolute spirit is the final phase of the human spirit means no more than that the human spirit is of essentially the same kind as the spirit of God, and that every man is potentially divine. (Stace, *The Philosophy of Hegel*, p. 119)

If we do *not* use religious language we discover that we are talking about a picture of man in which, finally, a unity is achieved between himself (his consciousness) and some sort of absolute. This unity is strikingly akin to the object of man's 'useless passion' according to Sartre. A unity between self-consciousness and the absolute would be the impossible pour-soi/en-soi entity called God. (So we have not been able to stay away from religion for very long.) But this unity is displayed artistically in all its ambiguity in later Beckett who, at his most obscure and paradoxical, seems to be struggling to find a parable that will fit the Hegelian view.

Hegel's *Phenomenology*, which was the subject of Chapter 4 has been described by Richard Kroner as

> A modern *itinerarium mentis ad Deum*, 'the journey of the mind to God.' The knowledge of God, or the Absolute, is the final goal of this voyage. (cf. Hegel, *Early Theological Writings*, trans. Knox and Kroner, University of Chicago Press, 1948)

This progress is somewhat parallel to Beckett's own. He, too, moves towards the absolute, or rather towards an adequate analogy for it, sloughing off surface detail and becoming progressively more abstract as he tries to find the absolute simultaneously entirely outside and entirely inside himself. The *Phenomenology* concludes with two sections ('Religion' and 'Absolute Knowledge') which are concerned with Absolute Spirit and offer a triad of which this Absolute Spirit can be said to be composed: religion, art and philosophy. What is most striking, from our Beckettian point of view, is that Hegel here proposes an increasingly close identity between individual consciousness and absolute spirit.

> The 'beautiful soul' is its own knowledge of itself in its pure transparent unity – self-consciousness, which knows this pure knowledge of pure inwardness to be spirit, is not merely intuition of the divine, but the self-intuition of God Himself. (PM,795)

> This last embodiment of spirit – spirit which at once gives its complete and true content the form of self, and thereby realizes its notion, and in doing so remains within its own notion – this is *Absolute Knowledge*. (PM,797)

This Absolute knowledge, the goal of art, religion and philosophy, depends on a relationship between Self and Spirit, between consciousness and Substance (in Beckettian terms, between 'I' and 'He') so intimate that even Hegel's dialectical method of showing how antitheses 'pass into' one another seems inadequate to describe it. In the end he has to invoke the metaphor of religion – man can achieve not merely an intuition of the divine but also a partaking in the Self-intuition of God himself. This sounds rather too satisfactory, too

pleasantly closed a system to be a true parallel with Beckett. Mure
explains it in almost mystical terms:

> God creates man's consciousness as an element in his own
> (God's) self-consciousness and therefore man's consciousness of
> God is self-consciousness, consciousness of himself as a constituent
> element of self-conscious God. (Mure, p. 3)

The important thing to remember, however, is that consciousness
is radically and in principle separated from its objects, including
itself. Thus the final step of union with God is precluded, for all
Hegel's attempts at bridging the gap, and we are left with choosing
between the proposition that God (the Absolute) *is* human self-
consciousness and nothing more and the proposition that God is still
an object for human self-consciousness, in which case he is Other
and not 'me'. For Hegel, paradoxically, man is as much God as it is
possible to be without being God. Put another way, human consciousness approaches the absolute and is made of the same stuff as
the absolute but remains one step away from being the absolute.

Here we have a philosophical version of a central problem which
Beckett gnaws at in all his work and which appears quite starkly in
his third period. Progressively he takes his eyes off the world and
tries to confront the Absolute; in Hegel's own way he finds himself
bereft of all save himself and having been washed up against that
rock (he cannot get rid of himself in order *himself* to meet the
Absolute) he is dragged back like the sea only to form another wave
that will uselessly break again against the unforgiving rock. Having
'ended' he has never ended and he must end yet again.

In his earlier work Beckett objectifies God in the manner of daily
religion. (Hegel sees religion as a stage in the development of spirit,
an objective and concrete prototype of the Absolute; at a later stage
he suggests that philosopy, like later Beckett, can try to do without
this concretization.) Most of Beckett's references to religion here are
satirical, as in the case of Watt and Sam feeling most like God when
they are feeding rats to other rats. Sometimes he verges on the
mystical, as in the case of Murphy's version of Nirvana or Watt's
view of Mr Knott. What is more important for our discussion of this
early work, however, is the presence of the author because this,
above all, is what will lead on to our Hegelian view; the satirical
references to things Christian (and, especially, Catholic) are more to
be taken as sallies of wit.

In reading *Murphy* and *Watt* we have no difficulty in identifying the author as Mr Beckett. His are the footnotes, the question-marks, the asides to the reader. When we come to the major, post-war work a change is apparent. *Godot* and *Endgame* retain a vestige of the old objectification of the divine but it is only superficial and it is certainly negative; Godot does not come; 'the bastard', in Hamm's phrase, 'doesn't exist'. The point is that by this time Beckett has started to withdraw from the outside world and there is considerable doubt cast on all 'off-stage' existence. Similarly, in the trilogy, there is a marked tendency to get rid of the level of existence on which we come across policemen and bicycles and to move inside. What is happening in these plays and novels is happening 'in here', that is, on stage, in Malone's mind, within a skull, between the reader's hands. Under these circumstances the presence of the narrator, or Mr Beckett, takes on new significance. At least he, as its creator, is outside the world of the work of art. Of his existence as an external entity there can be no doubt even if everything else is dubious. Thus Beckett moves towards a style of writing in which what he creates is hermetically sealed off from the outside except in so far as the narrator/author acts as a kind of safety-valve.

Beckett gradually shuts the exit-doors and by the time of *The Unnamable* there is only one door left open – the door to himself as author without which, in a celebrated phrase, nix. This explains why the *Texts For Nothing* never rose to the status of a novel and were published with less alacrity than the trilogy. They do not represent any advance over the trilogy from the point of view of the process I am describing. One of the *Texts* even descends to the specificity of 'the South-Eastern Railway Terminus' (NK,104), another raises its eyes to 'the beauty of the skies'. (NK,117) These impurities represent external elements, other ways out, although it must be admitted that in these *Texts* the 'no exit' signs go up often enough, as for instance:

> There's a way out there, there's a way out somewhere, to know exactly where would be a mere matter of time, and patience, and sequency of thought, and felicity of expression. But the body to get there with, where's the body? (NK,117)

In *How It Is*, as we have seen, the references to any external possibilities, slender as they are, are undercut by the repetition of 'I quote'. This is a writer writing the words he hears in his head, what he writes of is a sealed world, a hermetic picture of a perfect, if perfectly monstrous, reality belonging to and depending on an I, an eye, a perceiver.

In this sealed world we are offered lost ones, people and things cut off from the light of the sun and the other stars and illuminated by the only remaining source of light, the only exit, the author's consciousness. This situation is a parable for a Hegelian ontology. In Hegel absolute reality, an all-encompassing concept outside of which there is nothing, is connoted by human consciousness ('I') in Absolute Knowledge. In *The Lost Ones* there is a complete world with no way in or out, but Beckett (or a narrator) is looking in. Consciousness is essential to the Absolute but radically divorced from it; Beckett's narrative (sometimes 'I') is essential to the cylinder of the lost ones, it *is* the cylinder, but the cylinder is not it.

For To End Yet Again (1976) offers a parable for this Hegelian 'last state'. (The phrase 'last state' is frequent in the texts of Beckett's third period and can perhaps be taken as an equivalent to the extreme point in Hegel's dialectic, the arrival of human spirit at Absolute Knowledge.) The world of the text is a world nearly finished and a world still just dimly perceived by an author/narrator represented by a skull. At first the skull is somewhere (in a 'dark place') and is bent over a 'board' but the place and the board 'fade'. The skull is the writer, bowed over his table, the place is the world, external reality. This reality fades leaving only 'remains', memories, the internal reality of the writer's mind, 'remains of the days of the light of day' which are made to 'glimmer' so that 'all at once or by degrees there dawns and magic lingers a leaden dawn.' The narrative consciousness, like all consciousness, cannot rest at the end, in the darkness; whatever has been jettisoned or has faded the skull will be filled again with images and another text, such as *For To End Yet Again*, will uncoil its world. Here is the opening section of the text which this paragraph has summarized and interpreted:

> For to end yet again skull alone in a dark place pent bowed on a board to begin. Long thus to begin till the place fades followed by the board long after. For to end yet again skull alone in the dark the void no neck no face just the box last place of all in the dark the void. Place of remains where once used to gleam in the dark on and off used to glimmer a remain. Remains of the days of the light of day never light so faint as theirs so pale. Thus then the

skull makes to glimmer again in lieu of going out. There is the end
all at once or by degrees there dawns and magic lingers a leaden
dawn. (FTEYA,11)

The skull in the void seems an adequate preliminary symbol for consciousness confronting the absolute. And then, from consciousness,
because of consciousness, a world emerges; faced with the void man
must fill it, or, as Hegel has it, human spirit, aspiring to Absolute
Spirit, must connote Absolute Knowledge.

The sense of aloneness, of a flickering speck isolated in the vast
dark, is clearly symbolic of consciousness in its own radical subjective isolation. What makes a text such as this so particularly
appropriate as a metaphor for a metaphysical view is that the
position of consciousness before the Absolute is not only symbolized
by the skull in the void and the glimmer in the dark, it is also
symbolized by the writer (author, narrator) in the act of creation;
he, too, is an isolated moment confronted with the absolute demand
of the blank page.

The world of *For To End Yet Again*, the world created by
Beckett, perceived by the skull, is an 'ocean of dust' in which 'the
expelled' stands 'stark erect amidst his ruins'. (FTEYA, 11 and 12)
Here are remains indeed: 'the expelled' reminds us of the story of the
same name and the dust and the ruins remind us of *Lessness* and
other texts. Into this grey world walk two white dwarfs who carry a
litter. They seem to collect 'the expelled' and bear him away, a mark
of whiteness to be deciphered in all the grey. He falls out of the litter
onto his back and the dwarfs, too, collapse and lie still. Their 'ruins'
are now 'marble'. The skull is 'sepulchral' there is 'no fear of your
rising again.' (FTEYA, 14) Death seems to have overtaken them,
but there is still a blue eye open in all the whiteness and greyness,
enough consciousness left for the narrator to interpolate the word
'hell': this is the 'last state' for the 'expelled' and for the 'dwarfs' and
they are buried in the skull, which explains why it is 'sepulchral'.
They have been condemned to the hell within. Now the text ends
with a difficult passage. In it we are given a picture of the skull (consciousness) dreaming of a real end (though it is ironic that it is
dreaming for that is another form of consciousness and thus no
end). This corresponds to the author/narrator's attempt to 'get it all
said', to Mr Beckett's desire to be released from his 'hell of stories'
and to man's hopeless desire for an end to mere knowledge and a
union with the absolute.

And dream of a way in a space with neither here nor there where all the footsteps ever fell can never fare nearer to anywhere nor from anywhere further away. No for in the end for to end yet again by degrees or as though switched on dark falls there again that certain dark that alone certain ashes can.

Through it who knows yet another end beneath a cloudless sky same dark it earth and sky of a last end if ever there had to be another, absolutely had to be. (FTEYA,15)

The 'space with neither here nor there' is the absolute space (and time) known as infinity. Only when all is absolutely destroyed, in the darkness of the ashes of all knowledge, will it be the end. And if beyond that there is another, if there *'absolutely* had to be' another, it too would be made of the 'same dark', the dark of the 'last end'.

The aspiration here is not towards literal death. The text is laden with the imagery of death and decay but it is not a literal horror-story. The text is a parable for the anguish of an unfulfilled consciousness, a parable for the last ontological gasp of the Hegelian dialectic.

*   *   *

ONTOLOGICAL PARABLES 4.BECKETT

In the most recent Beckett texts, *Company* (1980) and *Ill Seen Ill Said* (1981; English edition 1982) there is a marginal re-humanising of the abstract world we have come to know as Beckett country. *Company* harps on the relationship between an objectified 'one in the dark' and the voice that speaks to him as 'You' ('Use of the second person marks the voice' (C,9). It canvasses other possible companions – father, beggar, girlfriend, and tries out various approaches to the dark, supine and presumably moribund figure around whom the text revolves.

Ill Seen Ill Said conjures up an old woman and her environment and contains some marvellous natural description, albeit of characteristic spareness and with touches of horror, as in 'Leprous with white scars where the grass has receded from the chalky soil. In contemplation of this erosion the eye finds solace.' (IS,26) This is caught up, with typical allusiveness, later in the text: 'Moonless star-studded sky reflected in the erosions filmed with ice.' (IS,26) It is clear that this text is about the approach to death ('What but life ending' IS,16) and that here Beckett means literal, natural death.

However, to take these two texts only on the literal level would be wilfully to ignore the greater part of their content. *Company* formally blows itself up with its repeated insistence on a 'deviser' who is 'devising it all for company'. (C,45) Later this is extended: 'Devising it all *himself included* for company' (C,59. My italics), and this theme reaches its culmination in the wonderful formula 'Devised deviser devising it all for company'. (C,64) If we put this together with the naturalistic level of the approach to death we can see the text as a parable about the self-consciousness and self-creation of the dying man 'on his back in the dark'. The 'company' is existentialist in that it is chosen by the 'deviser', a fact emphasised by the apparent arbitrariness of the *author's* choices of company. The author is not very sure about his creature and suggests 'If this no better than nothing cancel', which is a profoundly Sartrean proposition for the creature who approaches his own cancellation. The idea is made clearer: 'If this finally no improvement on nothing he can always fall for good'. (C,67) Here the tension between the ontological element and the natural level is beautifully expressed and when we turn the page and read 'Then sooner or later on from nought anew' (C,68) and 'Till again with no dead end for his pains he renounces and embarks on yet another course' (C,69) we realise that we are back where we were at the end of *Malone Dies* and at the end of *The Unnamable* and in the ontological endlessnesses of the *Texts for Nothing*.

The last word of *Company* is 'Alone', printed as a single separate word, a final paragraph. This word must have a powerful effect on any attentive reader but if one had to explain its meaning, to understand both it and the text, one would be forced on to the ontological plane. Deviser and devised are 'alone', in spite of the company, because death approaches, death 'my ownmost possibility of being' (Heidegger) that cannot be shared with another. They are 'alone' because what they *are* is that most radically isolated of possibilities the 'nothing' of self-consciousness (Sartre). They are 'alone' because they are single, one, undifferentiated, self-substantiating: there is only one voice, whatever tense it may speak in. This voice, consciousness, cannot dwell in itself (its 'self' is nothing) but must forever project, strain towards being:

Why crawl at all? Why not just lie in the dark with closed eyes and

> give up? Give up all...But...as he lies the craving for company revives. In which to escape from his own. (C,76–7)

The 'company' is anything at all ('For example an itch beyond reach of the hand or better still within while the hand immovable. An unscratchable itch. What an addition to company that would be!' (C,77–8) 'Company' is being, the objective, the world, words, thought. The self that writes *Company* is demonstrated, validated and destroyed by company. This is an *ontological* proposition. If, in this fine text, Beckett has also achieved a viable naturalistic level, on which for instance 'Why not give up?' appeals simply to our tiredness with life, then perhaps he has at last brought about the marriage he has long been seeking.

Ill Seen Ill Said has an even stronger naturalistic and literal component. In making the proposals of the final section of this study I am greatly emboldened, however, by its conclusion. It reads like the very last gasp that we have been waiting for for so long, and it marries the positive and negative side of the philosophical approach we have taken.

> First last moment. Grant only enough remain to devour all. Moment by glutton moment. Sky earth the whole kit and boodle. Not another crumb of carrion left. Lick chops and basta. No. One moment more. One last. Grace to breathe that void. Know happiness. (IS,59)

The world, here, goes out with the consciousness. The last moment (though it obviously isn't because it never can be) is spent in a prayer ('Grace') that the void will be experienced, that the consciousness will be conscious of unconsciousness, that the nirvana ('happiness') of *being nothing*, of the nothing-self's catching up with the absolute nothing, will at last be achieved. For it will, at last, be happiness, that.

*   *   *

THE WELLHEAD

If our philosophical analogies work we have perhaps found a useful way of reading Beckett, particularly in his darker moments and particularly in the third period of his work. In addition we have tested the common assumption that Beckett is a special sort of writer connected in some way with philosophy, especially Existentialist philosophy. Having come so far it seems necessary to go a little further and to see if our reading implies a possible religious or mystical interpretation of Beckett. We have been employing concepts such as the Void, Being and the Absolute in a way that is suggestive of another step.

It is well established that Beckett is profoundly conscious of the detail, flavour and mystery of the Christian religion. One of the best recent studies to elaborate on this is Hersh Ziefman's 'Religious Imagery in the Plays of Samuel Beckett' (in Ruby Cohn's *Samuel Beckett: A Collection of Criticism*) written in 1975. This essay extracts all sorts of hidden religious references and undercurrents from several plays making a special *tour de force* when considering *Embers*. The religious texture of this play is often well-hidden, but Ziefman uncovers it suggesting, for instance, that Bolton's name is necessarily associated with Christ's being nailed (or bolted) on to the cross, and that Holloway's name is a reversal of Christ's claim to be the positive 'way', in a surprisingly convincing argument. Similarly *Endgame* and *Godot* are combed for their implicit religious content (the explicit content is clear enough) and the results confirm Beckett's near-obsession with the story of Christ, particularly of his death: the tramps support Lucky (Act One) and Pozzo (Act Two) one on each side like the thieves at the crucifixion; *Endgame* is set in a skull because the crucifixion took place at Golgotha – the place of the skull, and so on. This imagery, Ziefman says, constitutes 'a *Kyrie eleison* of suffering and despair.' (Cohn, op. cit., p. 93) I quote all this from this critic to suggest that Beckett's work is perhaps even more permeated by religious motifs than has been commonly thought, but my main purpose is negative: Ziefman's essay is most interesting but it does not get us much further with an overall interpretation of Beckett's meaning. For that a different sort of approach seems indicated and I would offer as a model for this the approach taken by Richard Coe in his essay 'God and Samuel Beckett' (*Meanjin Quarterly*, March, 1965, reprinted in J.D. O'Hara's collection in the Twentieth Century Interpretation series, *Beckett*). This opens:

> The universe of Samuel Beckett is certainly as complex as that of any other living writer. Yet it is not a dream universe, like that of

Jarry or Ionesco. It is a metaphysical vision of ultimate 'reality', constructed out of innumerable threads of logic tightly inter-woven, out of fragmented arguments from Proust and Descartes, from Geulincx, Malebranche and Schopenhauer, from Dostoiev-sky, Wittgenstein and Sartre, each seemingly irrefutable, each in its right and proper place, and each rushing headlong towards an inescapable impossibility. (O'Hara, op. cit., p. 91)

It is my contention, too, that Beckett's work is a vision of ultimate 'reality' and it is for this very reason that I have tried to connect him to certain philosophers.

The result of this approach is that the monstrous and cruel God revealed behind Beckett's works when they are read on Ziefman's level of religious imagery now stands a chance of appearing more positive. I believe that it is possible to offer some mitigation of Beckettian pessimism out of Beckett's own mouth and that this depends on a philosophical reading of his work.

The conventional reading of Beckett arises from the assumption, quite correct as far as it goes, that he provokes bitter laughter at the delusory props of religion and then, casting them away as much as he is able to, considering his obsession with Christ crucified, plunges into an ever-darker world. His tone becomes less humorous and more desperate, the mind of his narrator seems to be increasingly near the end of its tether.

This reading is obviously valuable. However, if we go more deeply into the question and try to probe the meaning of Beckett's imaginative constructs we find tentative answers in parallels with certain philosophers, and, where Beckett is at his most obscure particularly, where we feel the need for explanation most acutely, the appropriate philosophical analogues turn out to be surprisingly positive – Heidegger on the trail of Being, Hegel thinking through to the Absolute. It is for this reason that in this last chapter I have dealt with our three philosophers in a different order, starting with Sartre's Nothing and moving towards the more positive ontologies.

This alternative movement which I am suggesting, a movement that is actually towards a more positive world-view, works beyond the consolations of conventional religion and beyond the comforts of the sort of philosophy with which Beckett became acquainted academically. Thus normal Christianity is derided and Geulincx, Descartes and the others left behind. Like Heidegger, Beckett is trying to go beyond all that, beyond a world-view based on belief, beyond mere 'metaphysics' and beyond reasoning of an Aristotelian sort. But, like Heidegger, he has not thus left *philosophy* behind (we can think here of Heidegger's attempt to achieve a more 'funda-mental' ontology) and there is always left open the possibility of some profounder view of religion.

The road through and beyond conventional religion and some sorts of philosophy is followed by our three philosophers and by Beckett. Sartre limits himself to the road and nothing but the road – in fact it is towards Nothing that he travels. This Nothing looms large for Beckett but does not seem adequate as a description of his final meaning. As Coe puts it:

> Behind 'reality' lies the void, the Nothing, 'than which naught is more real'; and it is from this concept of the void that Beckett's people start out on their pilgrimage in search of a new and more acceptable version of God. (O'Hara, op. cit., p. 100)

This takes us beyond Sartre just as we are beyond Christian orthodoxy and Rationalism. Our next stage is Heidegger, who certainly seemed close to Beckett in our discussions of him in this Chapter and in Chapter 2. Heidegger's view of Being has been adopted, as is well known, by some modern theologians, notably Bultmann (cf. for instance John Macquarrie's *An Existentialist Theology*). Beyond this perhaps mystical possibility lies Hegel whose conception of the Absolute, although he himself would reject the label 'mystic', must appear mystical to atheistic materialism of the sort with which Beckett is normally credited.

We have left behind the well-known level of Beckett's anti-Christianity and we are trying to learn what is beyond this level of Sartrean pessimism and how far we can take Beckett into it. What we are trying to discover is, finally, what Beckett *means* on an ontological level. This is as far as a philosophical reading can take us and, indeed, as far as any reading can take us. In passing we might notice that we need some explanation that will satisfy the paradoxical fact that Beckett's work is often found to be strangely comforting. It is a hideous journey on which he takes us, to the edge of the abyss, and when he reaches the edge (the end, of *Endgame* perhaps) he plunges over. If there is something Dantesque about this image that is not accidental, but is it merely the dark of Hell beyond the void, or is there light?

Chapter 6 of *Murphy*, the famous disquisition on Murphy's mind, takes us into a cynical impasse which is the direct result of rationalist dualism. A way out is, however, suggested, and it is a mystical exit at least in tone, in that the third 'zone' of Murphy's mind allows Murphy to conceive of himself as 'a mote in the dark of absolute freedom.' (M,79) This religious-sounding claim is considerably developed and expanded in *Watt*. In this novel we find traces of mysticism in the visit of the Gall's to Mr Knott's house, in Mr Knott himself, in the picture in Erskine's room of a centre and a circle and in half a dozen briefer references. The earliest trace of the mystical in *Watt*, however, and also the longest and most convincing, is to be found in Arsene's 'short statement' which concludes part one of the novel. This is not the place for an extensive analysis of its twenty-five pages, but the following considerations may help to establish the more positive philosophical and religious view of Beckett that I am attempting.

Arsene's speech is packed with implicit Christian references which are not intended satirically or ironically. Christ crucified is not present here as a source of parody or bitter joking but in a more positive guise; in fact there is no escaping the conclusion that Arsene is talking about Watt (or any other newly-arrived servant of Mr Knott's) as though he, Watt, were Christ.

> The man arrives! The dark ways all behind, all within, the long dark ways, in his head, in his side, in his hands and feet. . .(W,37)

The juxtaposition of these parts of the body reminds one irresistibly of Christ with his crown of thorns, the lance in his side, the nails in his hands and feet. And Beckett offers a background for his picture which suggests some of the details of early Italian paintings of the crucifixion.

> The long blue days for his head, for his side, and the little paths for his feet, and all the brightness to touch and gather. Through the grass the little mosspaths, bony with old roots, and the trees sticking up, and the flowers sticking up, and the fruit hanging down. . .(W,37–8)

The trees are perhaps the crosses and the fruit their victims. Arsene remembers when he, too, was the man newly arrived:

> How I feel it all again, after so long, here, and here, and in my

hands, and in my eyes, like a face raised, a face offered, all trust
and innocence and candour, all the old soil and fear and weakness offered, to be sponged away and forgiven. (W,38)

Surely behind this picture stands an image of Christ, innocent but
offering himself so that sin, the 'old soil', may be forgiven.

My present purpose is to go beyond this, beyond Beckett's playing
with the detail of Christianity, to a more direct confrontation of the
absolute, but it is worth reflecting for a moment on the significance
of this passage. Arsene, Watt, and other men, as servants of Mr
Knott are specifically likened to the suffering Christ. Beckett's
motivation here seems to be an extreme and radical version of
Christianity: what is so terrible about the suffering of the Son of
Man is that it is undergone not by God but by man. Arsene,
however, as we have said, goes beyond this.

The man has arrived at Mr Knott's house, having found the door
he has 'passed beyond it', Mr Knott's house is the beyond. In this
place he is 'in his midst at last' and can taste 'the long joys of being
himself' for here, although he may at first be indignant at having to
work, he comes to see that work for Mr Knott is also ('and indeed
chiefly') for himself. 'Calm and glad' he goes about his work, 'calm
and glad he witnesses and is witnessed.' (W,39–40) But Mr Knott's
servants do not rest here; one day something slips. Once they have
reached the point where what is 'inside' them and what is 'outside'
them have become indistinguishable, in other words once the
Sartrean-Hegelian identity of man with God has been established, a
profound feeling of alienation erupts.

> My personal system was so distended at the period of which I
> speak that the distinction between what was inside it and what
> was outside it was not at all easy to draw. Everything that
> happened happened inside it, and at the same time everything
> that happened happened outside it. (W,41–2)

Here Beckett offers us a man who has become the man-God, the
pour-soi-en-soi, who has connoted Absolute Knowledge. But he goes
beyond this; something changes even in the absolute, something
slips. Arsene observes that the old yearning was in fact happiness
and that to have arrived at last is not happiness.

The glutton castaway, the drunkard in the desert, the lecher in prison, they are the happy ones. (W,43)

This could be taken as a symbol of Beckett's whole endeavour: to fall silent in the bosom of God is the goal but no answer, the end but no conclusion, something impossible and, although desired, actually less good in attainment than prospect.

Arsene feels he has to offer an explanation of the 'change' that takes place, and we await his explanation with impatience as it will offer, perhaps, Beckett's conception of what is beyond the absolute, beyond God. Arsene says this:

In my opinion it was not an illusion, as long as it lasted, that presence of what did not exist, that presence without, that presence within. (W,43)

This conforms to the theme of negativity in *Watt*; Mr Knott is not; resting in his establishment is only the first step, the second leads man to see that the master for whom he works is absent, but this absence is not a simple absence: beyond man's quotidian conception of God lies an ineffable mystery, a 'presence which does not exist.' The servants revolve about Mr Knott 'in tireless love' (W,61) and they 'nest a little while in his branches' (W,56) but there is a problem about him in that he must have had a beginning and he must have an end or else how is time possible? The answer to this is the equivalent of the 'change' which offers the 'presence which did not exist.' Arsene wonders:

Or is there a coming that is not a coming to, a going that is not a going from, a shadow that is not the shadow of purpose, or not? (W,56)

This speculation is at once in keeping with the mystery of Arsene's 'change' and with the sort of paradoxical mysticism in which the *mysterium tremendum* both is and is not. Later in the novel, in the episode of the Galls father and son, Watt himself experiences the change and he describes it in these same paradoxical terms, terms expressive of God beyond God and of the identity between the Void and the Absolute: 'a thing that was nothing had happened.' (W,73)

After the Second World War, Beckett's work developed and matured as we have seen. One text stands out from this period as exploring further the theme of positive assertion of some exit, some beyond, some hope however empty and paradoxical. This is the significantly entitled *The Calmative* written in French in 1946. (NK,25–42)

This text contains the usual Beckettian miseries, which I shall take as read, and the usual uncertainties as to who is writing and whether the events narrated can seriously aspire to the status of existent entities or not. But it is also remarkable for its optimistic elements. The ancient (or dead) narrator enters a town by the Shepherd's Gate (the Good Shepherd's? anyway he sees not 'a soul' there, 'only the first bats like flying crucifixions') on a Sunday. He sits on a capstan at the waterside and gazes out to sea, but there is no help there (in this 'dead haven') and he looks at a flagstone because he has always found that help comes from the earth not from the sky. When he looks up he sees a young boy in biblical rags holding a goat; the boy offers him a sweet but departs before they can converse. When the narrator himself moves on he describes his 'getting back' (to where?) as 'not...quite empty-handed.' He goes into a church, which he prefers to call a cathedral, and he climbs a tower at high speed, coming out into the night. Back in the street he becomes acutely conscious of other people and he discovers to his surprise that he has 'no pain whatever' at this point. He falls asleep on a bench and wakes up to find a man beside him with whom he talks. The man, on discovering that the narrator has no money, seizes him but starts talking kindly to him in a way that generates a moment of optimism:

> Between the caressing voice and the fingers rowelling my neck the contrast was striking. But gradually the two things merged in a devastating hope, if I dare say so, and I dare. (NK,39)

After this the man offers him one of his one-and-sixpenny phials in exchange for a kiss, which is duly given. Then he departs 'with radiant smile.'

> My pains were back, but with something untoward which prevented my wrapping them round me. (NK,40)

The text ends with the dawn, for all this has taken place at night, but the dawn seems as much within him as without. He cannot see the stars:

> For the light I steeped in put out the stars, assuming they were there, which I doubted, remembering the clouds. (NK,42)

This can certainly be read as if the light is now emanating from the narrator. A comparison could be made with the dawn that rises on Watt, once Arsene has left, bringing in 'the day without precedent at last.' (W,63)

I think there is a suggestion in *The Calmative* that the narrator meets the young Christ, who behaves with characteristic charity. This boy is holding a sinner in the shape of the goat and is taking him away to look after him. Appropriately the narrator feels, after the boy has gone away, that he should have asked him what his father did. Once again we move from the presence, the existence, of the man who was Christ to the absence and ineffability of the nothing that is God. And for once, man, in the shape of the man on the bench, is kind and good and this immediately creates a 'devastating hope'. Interestingly this follows on a visit to a church and an attempt to ascend to God. God is not there at the top of the tower, but hope seems to be available at ground level, at the level of man. Yet the Cathedral is necessary, the Christian background is essential, humanism is certainly not enough, the absent God, God the Void, is paradoxically ever-present.

This more positive element in Beckett (though we have seen some reasons to qualify that adjective) is also present in the trilogy. Besides a large number of anticlerical and antireligious jokes in the Moran section of *Molloy* and many other veiled and overt references to Christianity, the trilogy contains some remarkably mystical and even optimistic moments. I shall limit myself to a discussion of one of the most striking of these. It is to be found in the closing section of the first part of *Molloy*. Here, more perhaps than anywhere in Beckett's mature work, the clouds lift for an instant and the narrator seems to have arrived.

The last forty-five lines of the first part of *Molloy* are an undoubted relief and the traces of light they contain must be looked at against the darkness of what precedes them.

And true enough the day came when the forest ended and I saw the light...I opened my eyes and I saw I had arrived. (T,90)

Molloy has fallen into a ditch and this has woken him up, it seems. He looks across the vast plain on to which he has emerged from the forest and on the horizon he sees the towers and steeple of a town. He relapses for a few lines into the old bitterness ('How could I drag myself over that vast moor?') but then the light returns with an optimism quite astonishing in Beckett.

Fortunately for me at this painful juncture...I heard a voice telling me not to fret, that help was coming. Literally...Don't fret Molloy, we're coming. (T,91)

This seems to be somewhat devalued by the ensuing sentence ('Well, I suppose you have to try everything once, succour included, to get a complete picture of the resources of their planet.'). But Molloy hears birds ('skylarks perhaps') and then, nearing the end of the one huge paragraph that constitutes his monologue, he says 'I did not fret.' Thus he obeys the voice. 'It must have been spring' he says. He remains in the ditch, he even longs to be back in the forest, but it is 'not a real longing', he has arrived somewhere.

The tone of this passage is a remarkable lightening of the Beckettian gloom, but one aspect of its specific content seems to demand analysis from a philosophical point of view. Whose is the voice?

In conformity with our earlier discussion in which the external voice in Beckett's prose is taken to be the author's I think we can see this voice as Beckett himself reassuring Molloy that he is getting to the end and that he will soon be relieved by Moran. However, also in conformity with that discussion, this relationship between creator and created is also that between God and creature. In *An Existentialist Theology* John Macquarrie summarizes this development in sentences which can easily apply to Beckett.

If man in the ocean of what is, possibility entangled in facticity, were the whole picture, the only logical outcome would seem to be that heroism of despair, the determination to be myself within and in spite of the limitations of a miserable existence, which we associate with Heidegger and Sartre...But on the other hand, if anxiety discloses the possibility of a ground of being, being itself, beyond the contingency of both *Vorhandenheit* and *Existenz*, that is, divine Being, man's finitude may be interpreted as creatureliness. (Macquarrie, op. cit., p. 80)

With the introduction of the external voice, especially the voice bringing comfort and succour, Beckett is opening the door to 'being itself' and to a view of man not as self-dependent, as has often seemed the case in other parts of his work, but as 'creaturely'.

Enrico Garzilli, in *Circles Without Center* (a pregnantly Beckettian title if we think of the picture in *Watt*) suggests that we can take this a stage further to a synthesis of an atheistic view with a

Christian view in an overall interpretation of Beckett. This is based on the Prologue to St John's Gospel in which Logos and Theos are seen as created (and, especially, created *word*) and creator. This duality underlies the relationship between God and Man, between God the Father and Christ, between the narrator and the narrated, between self-consciousness and the self. Here we have a development of the Sartrean slogan about man making himself: 'The person is most himself when he creates... The person ultimately is one who is creating himself as he lives' (Garzilli, 1, 144–9) This brings in Heidegger, Sartre and a Christian view and in fact also echoes Hegel. Consciousness, for Garzilli, 'looks back' at its creator just as human spirit, in Hegel, looks at Absolute Spirit.

Thus the 'voice' of Molloy is God, the Absolute, the author, the self, consciousness. Under a certain light all these are identical. This mystical intuition is perhaps the final depth in Beckett, the mystery towards which his parables aspire but which they never attain for the end of all these attempts, if they are unsuccessful, is failure, and, if they are successful, is nothing. As Coe puts it

> Just as the Self is the inconceivable *Néant* of silence behind the works of language, so also 'God' is the Total Nothing behind the word which is Creation. (O'Hara, op. cit., p. 111)

Or, as Charles Glicksberg has it in *Modern Literature and the Death of God*,

> When literary nihilism... is carried to an extreme, it then comes full circle and approaches the condition of 'negative theology' ... The literary nihilist... is a mystic *manqué*. (Glicksberg, op. cit., p. 99)

Beckett strenuously attempts the impossible and his task is profoundly human, whence perhaps the consolation to be derived from his work. Nietzsche expresses his position with strange accuracy:

> But that 'other world', that inhuman, dehumanized world which is a heavenly Nothing, is well hidden from men; and the belly of being does not speak to man, except as man. (*Thus Spake Zarathustra*, p. 59)

It is in the impossible going-on that Beckett, as man, speaks to us as man and it is within that discourse that Being is to be found, if anywhere. Like all metaphysical entities, Being, God, the Self, the Absolute, 'are brought into being by someone's wielding them in discourse.'[10] Beckett creates the conditions of metaphysical possibility in his discourse, and at times this is quite specific. I can conclude with two examples.

The Voice (appropriately enough) in *Cascando* speaks this over the Music:

> no further...no more searching...to find him...in the dark...to see him...for whom...that's it...no matter...never him...never right...start again...in the dark...done with that...this time...it's the right one...we're there...nearly... finish – (CA,44)

This voice, the voice of philosophical discourse, the foundation of the possibility of metaphysics, is Beckett's own and offers an abstract summary of his total project. 'Words', in *Words and Music* offers a more concrete, and therefore more metaphorical, summary of the same ontological process with its inevitable, but 'unattainable, mystical goal:

> Then down a little way
> Through the trash
> Towards where
> All dark no begging
> No giving no words
> No sense no need
> Through the scum
> Down a little way
> To whence one glimpse
> of that wellhead. (WM,35)

If it is true that the meaning of being can only be experienced and not explained it is perhaps the case that literature can come closer to it than philosophy. Samuel Beckett may in fact offer us a purer insight into ultimate reality even than those philosophers most nearly attuned to it.

NOTES AND REFERENCES

1. The most thorough chronology of Beckett's work that is readily available appears, on unnumbered pages, at the beginning of Ruby Cohn's *Back to Beckett*, (Princeton University Press, 1973).
2. Knowlson and Pilling talk of 'the more desiccated and more severely functional later texts.' (See *Frescoes of the Skull* (London: Calder, 1979), p. 16.
3. I give this date to stress the point that the *Three Dialogues*, although they are now printed with the *Proust* essay of 1931, are not in fact early Joycean work but belong to Beckett's second, post-war period and are the artistic theory of the man then writing the *Texts for Nothing*.
4. For information concerning this lost work cf. Deirdre Bair's biography *Samuel Beckett*, pp. 253–7.
5. Cf., for instance, the end of the 'Existenz' section of Chapter 2, above, pp. 16–17.
6. '*No Exit*' is, of course, one rendering of the title of Sartre's own play *Huis Clos*. It will have occurred to the reader to wonder whether Sartre's own literary works might not be his best parables. This possibility, discussed in, for instance, Edith Kern's *Existential Thought and Fictional Technique* (Yale University Press, 1970), is a very real one but it is not unreasonable to suggest that parables come out better when clearly divorced from the moral or metaphysical matter they illustrate. In Sartre's own case the parables are stronger where he avoids too much philosophising (as in *Les Mouches*) than they are where he sounds like his philosophical self (as in *La Nausée*).
7. The publishing-history of this piece emphasises the Beckettian nature of Heidegger's constant circling around his elusive goal. In fact *The Way Back* is a lengthy introduction to the essay *What is Metaphysics?* of twenty years earlier, an essay to which a postscript had been added in 1943. In the German text *What is Metaphysics?* runs to seventeen pages, the postscript to nine and the introduction to fifteen pages.
8. Heidegger is presumably speaking metaphorically here. There are languages that do not possess the verb 'to be', of course.
9. Knowlson and Pilling, in their account of *Lessness*, steer a careful course avoiding structuralism on the one hand and Existentialism on the other, preferring to see Beckett's writing as 'essentially *sui generis*'. I note, however, that their final word on this piece describes it enigmatically as 'a text for being'. (Knowlson and Pilling, op. cit., pp. 172–6)
10. This is from Elmer Sprague's lucid primer *Metaphysical Thinking* (New York: OUP, 1978), p. 4.

Bibliography

Alvarez, A., *Beckett* (London: Fontana, 1973).

Ayer, A.J., *Language, Truth and Logic* (London: Victor Gollancz, 1936).

Bair, D., *Samuel Beckett: A Biography* (London: Cape, 1978).

Beckett, S., *Waiting for Godot* (London: Faber, 1956).

——, *All That Fall* (London: Faber, 1957).

——, *Endgame* (London: Faber, 1958).

——, *Trilogy* (*Molloy, Malone Dies, The Unnamable*) (London: Calder, 1959).

——, *Murphy* (London: Calder, 1963) (1st. ed. Routledge, 1938).

——, *Watt* (London: Calder, 1963) (1st. ed. Olympia Press, Paris, 1953).

——, *How It Is* (London: Calder, 1964).

——, *Play* (*Play, Words and Music, Cascando*) (London: Faber, 1964).

——, *Proust* and *Three Dialogues* (London: Calder, 1965) (1st. ed. 1931 and 1949).

——, *Imagination Dead Imagine* (London: Calder, 1965).

——, *No's Knife* (London: Calder, 1967). (Includes *The Expelled, The Calmative, The End, Texts for Nothing, From An Abandoned Work, Enough, Imagination Dead Imagine* and *Ping*.)

——, *More Pricks Than Kicks* (London: Calder, 1970) (1st ed. Chatto, 1934).

——, *Mercier et Camier* (Paris: les Editions de Minuit, 1970).

——, *Lessness* (London: Calder, 1970).

——, *Breath and other shorts* (London: Faber, 1971).

——, *The Lost Ones* (London: Calder, 1972).

——, *Premier Amour* (Paris: les Editions de Minuit, 1972).

——, *For To End Yet Again* (London: Calder, 1976).

——, *Company* (London: Calder, 1980).

——, *Ill Seen Ill Said* (London: Calder, 1982).

——, *Eleuthéria* (unpublished typescript).

Bernal, O., *Language et fiction dans le roman de Samuel Beckett* (Paris: Gallimard, 1969).

Bochenski, I.M., *Contemporary European Philosophy*, trans. Nicholl and Aschenbrenner (Univ. of California Press, 1956).

Coe, R.N., *Beckett*, 'Writers and Critics' series (London: Oliver and Boyd, 1964).

——, 'God and Samuel Beckett' in *Meanjin Quarterly*, March 1965. (Reprinted in J.D. O'Hara, *Beckett*, Twentieth Century Interpretations, New Jersey, Prentice-Hall, 1971).

Cohn, R., *Samuel Beckett: The Comic Gamut* (New York: Rutgers University Press, 1962).

——, 'Philosophical Fragments in the Work of Samuel Beckett.' *Criticism*, writer 1964, reprinted in Esslin, M., below).

——, *Back to Beckett* (Princeton University Press, 1973).

——, *Samuel Beckett: A Collection of Criticism* (New York: McGraw-Hill, 1975).

Cormier, R. and Pallister, J.L., *Waiting for Death: The Philosophical Significance of Beckett's 'En Attendant Godot'* (University of Alabama Press, 1979).

Cruickshank, J. (ed.), *The Novelist as Philosopher* (London: OUP, 1962).

D'Aubarède, G., 'En attendant . . . Beckett' (in *Nouvelles Littéraires*, 16 Feb. 1961, trans. C. Waters in *Trace*, no. 42, Summer 1961.)

Doherty, F., *Samuel Beckett* (London: Hutchinson, 1971).

Driver, T., 'Beckett by the Madeleine', *Columbia Forum*, Summer 1961.

Edie, J.M. (ed.), *New Essays in Phenomenology* (Chicago: Quadrangle, 1969).

Esslin, M. (ed.), *Samuel Beckett*, A Collection of Critical Essays (New Jersey: Prentice-Hall, 1965).

Federman, R. and Fletcher, J., *Samuel Beckett*: His Works and His Critics (University of California Press, 1970).

Findlay, J.N., *Hegel: A Re-examination* (London: Allen and Unwin, 1958).

Finney, B., *Since How It Is* (London: Covent Garden Press, 1972).

Fletcher, J., *The Novels of Samuel Beckett* (London: Chatto and Windus, 1964).

——, *Samuel Beckett's Art* (London: Chatto and Windus, 1967).

Fletcher J. and Spurling J., *The Plays of Samuel Beckett* (New York: Hill and Wang, 1972.)

Garzilli, E., *Circles Without Center* (Cambridge, Mass: Harvard University Press, 1972).

Gessner, N., *Die Unzulänglichkeit der Sprache* (Zurich: Juris Verlag, 1957).

Glicksberg, C., *Modern Literature and the Death of God* (The Hague: Nijhoff, 1966).

Gurwitsch, A., 'Husserl's Theory of Intentionality' in Lee and Mandelbaum (eds), *Phenomenology and Existentialism* (Baltimore: Johns Hopkins, 1967).

Hassan, I., *The Literature of Silence* (New York: Alfred A. Knopf, 1967).

Hayman, R., *Samuel Beckett* (London: Heinemann, 1968).

Heidegger, M., *The Way Back into the Ground of Metaphysics*, trans. W. Kaufmann Appears in Kaufmann, W. (ed.), *Existentialism From Dostoevsky to Sartre* (New York: The World Publishing Co., 1956), pp. 206–21.

——, *What is Philosophy?*, trans. Kluback and Wilde (London: Vision Press, 1958).

——, *An Introduction to Metaphysics*, trans. Ralph Manheim (New York: Anchor Books, 1961). (First English ed. idem, Yale University Press, 1959.)

——, *Being and Time*, trans. Macquarrie and Robinson. (London: SCM Press, 1962). (Appears as 'BT' in this study.)

——, *Poetry, Language, Thought* (New York: Harper and Row, 1971.)

——, *Basic Writings* D.F. Krell (ed.) (London: Routledge, 1978). (Includes a translation of 'What Is Metaphysics?' of 1929.)

Hegel, G.W.F., *Encyclopaedia*, trans. as *The Philosophy of Mind* by W. Wallace (Oxford: Clarendon Press, 1894).

——, *Early Theological Writings*, trans. Knox and Kroner (University of Chicago Press, 1948). (New ed. University of Pennsylvania Press, 1971.)

——, *The Phenomenology of Mind*, trans. J.B. Baillie (New York: Harper, 1967). (Appears as 'PM' in this study.)

——, *The Phenomenology of Spirit*, trans. A.V. Miller (Oxford: Clarendon Press, 1977).

Hesla, D., *The Shape of Chaos* (Minneapolis: University of Minnesota Press, 1971).

Hoffer, J., 'Watt' in *Perspective*, vol. C.I. no. 3, Autumn 1959. Reprinted in Esslin, 1, above.

Hoffman, F.J., *Samuel Beckett: The Language of Self* (Southern Illinois University Press, 1962).

Janvier, L., *Pour Samuel Beckett* (Paris: Editions de Minuit, 1966).

Kaufmann, W., *From Shakespeare to Existentialism* (New York: Beacon, 1959).

——, *Hegel* (London: Weidenfeld and Nicolson, 1966).

Kenner, H., *Samuel Beckett: A Critical Study* (London: Calder, 1962). (1st. pub. New York, 1961.)

——, *A Reader's Guide to Samuel Beckett* (London: Thames and Hudson, 1973).

Kern, E., *Existential Thought and Fictional Technique* (New Haven and London: Yale University Press, 1970).

Kierkegaard, S., *The Concept of Dread*, trans. Walter Lowrie (Princeton University Press, 1944).

Knight, E.W., *Literature Considered as Philosophy* (London: Routledge, 1957).

Knowlson, J. and Pilling, J., *Frescoes of the Skull: The Later Prose and Drama of Samuel Beckett* (London: Calder, 1979).

Lee E.N. and Mandelbaum M. (eds.), *Phenomenology and Existentialism* (Baltimore: Johns Hopkins, 1967).

Levy, E.P., *Beckett and the Voice of Species* (Dublin: Gill and Macmillan, 1980)

Macquarrie, J., *An Existentialist Theology* (London: S.C.M. Press, 1955).

——, *Existentialism* (Harmondsworth: Penguin, 1973). (1st. ed. New York, 1972.)

Melèse, P., *Beckett* (Paris: Editions Seghers, 1966).

Mooney, M., 'Molloy, part 1: Beckett's *Discourse on Method*' in *Journal of Beckett Studies*, no.3, Summer 1978.

Mure, G.R.G., *An Introduction to Hegel* (London: OUP, 1940).

——, *The Philosophy of Hegel* (London: OUP, 1965).

Murray, M., *Heidegger and Modern Philosophy* (New Haven: Yale University Press, 1978).

Murray, P., *The Tragic Comedian* (Cork: The Mercier Press, 1970).

Naess, A., *Four Modern Philosophers*, trans. A. Hannay (London: University of Chicago Press, 1968).

Nietzsche, F.W., *Thus Spoke Zarathustra*, trans. R.J. Hollingdale (Harmondsworth: Penguin, 1961).

O'Hara, J.D., *Twentieth Century Interpretations of Molloy, Malone Dies, The Unnamable* (Englewood Cliffs, New Jersey: Prentice-Hall, 1971).

O'Hara, Sister M.J., *The Unfulfilled Search For Identity in the Poems and Novels of Samuel Beckett*. Thesis submitted at University College, Galway, 1974.

Onimus, J., *Beckett* (Paris: Desclée de Brouwer, 1968).

Powys, J.C., *Wolf Solent* (London: Macdonald, 1929).

Reid, A., *All I Can Manage, More Than I Could* (Dublin: Dolmen Press, 1968).

Rickels, M., 'Existential Themes in Beckett's *Unnamable*' in *Criticism*, Spring 1962.

Robbe-Grillet, A., *Pour un nouveau roman* (Paris: les Editions de Minuit, 1963).

Robinson, M., *The Long Sonata of the Dead* (London: Hart-Davis, 1969).

Rosen, S(tanley), *Nihilism* (New Haven: Yale University Press, 1969).

Rosen, S(teven) J., *Samuel Beckett and the Pessimistic Tradition* (New York:

Rutgers University Press, 1976).

Sartre, J-P., *La Transcendance de l'Ego: Esquisse d'une description phénoméno-logique* (Paris: Vrin, 1965). (1st ed. 1936).

——, *Being and Nothingness*, trans. Hazel E. Barnes (London: Methuen, University Paperback, 1969). (Appears as 'BN' in this study.)

Schulz, H-J., *This Hell of Stories: a Hegelian approach to the novels of Samuel Beckett* (The Hague: Mouton, 1973).

Scott, N.A., *Samuel Beckett* (London: Bowes and Bowes, 1965).

Sprague, E., *Metaphysical Thinking* (New York: OUP, 1978).

Stace, W.T., *The Philosophy of Hegel* (1st. ed. London, 1924, reprinted Toronto: Dover Publications Inc., 1955.)

Tagliaferri, A., *Beckett, ou la surdétermination littéraire*, in 'Traces' series (Paris: Paysot, 1974).

Tindall, W.Y., *Samuel Beckett* (New York: Columbia UP, 1964).

Webb, E., *Samuel Beckett, A Study of His Novels* (London: Peter Owen, 1970).

Worth, K., *Beckett The Shape Changer* (London: Routledge, 1975).

Index

211